Rethinking School

Rethinking School

HOW TO TAKE CHARGE OF YOUR CHILD'S EDUCATION

Susan Wise Bauer

W. W. NORTON & COMPANY
Independent Publishers Since 1923
NEW YORK | LONDON

For information about permission to reproduce selections from this book, write to
Permissions, W. W. Norton & Company, Inc., 500 Fifth Avenue, New York, NY 10110

For information about special discounts for bulk purchases, please contact
W. W. Norton Special Sales at specialsales@wwnorton.com or 800-233-4830

Manufacturing by Berryville Graphics
Book design by JAM design
Production manager: Julia Druskin

ISBN: 978-0-393-28596-3

W. W. Norton & Company, Inc., 500 Fifth Avenue, New York, N.Y. 10110
www.wwnorton.com

W. W. Norton & Company Ltd., 15 Carlisle Street, London W1D 3BS

1 2 3 4 5 6 7 8 9 0

To my colleagues and friends at the Well-Trained Mind enterprises:
Kim, Jackie, Mel, Justin, Kevin, Pattie, John, Elizabeth,
Julia, and Steve. It's a joy to talk education with you.

Contents

About This Book

American K–12 school is a modern product of market forces.

Its grades and subjects are largely arbitrary. It isn't a good fit for all (or even most) students. It prioritizes a single way of understanding over all others, and it pushes out other important things that children under eighteen should be doing (like daydreaming, exercising, drawing, working, and sleeping).

You have to put your kids into it anyway.

Even if you're a home educator, you're still in the K–12 system. You've still got to usher your child through twelve grades and an artificial array of subjects, and provide proof that you've done so.

But all parents can learn how to flex our K–12 system so that it fits our children—rather than forcing our children to conform themselves to school.

This book is a guide to one aspect of sane, humane parenting: negotiating our twelve-grade school system in a way that nurtures and protects your child's mind, emotions, and spirit.

Part I, The System, introduces you to the current state of American education.

Part II, Mismatches, identifies possible misalignments between children and the system that tries to educate them.

Part III, Taking Control, gives specific strategies for dealing with those mismatches, while still staying within the traditional K–12 framework.

Sometimes our K–12 system isn't just a pair of shoes that pinches and needs to be cobbled, though; it's such a bad match that stepping out of the shoes completely (and running away barefoot) is the only thing that will keep both you and your child sane.

So Part IV, Rethinking the System, offers you a series of thought experiments, ways to re-envision what education *could* look like.

Part V, Opting Out, follows up with guidance on how to begin to put that education into place.

There's no one strategy that works for every family. Your child may be working above or below grade level, struggling with a diagnosable difficulty, stranded in a bad classroom, or simply being taught in a way that doesn't fit the way he thinks—and the answer may be any one (or more) of the strategies offered across the entire book.

And even if you don't think you're ready to abandon the system-as-you-know-it, try out the thought experiments in Part IV. You might find yourself seeing school with new eyes.

Author's note: The italicized quotes are all from real parents of real K–12 students. I have occasionally changed inessential identifying details.

PART I

The System

CHAPTER ONE

The Way We Do School

Children are infinitely varied: made up of a riotous myriad of aptitudes, ways of understanding, physical and intellectual and emotional talents; maturing on a huge spectrum of readiness, from those who were born old souls to the recklessly heedless young adult; some finding a clear path forward very early, others still struggling to find purpose into their twenties.

School varies little. Less, as each grade ascends.

■ ■ ■

Children change constantly. Between the ages of five and eighteen, their minds develop endless connections—major thoroughfares and fascinating side streets, byways and overpasses and intriguing little cobbled alleys, roadblocks and work-arounds: in Edith Wharton's words, *throwing out countless tendrils of feeling and perception,* changing month by month (sometimes week by week) into something new.

From first grade on, school barely changes—except to become more restrictive, and even more narrowly focused on arbitrarily selected important skills.

■ ■ ■

Children are (as C. S. Lewis might have put it) amphibious: half animal, half spirit. Their bodies mature on a timeframe they can't control.

They don't know why (and sometimes aren't even aware of *when*) they are hungry or restless or yearning or sleepy. These physical currents intertwine with and disrupt their emotions and imaginations and intellects. Their eyes, or ears, or brains, or hands, don't always work with the polished efficiency of a factory-tooled machine. Blocks and problems get in the way.

School has no body. School serves a Platonic child, one who doesn't suddenly melt down, or get overwhelmed by a tidal wave of hormones, or unexpectedly need fourteen hours of sleep.

■ ■ ■

By "school," I don't simply mean the buildings where children go to sit in a physical classroom and learn.

I mean our entire K–12–plus system, the one that we tend to think of as normal: Classify yourself by the month and year in which you were born; group yourself with those born within twelve months of you; study seven or eight unrelated subjects in blocks, four or five times per week; do this for twelve or so years, but not usually during the summer; at least once a year (usually much more often), fill out lots of bubble sheets with a #2 pencil; after twelve years of this, go away and live in a group home with others born within four years of you, while attending lectures and choosing a major that doesn't necessarily line up with any particular adult pattern of life.

The physical institutions of local elementary, middle, and high schools add an additional layer of artificiality: Leave home and travel to a *place*, where you sit in a room with that group of others who were born within twelve months of you; do this from September to June, unless it snows; study your subjects in fifty-minute blocks, four or five times per week; listen to someone at the front of the room, and then go home and complete a series of randomly assigned tasks.

Oh, yes: Fill out lots of bubble sheets with a #2 pencil.

This has nothing to do with the way that actual human beings acquire knowledge.

In this book, I'll offer you a whole array of strategies to help your child not just survive, but *prosper,* in the K–12 years. But none of them will work unless you can first perform a mental somersault and change your point of view.

Realize that the way we do school is *entirely unnatural.*

And when your child struggles, think about how to flex the system, *before* you start trying to adjust the child.

■ ■ ■

I have three sons and a daughter, and one of my sons is an outlier.

Physically, he was always different: a strong resemblance in features to the others, but much taller and thinner, constantly moving, a child who slept far less and did much more than his siblings. He was an early talker and walker, physically coordinated, clearly smart.

But when he was three years old, he still didn't seem to know his colors. "What color is this?" I'd say, holding up a blue block, and he'd randomly yell out "Yellow! Green! Yellow!"

"I think he's color blind," I said to my father, who's a board-certified pediatrician.

"No, he's not," my father said. "He just doesn't care. He's saying the first thing that comes to mind just to shut you up."

As it turned out, yes, that's exactly what he was doing. He had his own agenda, and telling me the color of the random block I was waving in his face was way low on his priority list.

In fact, he rarely did *anything* that he couldn't see the point of. My other children would finish essays, complete worksheets, and perform math drills—sometimes accompanied with loud complaints, but they would *do* the work, and remember it afterward. This child seemed unable to retain anything learned in isolation. If I could browbeat him into actually finishing a worksheet in one subject, he often remembered *nothing* about the assignment once he'd moved on to the next.

Fast forward (past a lot of parental hair-pulling) to age fourteen. I'm a writer, so grammar is particularly important to me. I drilled my kids in grammar from first grade on. We did grammar drills and grammar exercises. We memorized grammar rules. We diagrammed sentences. We never did *not* do grammar.

So on the first day of seventh grade, I pulled out the previous year's grammar book for a quick review.

My son looked at me like a newborn fawn contemplating a bow hunter. He remembered *nothing*.

"How can you not know what a *noun* is?" I demanded.

"Well," he said, "maybe it's because we've never really done grammar before."

Looking back, I realize the extent to which I was always trying to force this kid to fit the system, rather than the other way around. I was using a grammar program with which I'd had great success—but I should have put it away and worked out another plan. He needed to learn principles of language in another context, one that made sense to him. He didn't remember what a noun was, because the definition was floating out there in his mind, unconnected to anything he cared about.

Despite my years working in education, I didn't do that. I kept plugging along with the grammar book. And I was homeschooling, no less. I was *already* outside the borders of what most people think of as school.

But I was still having trouble seeing beyond "subjects" and "grades."

That's because artificial systems, like our K–12 educational system, are *powerful.* They evolve just as inexorably as natural systems. They acquire a life of their own and become the framework that organizes our existence.

In other words, the way we currently do education has become a paradigm (as academics would call it), or a matrix (in movie-speak): an invisible pair of glasses through which we view everything else.

Our educational system told me that my son needed to be able to complete his grammar exercises in order to be educated. It tells us that students have to all be reading the same texts in third grade, writing five-paragraph essays by fifth grade, doing pre-algebra *no later* than sixth grade.

This is an illusion.

Mind you: Artificial systems aren't necessarily *intrinsically* warped. Smallpox was eradicated by an artificial system. Cell phone networks are artificial systems. Sewage disposal and treatment systems are very definitely artificial. These are all good things.

But here's why it's absolutely essential to at least *begin* imagining a life outside of this paradigm, this matrix, this framework: When an artificial system classifies and segregates *people* (as opposed to cell phones, say, or sewage), some people will inevitably fit into the system better than others.

"Only a few children in school," wrote John Holt, the year before I was born, "ever become good at learning in the way we try to make them learn. Most of them get humiliated, frightened, and discouraged."[1] And in this lies the problem with this particular artificial system: When children struggle with it, "school" pushes us, with overwhelming force, toward fixing the child—figuring out what's wrong with that little psyche that's causing them to feel humiliation, fright, discouragement, boredom, disengagement—rather than questioning the system.[2]

Some children respond to our educational matrix with *This is my natural home*. But there's a whole range of mismatches between that matrix and the rest of the actual human beings who are funneled into it. Just past *I'm good at school*, we find *I can do this, it's just boring*, progress through *I can do some of this, but other parts of it are a complete mystery to me*, continue on to *If I grit my teeth I can probably squeak by*, and end with *I am stupid. I can't do this. It's just unending torture that I can't get out of until I graduate.*

If your child falls anywhere on this mismatch spectrum, there's a very good chance that the problem is school, not your child.

And this is most definitely *not* the message that most struggling learners receive.

Our current school system, as Sir Ken Robinson explains in his wildly popular TED talk "Do Schools Kill Creativity?,"[3] was designed to produce good workers for a capitalistic society. Built inextricably into that model is the assumption that "real intelligence consists [of a] capacity for a certain type of deductive reasoning . . . what we come to think of as academic ability." Deep in "the gene pool of public education," Sir Ken concludes, is the unquestioned premise that "there are only two types of people—academic and nonacademic; smart people and non-smart people. And the consequence of that is that many bril-

---

1 John Holt, *How Children Learn* (New York: Pitman, 1967), p. viii.

2 As my own experience should show, if you happen to already be homeschooling, you're still not off the hook. The majority of home educators I've come into contact with are still a long way from questioning the system. Keep reading.

3 As of this writing, Sir Ken's talk, given in 2006, has racked up 41 million views and is the most frequently viewed TED talk ever. If you haven't listened to it, you can access it through his website, sirkenrobinson.com. While you're navigating there, consider these three things: (1) His answer is an extremely convincing "Yes"; (2) 41 million views suggest that the topic hit an international nerve; (3) Most of those 41 million viewers are still stuck with exactly the same school system that Sir Ken condemns.

liant people think they're not, because they've been judged against this particular view of the mind. . . . [T]his model has caused chaos in many people's lives. It's been great for some; there have been people who have benefitted wonderfully from it. But most people have not. Instead, they suffer."

■ ■ ■

Early in 2016, Jeremy Ford exercised a combination of high-level cooking skill and cool-headedness to win *Top Chef*, Season 13. He came into the reality show competition as executive chef of the Matador Room in Miami, a position that requires immense management and organizational ability, not to mention high-level multitasking; he has since taken on the task of running a second Miami restaurant, Market at Edition. In a ridiculously competitive profession, Ford is rising rapidly toward the top.

This is brilliance.

Yet Ford learned, in school, that he was stupid. Twelve episodes into the *Top Chef* season, having excelled at challenges that sent other exceptional chefs home, Ford finds out that his daughter has gotten onto the honor roll at her elementary school. "She had to read 125 books," he explains to the *Top Chef* camera. "At eight years old, you know, that's really hard to do. But she nailed it."

Those 125 books seem to awe Ford: "Daddy never got honor roll," he tells his daughter. "You're smarter than Daddy." "Are you sure about that?" she replies (which just shows that she's still in elementary school; in about ten years, he's going to seriously regret saying that).

At the top of his field, successful and accomplished, Jeremy Ford still questions his intelligence, to the point of yielding his place to an eight-year-old. His years in school indoctrinated him with a damning message: *There is only one kind of smart, and you are not it.* And that message still echoes in his head.

Instead, Sir Ken says, *they suffer.*

■ ■ ■

In the 1960s, as a second-grader, my husband was diagnosed with petit mal epilepsy, put on drugs, and placed in a special education classroom with profoundly disabled students.

Pete is not, as it happens, epileptic. No abnormality in his brain waves was ever found. But he spent much of first grade staring out the window (probably with his mouth hanging open, if I'm correct in thinking that my sons take after their father), his mind so busy with dreams, plans, and wishes that his teacher couldn't keep his attention. The mismatch between his intelligence and the K–12 system was so vast that the school could find no way to teach him except to drug him.

The damning message he's carried with him for decades? *There is only one kind of smart, and your brain is too defective to achieve it.*

"We're getting our children through education by anaesthetising them," Sir Ken says, in his TED talk. He's talking about Adderall, but he could be looking at Pete's elementary grade report. "And I think we should be doing the exact opposite. We shouldn't be putting them asleep; we should be waking them up to what they have inside of themselves."

At fifty-five, my husband is an accomplished professional who's done well in his chosen field. But it took him forty years to recover from his K–12 education; forty years before he dared to apply to a doctoral program to complete his professional education; forty years of listening to the internal message of failure; forty years to wake up.

This model has caused chaos in many people's lives.

■ ■ ■

Some children suffer from actual brain dysfunctions that can be helped with medication; I am not questioning that reality. But there are *many* brain wirings that are not *mis*-wirings. They just don't fit well with the way classrooms work.

Those brains do not need to be treated as disabled. Those brains do not need to be drugged into compliance. Classrooms, not children, should change.

This is so basic that reformers have been pointing it out for decades. In 1964, John Holt described a research study that examined five highly successful schools. Two qualities stood out in all five. First, "if the students did not learn, the schools did not blame them, or their families, backgrounds, neighborhoods, attitudes, nervous systems, or whatever. . . . They took full responsibility for the results or non-results of their work." Second, if something in the classroom didn't work, "they stopped doing it, and tried to do something else. They flunked unsuccessful methods, not the children."[4]

Yet more than fifty years later, the vast majority of classrooms, even the well-intentioned ones, still resist change; even when parents come to them with actual diagnoses of learning differences.

By seventh grade, none of my son's schools had accommodated his documented vision and executive function issues. They told us since he was passing classes there was no problem. No, he could not have written notes of the class lectures, because that would be unfair to other students. No, they could not accommodate his documented dysgraphia. No, he could not hand in typed work as this would be unfair to students who could not afford a computer at home. —ROSIE

My daughter felt overwhelmed with all of the distractions and fast transitions in her classroom. I sat with my daughter in her math class and I was overwhelmed. The class has twenty-seven kids in it, walls filled with stimuli and words all over the room—up to the ceiling actually. My daughter was in the very back, next to a kid who constantly interrupted her. So many kids were off task. The teacher simply couldn't accommodate her need for quiet and concentration. —KATE

The system, even when excellent teachers are laboring within it, defies adaptation.

Of course, thousands of educators, policy-makers, and thinkers are at work on school reform. Scores of voices are calling for change, from relatively minor adjustments (No Child Left Behind) to major new curriculum goals (Common Core) to massive structural overhauls (Seth Godin, Ken Robinson, and many others).

But our school system is so huge that reform movements are equally huge, dispersed, and unfocused. (Did you know that there's actually a national initiative, sponsored by the Harvard Graduate School of Education, dedicated to studying "The Futures of School Reform"? Not actual reform itself, you understand, or the schools in which reform needs to happen, but the reform *movement* and where *it* might be going. At least two removes from getting anything done in *your* child's classroom.)

4 John Holt, *How Children Fail* (New York: Pitman, 1964), p. 4.

Conversations about school reform have to keep happening. But as of right now, only a few innovative schools seem able to move ahead with them. If your twelve-year-old, or nine-year-old, or even five-year-old is, right now, weeping in frustration over homework, or staring blankly into space, switched off, I can guarantee you that school reform isn't going to happen soon enough to make a difference to you and your child.

Instead, you're going to have to take control of the K–12 years yourself, and use your own ingenuity to bend the system to fit your child.

Many of the insights in this book are drawn from my experience with homeschooling. In the United States, thirty years of legalized home education have made scores of useful tools available to parents and students—tools that probably weren't accessible when you were in elementary school. And many parents with kids who are mis-wired for the classroom, or whose only school options are substandard or toxic, do eventually find themselves home educating; sometimes for a short time, sometimes longer, and often with a fair amount of surprise.

I sent my daughter to kindergarten. It was a full academic day with lots of deskwork, and she frequently lost the meager fifteen minutes of recess the kids got for "talking too much."

I sent her on to first grade, because that's what people do. It was more of the same—only this teacher also gave her a "demerit" for talking too much (she came home one day, sobbing, and said: "I got a demerit, Mommy. And I don't know what that is, but it's BAD!").

I sent her on to second grade, because that's what people do. Her teacher was very nice, and at seven she was more able to keep still and quiet than she had been at five. But they were ridiculously long days. She came home with an hour of homework at LEAST and had no time to just be a kid.

I sent her on to third grade, because that's what people do. Now came the standardized testing year, and that was ALL the school focused on. My daughter had nervous stomach aches nearly every single day because she thought she was going to "fail."

I finally just had enough. I read everything I could about homeschooling, then talked to the moms I knew who homeschooled . . . and finally, toward the end of third grade, in March of that year, I pulled her out of public school and never looked back. —NANCY

But homeschooling is not the only way to push back against the rigidity of the classroom.

You can also opt out of the "expert" plan by working with your child's teachers, suggesting alternative plans, taking on one or more subjects yourself—or adopting one of the many other strategies in this book.

CHAPTER TWO

The Three Biggest Myths About School

E veryone goes to school. (There are at least twenty children's books that explain this: Daniel Tiger goes to school. Spot goes to school. Dora goes to school. Even Elmo goes to school.)

First grade starts at six.

My child needs a high-school diploma.

A good school is accredited.

That seventh-grade C– in English matters.

These are myths.

Monolithic systems need myths: things that are accepted as deeply true and so remain unexamined. But a little closer examination shows that K–12 education is anything but monolithic. It's more like a Jenga tower: you can pull out and discard multiple pieces without anything particular happening to the entire structure.

Over the course of this book, we'll be discarding quite a few myths. (Age and grade actually have nothing to do with each other. Testing isn't mandatory. You can decline to do homework. No one really needs to go to Stanford.)

As preparation for all of this rethinking, let's take a minute to blow away three of the biggest assumptions that parents make.

My kids should attend an accredited school.

"Accreditation" simply means that an outside agency has certified that the school meets certain standards. These could range from a set percentage of teachers having completed master's degrees to a minimum number of books in the school library.

But the U.S. Department of Education doesn't recognize, on a national level, *any* K–12 accreditation. Accreditation of elementary and secondary schools is purely a state issue.

Public school districts are accredited when their state recognizes that they've met minimum standards.

Sometimes, this is done through a so-called Regional Accrediting Association. These associations (for example, the Middle States Association and the Southern Association) have been around for a long time, and accredit universities as well as high schools.

However, not all states use the associations. Some of them simply set their own standards (state Standards of Learning) or use Common Core standards, and then require public schools to report directly to the state Department of Education.

A public school that loses accreditation (as happened with our local public school some years ago, thanks to low test scores) may face state consequences, such as stricter state oversight and less local control. But while it's unaccredited, it goes right ahead giving diplomas and functioning in *exactly the same way that it did before.* Check your state's Department of Education website, and you'll find that in most cases students from unaccredited districts can transfer into other districts, receive diplomas, and qualify for scholarships, just as if they were in an accredited district.

Furthermore, no state *requires* private schools (or home educators) to be accredited, which means private and home schools do *not* have to meet state or Common Core standards of learning. (See Appendix B for a longer explanation.)

In fact, because getting accredited by one of these associations costs tens of thousands of dollars plus ongoing yearly fees (these include paying association representatives up to two thousand dollars per day for onsite visits), many private schools just don't bother.

Or they apply to one of dozens of private accrediting agencies, such as the National Association of Private Catholic and Independent

Schools (Standard One: "The school adheres to the tenets of the Catholic Faith in recognition of and obedience to the Pope and Magisterium"—Middle States definitely doesn't apply that particular standard). If you're a school, you can cherry-pick private agencies, choosing the one that best suits you.

Or, alternatively, like-minded schools can get together, create their own private accrediting associations, set their own standards, and award each other accreditation for what they're already doing.

The result: Saying that you're accredited doesn't mean a whole lot.

My child has to take English, math, science, and social studies every year.

Actually, it doesn't matter what specific classes your student takes before high school. (And there's a fair amount of flexibility in high school too; see Appendix A for more.)

Nor does it matter what the final grades are.

Or even if there *are* grades.

Transcripts and records from grades 1–8 are only useful for students and teachers within the secondary system, as a way of evaluating whether students are ready to move on to the next level. A private high school that admits students by application may also use these grades, but most rely on standardized test results (since an A from one school system can represent an entirely different level of achievement than an A from another).

And no college, or employer, will *ever* ask for K–8 grades—or care if your child's preparation is a little bit on the nontraditional side.

In pragmatic—and transcript—terms, the purpose of middle school is simply to prepare students for the more difficult work in high school. Particular states, or districts, or individual schools, may list a course as *required* for public middle-school students. (Texas calls for a one-semester health course; Florida mandates a one-semester class in civics; at the Bath-Haverling Middle School in New York, sixth grade students *have* to take either band or chorus.) But required courses are few and far between, and only apply to public school students. Even state and Common Core standards of learning don't mandate particular classes—they only define *skills* that students should master, not *courses* that need to be taken. (See Appendix B, Skills vs. Content.)

Elementary school is even simpler.

Elementary students need to know how to read, write, do arithmetic, and carry out basic critical thinking skills (knowing the difference between fiction and nonfiction, for example, or understanding that countries on a globe are far apart in real space).

There are no particular classes that elementary students have to take. That's it.

My high-school student needs to earn a diploma.

A diploma is supposed to certify that you've fulfilled standards set for graduation—but the United States has no national high-school graduation standards. Not only do graduation requirements vary from state to state,[1] but they shift from year to year in any given state. (You can find links to your current, and probably temporary, state requirements at our home page, welltrainedmind.com.)

College admissions officers look at transcripts and test scores. They don't give a flip whether a diploma has been issued. (And they also don't bother to hunt down whether or not the high school that issued that transcript is, or has ever been, accredited.)

The diploma is just shorthand for "The student completed required courses." Given that there's no agreement on what "required" means, the college wants to see the courses themselves, not the shorthand.

What's *really* important, at the end of high school, is having a clear transcript with a proper array of courses on it. Any unaccredited private school can do this. Any *parent* can do this (I wrote out transcripts for all of my kids, which is how they got into college. See Appendix A, High School and the Transcript, for all the technical details.)

So when do you need a diploma?

Hardly ever. I have a bachelor's degree, two master's, and a Ph.D., but I don't actually have a high-school diploma at all. Since I was homeschooled, I used my mom-generated transcript to get into college. No one's ever asked me for my diploma.

---

1 Just a few random examples: As of 2016, Virginia requires three years of lab science, but Washington requires two years of science, of which only one needs to be a lab. Wisconsin only requires two years of math (and doesn't specify what they are, as long as there is *some* instruction in algebra and geometry); South Carolina requires a full four years. Oklahoma has no P.E. or health requirement, Louisiana has no arts requirement, Delaware awards high school credit for community volunteer work, Mississippi categorizes computer technology under the arts (?), and as of this writing *no* state requires a foreign language for graduation—which is ridiculous.

My older brother had to present one at some point, though; it was for some sort of society (I can't remember which one now) that he joined after high school but before he had a college degree. They insisted on seeing a piece of paper that looked like a diploma. My mother went to Staples, bought a diploma form, filled it out, and signed it.

He got into the society.

PART II

Mismatches

CHAPTER THREE

You Can't Make the Earth Go Around the Sun Faster

Your first task in making school fit your child, rather than the other way around: Identify possible mismatches.

We'll start with a relatively straightforward one:

If your child is struggling, there may simply be an incompatibility between the child's maturity level, and the grade/year of school in which they're placed.

Even the most rudimentary observations of the natural world reveal that biological organisms mature at widely varying rates. On my Virginia farm, I raise livestock; lambs and kids born on the same date rarely clock in at the same size, wean themselves, or eat the same amount of hay and grain on any given day. Daffodils bloom, baby birds fly, and puppies stop chewing on chair rungs when they're ready—not when the calendar dictates.

But we generally don't extend this same consideration to our children.

We've been so conditioned to accept the pattern of *infancy, toddler, preschool, elementary, middle, high school, college* that it's almost impossible for us to break out of it and think: *What makes me think that this tiny human being should mature on the exact same schedule as the rest of the tiny human beings born at the same time?*

Why do four- and five-year-olds go to kindergarten?

Why should all seven-year-olds be able to do second-grade work?

Why should all fourteen-year-olds do high-school work?

As a home educator myself, I never paid much attention to my children's grade level before the high-school years—but I learned early on that I had to teach my children what grade they were in, just so that we didn't look like idiots at the pediatrician's office or grocery store. ("What grade are you in?" I'd say, before we saw the nurse. "Um . . ." the kid would say, uncertainly. "Third grade! You're in third grade! Say third grade!")

The age-grading system that shoves six-year-olds into first grade, seven-year-olds into second, and so on is so normal, to most people, that "How old are you?" and "What grade are you in?" seem to be the same question.

But this system isn't remotely natural. It's not even based on sound educational principles.

WHY AGE = GRADE
(It's Prussia's Fault)

Before about 1850, teachers in American schools taught mixed-age groups together, in one room, with no standard curriculum. Students just moved to more difficult material when they were ready, at widely varying times. (The medieval predecessor of the American one-room schoolhouse, the European cathedral school, might have had students from age eight up to twenty-one or twenty-two, all chanting the same lessons until they were learned.)

But over in Prussia, a new system had been instituted in the early 1800s: smaller classrooms where students were grouped by age and led by a single teacher.

This strategy wasn't driven by educational research; it was an attempt to try to restore Prussian military might, after a humiliating defeat by Napoleon.[1] Struggling to rebuild, Prussian statesmen decided to organize schools like military units, in order to instill the will to fight and build pride in Prussia's historically pugnacious national culture. Students were organized into platoons by age and assigned to a

---

1 At the battles of Jena and Auerstadt, in 1806, France destroyed the Prussian army and claimed half of Prussia's territory.

single "squadron leader," a system that made the transition into military service quite straightforward.[2]

In 1843, Horace Mann, Secretary of Education for the state of Massachusetts, visited Prussia to tour its schools.

At the time, no American state had anything like a unified education system—but all the states were dealing with a huge swell in immigration, and the need to somehow assimilate these thousands of newcomers. Mann had long hoped to see a "common school" introduced into America, a school that all students, native-born and immigrant, would attend together. This school, accessible to all, would help give Americans a common language and purpose: "Education," he wrote, in one of his annual reports, "beyond all other devices of human origin, is a great equalizer of the conditions of men."

But drawing the masses of the foreign, and native uneducated, into America's current multi-age classrooms was a daunting task. Multi-age classrooms required huge resources, and scores of talented, energetic, and flexible teachers.

The Prussian system (complete with compulsory attendance, not at that time an American practice) struck Mann as the perfect answer: the very best way to channel a large number of diverse students into a single institution with maximum efficiency. With minimal training and a set curriculum, one teacher could corral and indoctrinate dozens of students at a time, as long as they were of roughly the same age and ability.[3]

With Mann's support, the Prussian system was introduced to Massachusetts in 1847, when the Quincy Grammar School was built with twelve separate classrooms, each room for a single, age-graded class, led by a single teacher.

The new plan did indeed turn out to be highly efficient (factories generally are), and age-graded schools were soon spreading—into the rest of New England's urban centers, westward to other cities, and then out into rural areas as well. By the turn of the century, age-grading was

2 Randall Collins, "Comparative and Historical Patterns of Education," in *Handbook of the Sociology of Education*, ed. Maureen T. Hallinan (New York: Springer, 2006), p. 213; Thomas C. Hunt, *Encyclopedia of Educational Reform and Dissent*, Vol. 1 (Thousand Oaks, CA: SAGE, 2010), pp. 33–34.
3 Sonia Nieto, *Language, Culture, and Teaching: Critical Perspectives* (New York: Routledge, 2009), p. 89.

the norm in almost all of the nation's "common schools." (Compulsory attendance laws, also modeled after the Prussian system, followed shortly after; Massachusetts again led the way, passing the first regulations in 1852.)[4]

So our strong identification of age with grade is the result of (in the words of Rick Hess) "our peculiar devotion to a model that defeated Prussian leaders developed in order to salvage the last vestiges of their shattered national pride."

Yet it continues to govern our ideas about when children learn; six-year-olds should be capable of first grade work, fourteen-year-olds of high-school work, regardless of individual maturity.[5]

Here's your first task: Try to put aside your Prussianized assumptions about grade level, and ask yourself, "Does my child belong in another grade?"

THREE QUESTIONS FOR EVALUATING MATURITY

When confronted with schoolwork, does your child shut down, show anger, cry?

The prime symptom of immaturity—working at a grade level too high for physical maturity—is nonverbal frustration. Children confronted with work that is too advanced for them are usually incapable of saying, "I'm sorry, but this is developmentally inappropriate and my mind isn't yet able to grasp it."

In fact, a child who says, "This is too hard!" is probably actually working at close to grade level, because she's able to understand the task well enough to know that it's difficult. The child who just bursts into tears isn't ready to do the work in front of her. She can't yet comprehend *how* to do it, or even find a way into it.

So consider that a child who weeps, or resists but won't say why, or

---

4 Calvin Ellis Stowe, *The Prussian System of Public Instruction: And Its Applicability to the United States* (Cincinnati: Truman and Smith, 1836), pp. 22, 71; Frederick Dean McClusky, "Introduction of Grading into the Public Schools of New England," in *The Elementary School Journal* 21, Sept. 1920–June 1921 (Chicago: University of Chicago Press), pp. 144–45.

5 Frederick M. Hess, *The Same Thing Over and Over: How School Reformers Get Stuck in Yesterday's Ideas* (Boston: Harvard University Press, 2010), p. 83.

slouches and refuses to make eye contact, or displays anger (balling up paper and throwing it, breaking pencil points) is signaling that something is wrong—but is too immature to articulate what it is.

A child who is working right at the top level of his maturity can also be derailed by physical factors—allergies or a bad case of flu or suddenly expending a lot of physical energy in a new sport. (Or puberty.) What was once difficult suddenly becomes impossible. If a child suddenly begins to show frustration with work that had previously been doable, consider that he might be bumping up against a maturity ceiling.

When learning stalls, particularly if it's across the board, always consider evaluation by a learning specialist (see the next chapter). But in many cases, a child who's struggling simply needs the earth to circle the sun one more time.

Does your child struggle in some areas and sail through in others?

You could still be dealing with a maturity mismatch. Abilities don't develop evenly in children, any more than their bodies grow at an even rate. In our highly structured school system, students are expected to be at grade level in math, science, reading, and writing. But these subjects require very different thinking skills, and it is far more common for students to be working at two or more grade levels across the curriculum.

That's called asynchronous development, and it is the norm, not the exception. It is *normal* for a fifth-grade aged student to be writing at a third-grade level, reading at a fifth-grade level, and doing math at a seventh-grade level. A child who succeeds at two subjects and cries over the third may still be showing immaturity—and the answer may be to drop back to a lower level in *only* the third subject.

On the most basic level, most students find either language-based (reading- and writing-based subjects) or symbolic (math and related subjects) learning to be more natural, and will progress more rapidly in their preferred subject type. Don't use either the "slower" or "faster" subject as a way to locate the child within an entire grade.

I've often spoken to parents who are frustrated (for example) because their fourth-grade aged child is reading at a high level, but is struggling with second- or third-grade math skills. The tendency is to focus on the child's *slower* areas, to spend more time on those in order to move the child into a higher grade. But the result can be that the child ends up evaluating himself by his *weaknesses,* not his strengths. And this can obscure natural gifts, requiring children to spend untold hours laboring away at subjects they dislike, at the expense of learning in which they excel.

A century ago, Montessori educator Dorothy Canfield Fisher wrote a popular children's novel called *Understood Betsy* in which nine-year-old Elizabeth Ann leaves the big city and her urban school, where age-grading has been thoroughly instituted: "In the big brick schoolhouse," Canfield Fisher writes, "nobody *ever* went into another grade except at the beginning of a new year, after you'd passed a lot of examinations. She had not known that anybody could do anything else."

Instead, she goes to live with country cousins and attends their tiny rural school, still one room and multi-age, led by one teacher who praises her reading skills, but realizes that she needs work in math:

After the lesson the teacher said, smiling, "Well, Betsy, you were right about arithmetic. I guess you'd better recite with Eliza for a while. She's doing second-grade work. I shouldn't be surprised if, after a good review with her, you'd be able to go on with the third-grade work."

Elizabeth Ann fell back on the bench with her mouth open. She felt really dizzy. What crazy things the teacher said! She felt as though she was being pulled limb from limb.

"What's the matter?" asked the teacher, seeing her bewildered face.

"Why—why," said Elizabeth Ann, "I don't know what I am at all. If I'm second-grade arithmetic and seventh-grade reading and third-grade spelling, what grade AM I?"

The teacher laughed at the turn of her phrase. "YOU aren't any grade at all, no matter where you are in school. You're just yourself, aren't you? What difference does it make what grade you're in! And what's the use of your reading little baby things too easy for you just because you don't know your multiplication table?"

"Well, for goodness' sakes!" ejaculated Elizabeth Ann, feeling very much as though somebody had stood her suddenly on her head.

"Why, what's the matter?" asked the teacher again.

> This time Elizabeth Ann didn't answer, because she herself didn't know what the matter was. But I do, and I'll tell you. The matter was that never before had she known what she was doing in school. She had always thought she was there to pass from one grade to another, and she was ever so startled to get a glimpse of the fact that she was there to learn how to read and write and cipher and generally use her mind. . . . [I]t made her feel the way you do when you're learning to skate and somebody pulls away the chair you've been leaning on and says, "Now, go it alone!"[6]

Grasping this thoroughly yourself, and then *articulating* this reality to the child—giving her a sense of normalcy over the variety in her abilities—can begin to defuse frustration.

Is your child small or large for his or her age?

Age-grading is based on a mean—and if you're not a math person, "mean" is simply one way to express "average." In math, you find the mean by adding a list of numbers together and dividing them by the number of numbers. Here's what's important about that: Often, the mean is a number that didn't even appear on the original list.

> 13, 17, 28, 52, 71
> Added together: 181
> Divided by 5: 36.2 (the mean)

The "average" fourth grader is 4' 3¾" tall and weighs 70.5 pounds. In any given fourth-grade class, there may be *no* students who are actually this height and weight, plus ten-year-olds who weigh anything from 40 to 90 pounds and range between four and five feet in height.

Physical development affects learning. Children who are on either end of this completely normal range often struggle with "grade-level" work. Very small children need time to catch up; children who are on the larger side often need the same amount of time to figure out how to manage their bodies; they can be like large uncoordinated puppies, growing toward an imposing presence but with no idea how to man-

6 Dorothy Canfield Fisher, *Understood Betsy* (New York: The Century Co., 1916), pp. 104–6.

age their limbs. When you're trying not to trip, struggling to keep your pants up and zipped, and having a hard time fitting into your desk, your attention isn't going to be on your essay assignment.

If your child is on the low or high side of the average for his or her age-grade, consider that you may have a serious maturity mismatch.

ACTION PLAN

Forget about a single age-grade calculation, and take some time to think carefully about your child's maturity levels.

For the following activities and categories, check "immature," "average maturity," or "unusually mature." Don't stop to overanalyze or explain; just follow your gut instincts. It's also worth polling adult family members (grandparents, aunts and uncles) and others (regular caregivers, tutors, teachers), keeping in mind that each grown-up in the child's life sees a different aspect of it.

Do you see any patterns?

"Giftedness" and "learning disabilities" (which we'll discuss in the next two chapters) often shade into issues of maturity and immaturity, so hold this action plan lightly; you'll probably find yourself rethinking as you continue reading. The goal here is simply to shake you out of considering your child as an *X*-grader.

	Immature	Average maturity	Unusually mature
Personal cleanliness/ hygiene	____	____	____
Keeping possessions and room tidy	____	____	____
Team sports ability	____	____	____
Physical coordination in games and individual sports	____	____	____
Ability to read social cues of adults	____	____	____

	Immature	Average maturity	Unusually mature
Peer-to-peer socialization skills	_____	_____	_____
Reading ability	_____	_____	_____
Writing ability	_____	_____	_____
Arithmetical/mathematical ability	_____	_____	_____
Ability to use technology	_____	_____	_____
Hand-eye and fine motor coordination (using scissors, stringing beads, etc.)	_____	_____	_____
Ability to deal with disappointment	_____	_____	_____
Reaction to stressful situations	_____	_____	_____
Coping with change	_____	_____	_____
Independence	_____	_____	_____
Sibling relationships	_____	_____	_____
Eating habits (willingness to try new foods, eat vegetables)	_____	_____	_____

Consider your options for single-subject acceleration or deceleration.

I discuss this option, in detail, in Chapter 10, but here's the basic principle for you to keep in mind: When you're dealing with a younger student, *be very careful about accelerating across the board.*

It's very tempting to jump a bored kid ahead by one or two grade levels as a quick fix, but consider this: The biggest maturity leaps tend to happen between six and ten, and again between thirteen and sixteen. If you leap your second grader ahead into third grade because she's more mature than the other second-graders, there's a very real possibility she'll find herself, at thirteen, in a group of more-mature students and struggling.

> *I made a huge mistake by starting my daughter early. She is an October birthday, and was after the cut off, so she started kindergarten at four, not five. She was a super-early talker, and also talked a blue streak. Was big for her age too. We had her in full day pre-K at the same private school and no one saw any red flags, so we just popped her into kindergarten. But when we transferred her to the public school, the testing culture got to her. She wasn't mature enough emotionally to handle the pressure, and I had no idea the impact that type of system was having on her until too late.* —MOLLY

It's the nature of our school system that it is much easier (and less emotionally fraught for the student) to move ahead than to drop back. Dropping back is traumatic, even when it's necessary. So think very hard about the wisdom of starting a child early or accelerating them before they reach puberty, realizing that this may put you in the position of forcing a child to drop back later on—an action that too often conveys a message of failure.

Also consider the nonacademic results of accelerating: A student who reaches high school early will not be old enough to drive (when all of his friends are), or take part in other age-graded activities.

> *My oldest son's birthday is so near the cutoff that I allowed him to start a little early. While not a problem academically, it's turned out to be a problem with age cut-offs for programs. He wanted to apply to a foreign language program, but participants must be fifteen by June 1, and he won't be. He wanted to go to an anthropology camp for grades 9–12— same deal, he couldn't go because he wouldn't be fifteen by the deadline. He can't get a permit yet, so he can't take driver's ed with his buddies this summer.* —STEPHEN

You may also end up with a sixteen- or seventeen-year-old college freshman. Some students are mature enough to benefit from college at those ages, but fifteen years of university teaching has convinced me that most are not. You need to be not just intellectually, but *emotionally* mature to benefit from college—and emotional maturity can't be rushed; it happens when the earth has gone around the sun the appropriate number of times.

I was a sixteen-year-old college freshman. I was perfectly capable of doing the academic work, but I didn't know enough to relax, slow down, explore. I barreled through classes, taking twenty and twenty-two credits every semester, and graduated at nineteen. When I did my first master's degree, I was so young that I couldn't attend social gatherings where there was alcohol. I still didn't have the maturity to benefit from the intellectual puzzles being raised and grappled with. The most valuable degree I completed was my second master's—which I took at the age of twenty-four, the appropriate age for doing a graduate degree. And I didn't return to do my Ph.D. until I was in my thirties.

All that rushing did no good. It didn't put me "ahead." If I could do it again, I'd travel, work, read, and figure out how to be an adult, rather than charging headfirst into early academics.

Consider your options for "gapping" your child.

A gap year is a widely accepted post-high-school option, more common in Europe than in North America but gaining traction here as well: students take a year to work, travel, pursue interests, and generally get a better sense of who they are before beginning college.

As a university instructor, I've found freshmen who took gap years to be light-years ahead of their classmates in their ability to profit from their classes. Of my three children who've gone through college thus far, one took a gap year, working for six months and then traveling to do nonprofit work in Africa (primate rescue) and India (a refugee camp in the Narmada desert). It was a life-changing experience.

One resisted the idea to the point that I gave in, against my better judgment. After a disastrous freshman year, he dropped out before returning the following year—and ending up exactly where he would have been if he'd taken the gap year. Except that we were down a full year's tuition.

One didn't take a gap year because he was already almost a year older than his classmates. He had a late October birthday, so I'd started him in first grade the year he turned seven, not six—which just illustrates that the "gap year" principle can be applied well before twelfth grade.

The simplest "gap" option comes at the very beginning of the child's academic career: If your kindergarten or first-grade-aged student is right on the edge of being old enough for his or her grade (I'd classify this as a birthday in late August or after), simply wait to start. There are plenty of ways to challenge a child intellectually (use some of the methods and insights from Part V) without formally enrolling in a grade. Remember: It's always easier to move forward than to move back, and if it becomes clear later on that the student belongs with older peers, you can simply jump her forward.

Educator and entrepreneur Kenneth Danford has suggested that an "Eighth Grade Out!" year would be even more useful: "While some teens do thrive in a junior high or middle-school setting," he writes, "in general we expect these years to be the nadir of productive learning in school." Danford proposes that, during the eighth-grade year, students register as homeschoolers, and then spend the year investigating both their own interests and brand-new fields of study and experience that they haven't yet considered:

> A year's program might begin with some of the academic courses and local programs already structured for teen homeschoolers, including events such as literature groups, theater projects, and outdoor education. A full year's routine might include a foreign language intensive, involvement with a local nonprofit organization or museum, and other kinds of entrepreneurial work or family involvement.[7]

As Danford points out, since this—like any homeschooling effort—requires a massive adjustment of everyone's schedules, it isn't an option for everyone. (Although it may be simpler than you think; see Part IV.)

But the principle here is worth considering: It's much better, both for the child's self-esteem *and* overall development, if you can allow them to step completely out of the system for one year and do something else, and then guide them back into it with an additional year of maturity.

A gap year is not the same as being "held back"; it is a positive step forward.

7 Kenneth Danford, "Eighth Grade Out!," Huffington Post, http://www .huffingtonpost.com/kenneth-danford/eighth-grade-out_b_1501461.html (accessed November 15, 2016).

CHAPTER FOUR

Differences, Disabilities, and Disorders

Although it's not easy to step out of our Prussianized age-grading system, a maturity mismatch is a relatively simple problem: a child who's out of step with her grade will, eventually, grow up.

What's much more complicated is a systematic mismatch between your child and the learning situation she's in.

Most K–12 classrooms cater to one type of learner (linear, a natural processor of symbols), prioritize one type of knowledge (propositional—see Chapter 14 for a more detailed explanation), and favor one kind of personality (compliant, organized, in control of his/her physical impulses, that is, able to sit quietly).

This can create havoc for the child who doesn't fit the paradigm.

In the early seventies, it was estimated that 3 to 10 per cent of the school population had learning disabilities; and now responsible spokesmen are saying that up to 40 per cent of our youngsters are so afflicted. (1975)

One parent, discussing her daughter's difficulties in learning to read, mentioned to another parent that the child was suspected by school personnel of having learning disabilities. "My son's teacher thinks that he has learning disabilities, too," confided the second parent. "Both of my children have already been diagnosed as learning-disabled," interjected a third parent, who was nearby. . . . [C]hildren with learning disabilities [now] form the single largest category of students receiving special education services. (1998)

There were 783,000 children identified with LD in 1976, but by 1992–1993 the LD population totaled approximately 2.3 million. . . . In addition, approximately another 120,000 students each year are identified as LD, a number equal to all Americans who have contracted AIDS, hepatitis, and tuberculosis in 1995. (2000)

Attention Deficit Disorder increases as you travel east across the country. People start losing interest in Oklahoma, they can hardly think straight in Arkansas. And by the time they get to Washington they've lost it completely. (2008)[1]

More children than ever before are being diagnosed with disabilities that affect their learning. I don't wish to come across as a disability denier; processing problems absolutely exist, and affect the ability to learn.

But I also think that these mismatches have always existed and that, in the past, human beings whose brains worked in different ways were much more likely to simply find another way to work, learn, and be.

What has changed is our K–12 system. Over the last century, schools became age-graded, and so offered fewer possible tracks for students to fit into; shortly afterward, schooling became mandatory, thus sweeping an enormous number of new pupils into those rigid tracks. And just three decades or so later, the entire system exploded; baby boomers began to enter kindergarten around 1952, swelling the ranks of schoolchildren in a rising tide that lasted at least twenty years.

1 Sources for these four quotes, in order: Diane Divoky, "Learning-Disability 'Epidemic,'" *The New York Times* (January 15, 1975), p. 61; Louise Spear-Swerling and Robert J. Sternberg, "Curing Our 'Epidemic' of Learning Disabilities," *The Phi Delta Kappan* 79:5 (January 1998), p. 397; H. Lee Swanson, "Issues Facing the Field of Learning Disabilities," *Learning Disability Quarterly* 23:1 (Winter 2000), p. 37; Sir Ken Robinson, "Do Schools Kill Creativity?" TED talk, 2008.

And at the same time, schools lost funding, and struggled to educate more and more children with fewer and fewer resources.

It's no wonder that an entire new enterprise grew up alongside our K–12 system: a system for classifying and coping with the increasing number of youngsters who didn't flourish in the classroom.

In 1963, the psychologist and reading specialist Samuel Kirk used the term "learning disability" to describe students who could *not* be clinically diagnosed with an organic dysfunction or injury, but who nevertheless were simply not performing at the expected academic level. In coining this term, he gave us a way to classify learning differences that enabled us to *stop* thinking about how the system might need to change—and encouraged us to focus on the student, not *school,* as the problem.

The historical development of "learning disabled" as a category (encompassing an enormous range of mismatches between child and school) is a vast topic, far beyond my scope here; in Appendix C, I've suggested some titles for those who want to read up on this. But here's the most important fact to keep in mind: Over the last half-century, Samuel Kirk's definition has been tinkered with, but not substantially changed.

According to the definition provided by the U.S. Office of Special Education Programs, a "specific learning disability" is a disorder

> of learning and cognition that [is] intrinsic to the individual. SLD are specific in the sense that these disorders each significantly affect a relatively narrow range of academic and performance outcomes. SLD may occur in combination with other disabling conditions, but they are not due primarily to other conditions, such as mental retardation, behavioral disturbance, lack of opportunities to learn, or primary sensory deficits.[2]

Here's the plain English translation of this pronouncement:

> Children have a learning disability when they can't perform well in school, and their failure to perform can't be chalked up to an

2 Tonette S. Rocco, ed., *Challenging Ableism, Understanding Disability* (San Francisco: Jossey-Bass, 2012), p. 75.

identifiable, diagnosable physical problem, emotional condition, or social disadvantage.

Again, I'm not denying that learning disabilities are real phenomena. But I'm fairly sure that most parents don't realize that "learning disability" is a label that essentially concludes: *We cannot find any other reason why this child is struggling.*

Thanks in large part to Samuel Kirk, our national response to an underperforming or failing student isn't to question or rework the *system*. It's to slap a label on the *child*.

THE THREE LABELS

Let's think our way through three different labels that might be applied to a child who's not flourishing in his current academic situation: *Disorder, disability, difference.*

These are listed, not in order of severity (a mild disorder can be much less disruptive than a major difference), but from the most concrete to the hardest to pin down. A seizure recorded on an EEG or caused by a brain lesion visible on an MRI is a *disorder* that calls for an established medical treatment. A strong preference for aural over written information is a *difference*. It's real. It complicates learning, since in most classrooms, 80 percent of learning is based on written material. It's also impossible to capture on a brain scan, difficult to clearly quantify, and it resists straightforward solutions.

In this chapter, I'm going to use *disorder* to describe permanently damaged mind-body relationships that afflict people in every sphere of their existence; *disability* for mind-body relationships that *primarily* affect academic learning, although they may also affect social relationships and employability; and *difference* to refer to processing styles that wouldn't matter in the slightest if the child weren't stuck in our current K–12 system.

The borders between the three are vague and inconsistent, because people are organisms, not mathematical equations; our weaknesses always involve both mind and body, and the labels we put on them shade imperceptibly into each other. As a result, the massive literature on learning problems is an enormous thicket of overlapping definitions and classifications, some of which have been coined, used, discarded, and resurrected. To make things even more confusing, medical and educational workers rarely use the words "disorder" and "disability" in any consistent way.

So consider the following to be a starting place: a way to *begin* thinking about the problems your child might be experiencing in school. (See welltrainedmind.com for many additional links and resources.)

Disorders

A *disorder* (definition: malady, dysfunction) can be medically diagnosed. Vision problems, seizure disorders, cerebral palsy (which can be mild enough to escape diagnosis in a baby, but cause difficulty as the child grows), and hearing loss are disorders. Disorders can be measured on a scale that has nothing to do with academic experience, but they also affect learning—often severely.

While I obviously can't provide a full checklist of possible disorders, here are five of the most common general categories that are often overlooked or mistaken for learning disabilities.

Allergies are probably the most common disorder (often undiagnosed) that children suffer from. An allergy is an immune-system reaction to something that isn't actually a germ—something breathed, eaten, or touching the skin. Many allergies can be diagnosed by skin prick or intradermal skin tests, but food allergies are usually better diagnosed through an elimination diet.

Undiagnosed allergies can mimic learning disabilities (particularly ADHD, attention-deficit/hyperactivity disorder). An allergy can cause headaches, fatigue and inertia, upset stomachs, mood changes, difficulty hearing (thanks to clogged ears), and more. Children with allergies are often unaware that the way they're feeling *isn't* normal, but when they're asked to concentrate, they simply can't—their bodies are preoccupying them.

Vision function problems are potentially a huge block to learning. Most children get standard vision screening at their pediatrician checkups, but more subtle problems are often missed. Farsightedness, eye-teaming problems (both eyes cannot stay focused on the same point), and poor tracking (inability to keep eyes focused on a single line of print) are generally missed in standard vision tests, because most children can focus properly for short periods of time; when their eyes grow tired, though, vision acuity decreases.

A child with a vision function problem can pass a traditional eye test at the optometrist with flying colors, but still struggle to see text properly. The difficulty can show up as short attention span, daydreaming, or lack of interest—and is often misdiagnosed as a learning disability. Screening by a visual specialist who is a member of the College of Optometrists in Vision Development (www.covd.org) should always come before a child is labeled as dyslexic, dysgraphic, or having ADHD.

> It was our child's grandmother who insisted our daughter was far-sighted (like Grandma) despite our child passing school vision screenings. When we asked, our pediatrician recommended an actual child's eye specialist to get the most accurate idea about our daughter's acuity of vision, and the specialist not only confirmed the farsightedness but also spotted indicators of vision function problems. Before they informed me of this and requested we do further screening I had never even heard of vision function problems.
>
> Farsighted people, including kids, can actually force their eyes to focus on near objects for a short period of time (long enough to pass a typical vision screening). They cannot sustain such focus, though, and testing for farsightedness must test for sustained near-object focus in order to truly rule out this acuity issue. The usual vision screenings at an optometrist's office don't include this, and neither do the screenings done with kids at schools.
>
> The real kicker is the fact that our child's farsightedness cleared up as her vision therapy progressed. She now has vision near 20/20, and has had since the first several weeks of vision therapy (which was eight years ago). The vision function therapy took thirty-two weeks, less than a school year, and permanently fixed those vision function problems. This was life-altering both at school and at home. My child, who thought she was stupid and uncoordinated and hated school, started believing herself smart and able and loving school, simply because her vision was finally working properly.   —M.J.

Hearing loss can be equally subtle—and devastating. Although hospitals regularly test the hearing of newborns, mild loss, or loss in only one ear, is easily missed. And even if a newborn hears perfectly, loss can develop later in childhood.

A child with hearing loss may be slow to speak. But he may also appear to be functioning perfectly well at home and only have difficulty hearing when he's surrounded by the background chatter of a classroom. Because he can't hear the teacher well over other sounds, he may appear inattentive or disruptive. As pediatric ear, nose, and throat specialist Judith E. C. Lieu told *The New York Times*, "Hearing loss has often been thought of as the silent disability. It may look like not paying attention; they talk while the teacher is talking."[3]

Testing by an audiologist (this may also involve an MRI) can pick up this physical problem, which is often missed in standard checkups.

Mild cerebral palsy and seizure disorders can appear separately or together. Minor seizures can simply look like inattentiveness. Mild cerebral palsy can be mistaken for general development delay (slow walking, slow talking), dysgraphia (great difficulty with physical writing), dysphasia (difficulty talking and understanding spoken language), and a host of other learning disabilities. But brain imaging tests (CT scan, MRI, EEG, cranial ultrasound) can reveal damage or abnormalities in the brain itself.

> *We were told for years about our little boy: Don't worry. He will learn when he needs it. He is a late bloomer. It will kick in when he is ready.*
> *We heard this from our pediatricians.*
> *We heard this from friends, community, family.*
> *When our son was ten years of age, I finally told our pediatrician that enough was enough, I was demanding referrals for evaluations. We ended up getting a late diagnosis of mild cerebral palsy.*
> *Many of the related medical issues had been diagnosed and treated over the years, with doctors ignoring the elephant in the middle of the*

3 Perri Klass, M.D., "What to Do When a Newborn Can't Hear," *The New York Times* (May 10, 2010), p. D6, http://www.nytimes.com/2010/05/11/health/11klass.html (accessed November 22, 2016).

room. My son was just smart enough to keep the doctors from wor-
rying about his delays, his "wiggles," his inability to hold a pencil and
write. We lost precious years of treatment and therapy because of the
"wait and they will outgrow it" attitude.   —GREG

If you suspect a learning disability (or have been told that your child has one), I strongly urge you to rule out these disorders—even if it takes time and a lot of harassing of doctors for referrals to the correct specialists—before you accept the label. Remember: Learning disability is code for "Something's not working correctly but we can't find a physical cause." Do your very best to be sure that there *is* no physical cause—because if there is, treating it can absolutely transform the student's learning.

Disabilities and differences

And what if there is, apparently, no physical disorder?

In that case, a struggling student might indeed have a *learning disability*.

Or, the student might have a learning difference: a preferred way of collecting and processing information that doesn't line up with his or her learning environment.

The border between the two remains frustratingly elusive. Even learning disability specialists recognize that the absence of a physical cause makes diagnosing a learning disability a very inexact science. Three experts speak (italics are mine):

A . . . popularized belief about children who find learning to read difficult is that these children suffer a disability. Usually this disability is characterized in terms of neurological damage or difference that makes perceptual or verbal learning exceedingly difficult, if not impossible. *But evidence of a neurological basis for reading difficulties has been difficult to find.* If children with such conditions exist, they exist in incredibly small numbers—far too few to account for the range of difficulties now observed.

[T]here is consensus among contemporary researchers and practitioners that LDs are brain-based and heritable. However, *measuring brain dysfunction and heritability have proven elusive.*

Like the rest of us, children with learning disabilities are influenced by their biology. The point is that, in most cases of school identified learning disabilities, there is little evidence that these biological influences constitute actual abnormalities or defects; rather, they probably *fall along a continuum with the biological influences experienced by everyone.*[4]

In children who haven't been diagnosed with a disorder, such as cerebral palsy, a *learning disability* is rarely related to a clear physical abnormality. Which does *not* mean that learning disabilities are imaginary. Major depression, early Alzheimer's, and severe autism also can't be viewed on an MRI or diagnosed with a blood test. Yet they are clearly diseases, altering lives and requiring serious intervention.

But this is where we get to the question of a *continuum.*

It's a truism that many successful people have been diagnosed with (or seem to have suffered from) learning disabilities. Thomas Edison didn't speak until he was four and got pitched out of his classroom at the age of seven for persistently interrupting his teacher with unrelated questions (the teacher, in a note home, suggested that Edison's inability to pay attention, paired with his oddly shaped forehead, meant that his brains were "addled"). Albert Einstein seems to have been on the autistic spectrum—although he also suffered from early hearing loss that grew more severe as he aged, adding to his communication troubles. Steven Spielberg is dyslexic, Daniel Radcliffe has both dyslexia and dyspraxia (difficulty with motor coordination). Michael Phelps was diagnosed with ADHD in fifth grade.

But Edison's slow speech and apparent distractibility were signs not only of hearing troubles, but also of an original thinker: so consumed with his own internal thought processes (which eventually led to his claiming an unbelievable 2,332 patents on inventions) that he had no patience with external demands on his attention.

Einstein's social isolation and "perseveration" (an obsessive focus on a single thing or idea, usually considered a symptom of psychiatric ill-

4 Sources for these three quotes, in order: Bob Sornson, ed., *Preventing Early Learning Failure* (Association for Supervision and Curriculum Development, 2001), p. 7; Bernice Wong and Deborah L. Butler, *Learning About Learning Disabilities* (San Diego: Academic Press, 2012), p. 2; Spear-Swerling and Sternberg, "Curing Our 'Epidemic' of Learning Disabilities," p. 339.

ness) were central to his creative process. (Later in life, he also claimed his hearing loss as an advantage, pointing out that it insulated him from idle social chatter and the general noise of civilization.)[5]

Spielberg's struggle with written language is the flip side of a highly visual, image-rich thinking style.

Radcliffe auditioned for his first acting job at age nine because his mother thought he needed a boost in self-confidence, given that his handwriting was horrendous, he couldn't tie his shoes, and his classroom performance was way below par; none of these things mattered in the theater.

Michael Phelps was medicated with Ritalin because he couldn't sit still. Of course he couldn't. He is naturally designed to move, constantly, very fast.

I was home educated from first grade on, but if I'd been in a classroom I would very likely have been diagnosed with a disability. I was physically clumsy (I still crash into furniture), had an unusually low pain threshold, couldn't stand to wear a belt or anything tight. My clothes were always scratchy and I had to cut the tags out (I still do). I couldn't wear socks because the seam across the toe drove me crazy. I couldn't work if there was much background noise and hated being in a crowd. I pursued one activity or subject obsessively, and resisted being moved to the next. These are all symptoms of sensory processing disorder, or SPD. (A 2009 study in the *Journal of Abnormal Child Psychology* suggested that up to 16.5 percent of elementary school children could be diagnosed as suffering from SPD, which can "impede . . . academic skills" in a school setting, especially as "learning demands increase.")[6]

Yet I've been an academic all my life. My mother let me work in sweats and PJs, and fitted up an outbuilding on our farm as a study space so I could work entirely alone. She allowed me to spend as long as I wanted to on a subject before moving on to the next. (Sometimes this was weeks.) My oversensitivity to physical stimuli is the flip side of an unusually fast processing speed; solitude is essential to a writer (we

5 Harry G. Lang and Bonnie Meath-Lang, *Deaf Persons in the Arts and Sciences: A Biographical Dictionary* (Westport, CT: Greenwood Press, 1995), p. 109.

6 A. Ben-Sasson, A. S. Carter, and M. J. Briggs-Gowan, "Sensory Over-Responsivity in Elementary School: Prevalence and Social-Emotional Correlates," *Journal of Abnormal Child Psychology* 37 (2009), pp. 705, 713.

spend a lot of time in the sole company of our laptops); my obsessive concentration has made it possible for me to produce very large-scale books that require years of research and synthesis.

Differences can be strengths, given the correct context.

Clearly, a difference that causes struggle and angst across the whole of a child's life (a sensory processing style that makes leaving the house a challenge, for example; a speech disorder that affects communication with friends and siblings; trouble reading anything, signs and labels included) has become a true disability that needs careful and probably aggressive intervention.

But if a "disability" really only becomes a problem in one setting—our factory-model K–12 system—I'd challenge that label.

Yet accepting the label *learning disability* may be your best strategy, because it will allow your child access to learning disability specialists and therapies. In many cases, these simply allow your child to learn out of lockstep with traditional classroom methods.

Before we explore this distinction further, I've provided a noncomprehensive list of some of the most commonly diagnosed learning disabilities, along with a few of the more usual therapies.

(Note: The definitions in the table that follows reflect *only* how these terms are used within the K–12 system to describe learning disabilities. Some of them are also used, in medicine, in a more technical sense. For example, learning specialists often use the diagnosis of dysphasia for childhood impaired speech that is unrelated to brain injury; in an adult who has suffered a stroke, "dysphasia" is impaired speech brought on by physical damage to the brain's dominant hemisphere.)

(Further note: In the past decade or so, the phrase "twice exceptional" has become more common as a description of children who are intellectually gifted but also have been diagnosed with a learning disability. I'll address this further in the next chapter.)

With the exception of severe autism (more about that shortly), all of these disabilities have three things in common.

First, the labels assume—without proof or discussion—that there is a perfectly normal, although biologically unmeasurable, way for every brain to process reading, writing, hearing, speaking, even organizing.

Holding up this gold standard, classrooms shunt children who don't hit it in every area into some subsection of "learning disability." And the fact that boys are diagnosed with almost all learning disabili-

Specific Learning Disability (SLD)	Description/Definition	Common Therapies
"Academic" (reading, writing, and arithmetic) disabilities		
dyslexia	"[C]haracterized by difficulties with accurate and/or fluent word recognition and by poor spelling and decoding abilities. These difficulties typically result from a deficit in the phonological component of language that is often unexpected in relation to other cognitive abilities and the provision of effective classroom instruction." (*Journal of Child Neurology*, 2003)	Multisensory teaching of reading skills (Orton-Gillingham programs are the most common), "guided oral reading" (the student reads aloud with constant instructor feedback).
dysgraphia	"Dysgraphia . . . causes a person's writing to be distorted or incorrect. In children, the disorder generally emerges when they are first introduced to writing. They make inappropriately sized and spaced letters, or write wrong or misspelled words, despite thorough instruction. . . . In addition to poor handwriting, dysgraphia is characterized by wrong or odd spelling." (National Institute of Neurological Disorders and Stroke)	Occupational therapy to strengthen hand muscles, fine motor skills, body posture, and arm position; specialized hand-writing programs (such as Hand-writing Without Tears); early move to word processing programs instead of handwritten work.
dyscalculia	"Dyscalculia is a condition that affects the ability to acquire arithmetical skills. Dyscalculic learners may have difficulty understanding simple number concepts, lack an intuitive grasp of numbers, and have problems learning number facts and procedures. Even if they produce a correct answer or use a correct method, they may do so mechanically and without confidence." (Department for Education, United Kingdom)	Use of math curriculum specifically designed to teach the most basic math concepts explicitly; emphasis on additional practice and repeating skills; teaching in small groups; teaching math concepts individually.
Speaking and listening disabilities (also known as phonological, articulation, and CAP disorders)		
dysphasia	"Dysphasia is a language disorder that is characterized by impairment of speech, writing, and comprehension of spoken or written language. The affection may be mild or severe. Symptoms include difficulty in talking, writing, listening, and understanding." (Office for Americans with Disabilities)	Speech therapy, both individual and in groups. Speech therapy may involve many different exercises, including pairing spoken words with written and pictured versions of each word; practice chanting and singing words; motor programming (teaching students to build up words from single sounds and syllables); direct intensive instruction in phonological principles.

Specific Learning Disability (SLD)	Description/Definition	Common Therapies
articulation disorder	"An articulation disorder involves problems making sounds. Sounds can be substituted, left off, added or changed. These errors may make it hard for people to understand you. Young children often make speech errors. For instance, many young children sound like they are making a 'w' sound for an 'r' sound (e.g., 'wabbit' for 'rabbit') or may leave sounds out of words, such as 'nana' for 'banana.' The child may have an articulation disorder if these errors continue past the expected age." (American Speech-Language-Hearing Association)	Speech therapy, both individual and in groups. Speech therapy may involve many different exercises, including contrast therapy (practicing word pairs with contrasting sounds), core vocabulary approach (drilling the pronunciation of selected sets of words, as if they were spelling lists), speech sound perception training (teaching children to distinguish heard sounds from each other).
auditory processing disorder	"[T]he reduced or impaired ability to discriminate, recognize or comprehend complex sounds, such as those used in words, even though the person's hearing is normal. . . . Symptoms of APD include, but are not limited to: difficulty understanding in noisy environments; difficulty following multi-task directions; difficulty distinguishing between similar sounds . . . often requiring repetition or clarification . . . easily distracted or unusually bothered by loud or sudden noises . . . have trouble understanding jokes, riddles or idioms; show difficulty in expressive language . . ." (Auditory Processing Disorder Foundation)	Practice in sound discrimination; direct instruction in phonological principles; development of active listening skills; conversation practice; auditory training therapy (currently considered an unproven experimental strategy).
Social/developmental disorders		
ADHD/ADD	"A child with AD/HD [ADD or ADHD] is usually described as having a short attention span and as being distractible. . . . Symptoms of inattention, as listed in the DSM-IV, are: often fails to give close attention to details or makes careless mistakes in schoolwork, work, or other activities; often has difficulty sustaining attention in tasks or play activities; often does not seem to listen when spoken to directly; often does not follow through on instructions and fails to finish schoolwork, chores, or duties in the workplace; . . . often has difficulty organizing tasks and activities; often avoids, dislikes, or is reluctant to engage in tasks that require sustained mental effort (such as schoolwork or homework); often loses things necessary for tasks or activities (e.g., toys, school assignments, pencils, books, or tools); is often easily distracted by extraneous stimuli; is often forgetful in daily activities. Excessive activity is the most visible sign of AD/HD: often fidgets with hands or feet or squirms in seat; often leaves seat in classroom or in other situations in which remaining seated is expected; often runs about or climbs excessively in situations in which it is inappropriate; often has difficulty playing or engaging in leisure activities quietly . . . often talks excessively." (American Psychiatric Association, 1994)	Behavior therapy (replacing problematic actions with new actions; practicing how to express feelings; training in organizational skills); teaching parents and teachers how to respond to interruptions and disruptive behavior; medication (both stimulants and nonstimulants).

Specific Learning Disability (SLD)	Description/Definition	Common Therapies
autism spectrum disorder	"Autism spectrum disorder impacts how a child perceives and socializes with others, causing problems in crucial areas of development—social interaction, communication and behavior. . . . Each child with ASD is likely to have a unique pattern of behavior and level of severity—from low functioning to high functioning. Severity is based on social communication impairments and the restrictive and repetitive nature of behaviors, along with how these impact the ability to function. . . . As they mature, some children with ASD become more engaged with others and show fewer disturbances in behavior. Some, usually those with the least severe problems, eventually may lead normal or near-normal lives. Others, however, continue to have difficulty with language or social skills." (Mayo Clinic)	Because autism spectrum disorder ranges from crippling, life-altering disability to much milder cases of social awkwardness and difficulty reading the reactions of others, therapies are dizzyingly complex (and multiple). They involve: behavior therapy, communication therapy, targeted individual instruction in specific academic area, family therapy, and medication to deal with specific symptoms.
executive function disorder	"An inefficiency in the cognitive management systems of the brain that affects a variety of neuropsychological processes such as planning, organization, strategizing, paying attention to and remembering details, and managing time and space." (Learning Disabilities Association of America)	Explicit instruction in use of schedules, organizers, checklists, calendars, and to-do lists; establishment of routines.
nonverbal learning disability	"Characterized by a significant discrepancy between higher verbal skills and weaker motor, visual-spatial and social skills. Signs and symptoms: trouble recognizing nonverbal cues such as facial expression or body language; clumsy; seems to be constantly 'getting in the way,' bumping into people and objects; using fine motor skills a challenge: needs to verbally label everything that happens to comprehend circumstances, spatial orientation, directional concepts and coordination; often lost or tardy; has difficulty following multi-step instructions; asks too many questions." (Learning Disabilities Association of America)	Provide child with simplified worksheet formats; occupational therapy to improve motor skills; elimination of timed assignments; direct and explicit instructions for every assignment; establishment of routines; provide verbal explanations for all visual teaching materials; teach social skills directly.

ties at a much higher rate than girls suggests that "normal," for whatever reason, lines up with how girls, not boys, mature. (According to the Centers for Disease Control and Prevention, boys are diagnosed with ADHD at *three times* the rate that girls are. As a parent of three boys and a girl, I think that a lot of learning disability specialists don't realize how much preteen boys need to move around.)[7]

Second, all of the "symptoms" listed are perfectly normal for younger children. They only become "disabilities" when the behaviors and experiences persist past the span of time designated by pediatricians as "developmentally normal."

So "disability" shades imperceptibly over into differences in maturity (see Chapter 3), and some students who struggle are probably just being assigned tasks for which they're not quite ready.

Third, notice that in almost every case, the therapy involved is essentially: Teach in a different way, teach skills explicitly, target the area where the student needs more work and support.

Technically, that's not treatment. It's just good teaching.

Good teaching is responsive to the student, flexible, always experimenting, equipped with a full toolbox of strategies that make sense to different kinds of brains, and creative enough to find multiple ways to present information and train skills.

Yet no matter how gifted the teacher, it is practically impossible to offer this kind of teaching to a large, understaffed classroom of widely differing learners, particularly in a school where the curriculum is inflexible, test-centered, and/or tied to strictly defined outcomes at specific grade levels.

Louise Spear-Swerling (Ph.D. in cognitive psychology, Yale) and Robert Sternberg (currently Professor of Human Development at Cornell) point this out eloquently:

[W]e would like to see learning disabilities specialists become, simply, learning specialists. Learning specialists could specialize in knowledge about the cognitive processes involved in typical acquisition of academic skills, in knowledge about the ways in which children might go awry in acquiring important cognitive and aca-

7 National Center for Learning Disabilities, *The State of Learning Disabilities*, 3rd ed. (2014), p. 5.

demic skills, and in adapting instruction for children with a variety of cognitive and academic difficulties. Without some truly sweeping changes, the entire field of learning disabilities will continue to rest on a crumbling conceptual foundation. On the other hand, with the right kinds of changes, those in the learning-disabilities field have the capacity to make a real difference in the lives of low achievers.

That many children experience school failure is beyond dispute. However, the solutions to any problem may stand or fall on how we frame that problem. The concept of learning disabilities has not and will not provide a solution to the problem of school failure. To cure our "epidemic" of learning disabilities, we need to begin by dispensing with the concept of learning disabilities itself.[8]

While I'm in sympathy with this proposal as a way to reform the whole system, individual families need to take a different approach.

I suggest, instead, that if your child is struggling, you should vigorously pursue diagnosis of a learning disability.

Why? Because students who are diagnosed as learning disabled can potentially receive additional tutoring, targeted teaching, explicit instruction by specialists—in other words, good teaching outside of the set boundaries of the classroom (or curriculum) that's failing them.

The international Association for Supervision and Curriculum Development has already pointed this out (italics are mine):

> Studies supported by the National Institutes of Child Health and Human Development show that at least 20 to 30 percent of American students cannot read well enough to successfully complete school-work. Unfortunately, there are few remedial reading and writing services within regular education programs, especially at the middle and high-school levels. *The only remedial literacy services available are usually in special education programs, and students are often diagnosed as LD so that they may have access to these resources. Many of these students are not LD at all,* however; some are . . . "curriculum casualties" who never received appropriate instruction in the first place.[9]

8 Spear-Swerling and Sternberg, "Curing Our 'Epidemic' of Learning Disabilities," p. 401.

9 Sornson, *Preventing Early Learning Failure*, p. 21.

In case you're wondering, remedial reading instruction generally means "a change in instruction": Teaching in a different way so that the student can finally understand.

Which is how you should treat a learning difference.

In many cases, having a learning disability means that you don't come to an intuitive understanding of what others may pick up more easily. You need different, more explicit, instruction. Consider the following therapies for sufferers of executive function disorder, from the University of Michigan:

> Students need to learn how to develop and use organizers. These external systems include calendars, to-do lists, daily logs, and checklists. These can be in paper form or by cell phone, iPad, or other technology devices.
>
> Get enough sleep at night. Getting adequate amounts of sleep enables a student to be fully awake and have the mental energy to learn and perform in school. . . . Going to bed at the same time each night and establishing a bed-time routine, starting at dinner or just after dinner, will assist in maintaining appropriate levels of alertness throughout the day.
>
> Using highlighters and/or graphics can help to draw attention to important information.
>
> Take frequent breaks during the day and vary the length of work periods. Use stretching and walking as ways to revitalize your body, getting the blood flowing more evenly throughout the body. Use quiet time to rejuvenate mental energy.
>
> Become aware of your periods of lower energy; keep a diary or a log of the times during the day when this occurs. Plan on having a healthy energy snack in the afternoon.
>
> Learn to use textbooks efficiently, for example: how to use the table of contents and the index.[10]

Actually, those are pretty basic skills for *all* students, not therapies.

But some students may not have the natural tendency to adopt these

10 "Executive Function Problems," Dyslexia Help, University of Michigan, http://dyslexiahelp.umich.edu/professionals/dyslexia-school/executive-function-disorders (accessed November 25, 2016).

strategies. Or may never have been in a classroom, or family, where these skills have been demonstrated or taught.

If the label "executive function disorder" allows them to be directly instructed in these basic skills, they now have access to the information they need.

■ ■ ■

A word to those who may already be homeschooling: This applies to you as well.

When you're teaching your child at home, you're in the same position as a solo teacher in a classroom: You may not have all the teaching tools you need to adapt your instruction to your child's particular mode of learning—particularly if your child has a very different brain than yours.

I've seen far too many home educators push doggedly on with curricula and instruction styles that aren't getting good results, without stopping to reevaluate. In my years of homeschooling, I too often did this myself. This is the voice of experience: If learning stalls for more than six months or so, it is *never* a bad idea to get professional evaluation. Learning disability specialists *are* learning specialists; they can offer you a whole toolbag of strategies and techniques to get you, and your child, out of your learning rut.

Change your thinking: Regard the label "learning disability" as signifying "This child needs a different approach," rather than "Something is wrong with your child." Follow the action steps at the end of this chapter, as a way of steering your struggling learner (and yourself) onto a better path.

■ ■ ■

Given that autism can be a devastating, life-altering condition, you may wonder why it's on my disabilities list.

The label "autism" has, in recent years, ballooned to cover a range of behaviors that once were labeled differently, or not at all—and many of those behaviors occur primarily within a school setting, and mostly affect the child's classroom experience.

Currently, in the United States, one in sixty-eight children has been identified as having the condition now known as autism spectrum disorder, or ASD. At its most severe—the form most of us probably think of when we hear the word "autism"—sufferers cannot communicate with words, get trapped within repetitive motions, are destructive to themselves and their environments.

But the 2013 edition of the *Diagnostic and Statistical Manual of Mental Disorders* (DSM-5) offers the following definition for diagnosing children with the mild version, ASD-1 (Autism Spectrum Disorder, Level 1):

Level 1, "Requiring support"

Social communication

Without supports in place, deficits in social communication cause noticeable impairments. Difficulty initiating social interactions, and clear examples of atypical or unsuccessful response to social overtures of others. May appear to have decreased interest in social interactions. For example, a person who is able to speak in full sentences and engages in communication but whose to-and-fro conversation with others fails, and whose attempts to make friends are odd and typically unsuccessful.

Restricted, repetitive behaviors

Inflexibility of behavior causes significant interference with functioning in one or more contexts. Difficulty switching between activities. Problems of organization and planning hamper independence.[11]

In other words, these are children who have trouble reading social cues, tend to talk over others without paying attention to what they're saying, don't like change, and have difficulty making friends.

These difficulties can easily shade over into personality, relational style, and maturity.

Like executive function disorder therapies, the "behavioral therapies" suggested for children diagnosed with ASD-1 tend to be strategies that actually work well for all children. The Autism Speaks Autism Treatment Network publication for parents, "An Introduction to Behavioral Health Treatment," gives the following "overview of in-home strategies" to deal with ASD-1 related "problem behaviors":

11 "DSM-5 Diagnostic Criteria," Autism Speaks, https://www.autismspeaks.org/what-autism/diagnosis/dsm-5-diagnostic-criteria (accessed November 25, 2016).

- **Look for opportunities to teach and praise your child.** Teach and praise appropriate communication, sharing, waiting, etc. If problem behavior happens when your child wants to get out of a particular activity, you may teach your child to request a break.
- **Make requests of your child that you believe your child can meet. (Set your child up for success!)** Ask your child to do things you know he/she can do independently or with minimal assistance. Additionally, break tasks and assignments down into small parts and steps, or only ask your child to do part of a task (e.g., ask him/her to pick up one block, rather than all the blocks).
- **Communicate your requests clearly, in a manner your child understands.** Also, let your child know what he/she will receive for doing what you asked. Increase requests slowly as your child succeeds. Be sure to only make a request when able to follow through on it (e.g., you have time to wait for your child to do as you asked) and reward or praise your child for doing what you asked.
- **Plan ahead to set your child up for good behavior.** Find ways to change the environment where problem behavior typically takes place in order to improve your child's behavior (e.g., keep snacks with you if your child tends to be more aggressive when hungry).[12]

I have no training in psychology, so I won't announce that ASD-1 behaviors should *not*, in fact, be classified on the autism spectrum.

But as a mother of four and grandmother of one, I *can* say that so-called problem behaviors are a lot more likely to occur in children who aren't taught and praised, who are given unclear commands, who are asked to do tasks that they can't manage, and who aren't provided snacks when their blood sugar gets low.

■ ■ ■

To sum up: The skyrocketing percentage of students diagnosed with a learning disability has definitely been affected by a narrowing definition of *normal*.

12 Autism Speaks Autism Treatment Network / Autism Intervention Research Network on Physical Health, "An Introduction to Behavioral Health Treatments: A Parent's Guide" (Autism Speaks, 2012), p. 2.

Given that all parents (even home educators) have to operate within a K–12 framework that defines those "normals," we can use the term "learning disability" to our advantage in order to flex the system to accommodate our children. It may in fact be normal for a twelve-year-old to struggle with reading, or a ten-year-old to be unable to read social cues—but when children live inside a matrix that demands both of those skills at a particular age, we have to find ways for them to flourish.

And if your child is struggling, don't wait too long for maturity to kick in—particularly if your child needs to remain within our age-graded K–12 system for the foreseeable future. Instead, put the following steps into action.

ACTION PLAN

If a child is struggling, rule out physical difficulties first.

Ask your pediatrician for a full workup and follow up on anything that seems of concern by asking for a referral to a specialist.

This can be a shortcut toward pinpointing the problem, but even if the physical checkup is normal, I strongly suggest then going directly to the following specialists. Health insurance plans should cover most of the costs. If seeing these specialists is not financially feasible, return to your pediatrician and be more persistent: You know that something is wrong. Can other tests be done to rule out vision or hearing problems, allergies, or minor seizure disorders?

Consult a College of Optometrists in Vision Development member if child:

> while reading, skips or rereads lines
> reads and/or completes homework at a snail's pace
> has poor reading comprehension
> reverses letters or confuses similar letters
> has a short attention span while doing written/reading-based work
> rubs eyes, has headaches, says eyes are tired
> cannot write on lines, has poor copying skills

can answer questions orally but not in writing
has trouble with basic math concepts of size and position
tilts head oddly while reading words or numbers

Consult an American Academy of Audiology member if child:

is slow to speak
speaks with slurred speech or odd pronunciation
is inattentive, especially in a group setting
doesn't seem to hear/understand instructions (always, or
    sometimes)
can only concentrate on instruction for short periods
has very poor spelling (particularly if handwriting is acceptable)
is socially withdrawn
shows odd conversational patterns and responses
seems more attentive when looking you directly in the face
tilts head while listening
says "what?" or "huh?" continually

Consult an American College of Allergy, Asthma and Immunology
member if child:

is inattentive or hyperactive
complains of stomachache
is frequently fatigued, irritable, anxious, agitated, or nervous
acts impulsively and irrationally
seems depressed and lethargic
can only concentrate for short periods
often complains about light, touch, tastes, or smells
suffers from eczema, rashes, or "itchy skin"

Consult an American Academy of Neurology member if child:

is frequently inattentive
stares blankly during instruction
seems unusually disoriented at odd times
is unusually forgetful
seems to be frequently daydreaming

has frequent headaches

has vomiting spells without fever or other symptoms

often trips or falls but otherwise seems well-coordinated

Note that undiagnosed vision and hearing problems, allergies, and minor seizure disorders can *all* mimic the commonly diagnosed ADHD, unless careful testing is done.

Each of the above medical associations hosts informative websites with much more information, along with additional lists of possible symptoms.

Skip the IQ test.

So-called intelligence quotient tests were developed during the first quarter of the twentieth century as an attempt to better place children into age-graded classrooms. Work done by a series of late nineteenth- and early twentieth-century psychologists (including Alfred Binet and Théodore Simon of France, William Stern of Germany, and the American Lewis Terman) evolved into the IQ test we know today, in which a child completes a series of thinking tests. His success is then compared to the expected norm for his chronological age; this yields a number called the mental age, which is higher if he has more correct answers than the norm, lower if he completes fewer tests accurately. This mental age is then divided by his chronological age and multiplied by 100. Voilà: the IQ score.[13]

There are so many thoroughly documented problems with this method that I won't even bother going into them here; see the Brief Essential Bibliography in Appendix C, if you'd like to read more.

Binet himself argued against using an IQ score as a measure of intelligence; he believed that intelligence was always developing, and the tests merely gave a starting place for "practice, training, and above all, method," with the goal to continually increase attention, memory, and judgment: "literally to become more intelligent than we were before."[14]

This is *not* how the test is interpreted in American culture. It is

13 B. R. Hergenhahn and Tracy Henley, *An Introduction to the History of Psychology*, 7th ed. (Boston: Wadsworth Cengage Learning, 2014), p. 298.

14 Ibid., p. 299.

taken as a static value judgment, a flat measure of how "smart" a kid is. A high score immediately gives status as "gifted," and a low score represents a dimmer outlook on future achievement.

This is both perverse (given that IQ tests measure one very narrow type of problem-solving ability) and damaging. Children with lower scores immediately believe that they're not very smart, and children with very low scores earn the label "severely disabled"—something which can determine the course of a life.

But children with high IQ scores also suffer. Rather than being treated as individuals, they are often fast tracked, even if their emotional maturity and interests fit better with a lower grade.

As children grow older, if it becomes clear that they will need special services, an IQ test may be necessary to qualify them for particular programs. If it becomes necessary, schedule the test and hold the result very, very lightly.

But my advice is to avoid the test for as long as you possibly can. Forget being pigeonholed by others: IQ tests hold such an outsized influence in Western culture that knowing your number makes it almost impossible for you to avoid pigeonholing yourself.

Have your child evaluated for specific learning disabilities, but resolve to see these *only* as differences that require new teaching strategies.

A learning disability diagnosis can give children within school systems access to a whole new teaching network. Homeschooling parents can use the diagnosis as a pointer to entirely new learning strategies. So a diagnosis can be worth pursuing.

But only if *you* determine *not* to think of your child as "dyslexic," or "dysgraphic," or whatever the label turns out to be.

Labels point to solutions. Labels *cannot* become part of who the child *is*. And a label should never play a major part in deciding what *not* to do (where to *not* bother applying to school, what subject *not* to tackle, what sport *not* to try out for). A label should only provide a way forward.

The first step is to have the child evaluated by an educational psychologist, a licensed clinical psychologist who specializes in learning disabilities, or a neuropsychologist.

An educational psychologist (usually, this is what schools will have on staff) will focus primarily on the child's school and learning experiences, academic skill levels, and any difficulties in performing academic work. A licensed clinical psychologist has additional training in possible misfires between the brain and body, and will be able to do a more comprehensive exam that also evaluates processing skills and speed, memory function, and possible sensory problems. A neuropsychologist is a licensed clinical psychologist who has done yet more work on brain function and brain disease.

Unless a child is experiencing severe difficulty in several areas (not just school), beginning with an educational psychologist is a reasonable starting point. If the psychologist's recommendations don't seem to fit or help, ask for a referral to a neuropsychologist or licensed clinical psychologist.

Listen to the findings, review the recommended therapies, and then make up your mind whether or not to try them. You and the child have the final say.

For children who are in a school system, diagnosis of a learning disability opens the door for the school to make up an Individualized Education Program, or IEP—a document that spells out what individual, specialized services the child can receive.

In many areas, home-educated students can also qualify for school-based services with an IEP, which gives you affordable access to a range of learning specialists.

My son has severe dysgraphia. His IEP allows him to take a netbook with him to type class notes. His IEP also gives him extra time to do math tests because, if he writes the numbers very, very slowly, his teacher can read them. —RANDY

When our son was in kindergarten, he could hardly get out a complete sentence. He was a bright kid, but he stammered when trying to verbally express himself. He had real trouble transferring his thoughts from his brain to his mouth. The problem was severe enough that his public elementary school recommended a speech IEP. He had two sessions a week with his speech therapist at school and was improved enough to drop the IEP at the end of first grade. —GEORGIA

We are homeschooling, and my son's IEP is a part of the homeschooling. I choose my own curricula as I like. My son gets two half-hour sessions at school daily and a chance to use the high-speed computer and library. Sometimes members of his IEP committee, which includes me, discuss what we are doing at home so as to make things fit together (for example, not doing double spelling programs). It is a situation of working together to figure out how to deal with the problems—they don't know what our whole home program is, nor do they need to approve it.   —PEN

Getting an IEP can be amazingly helpful—or it can be a difficult process, particularly if your school is uncooperative. To hear from hundreds of parents who've worked with IEPs for their children, visit the Learning Challenges discussion board that I host at forums.well trainedmind.com.

In the absence of a physical disorder, be very careful about agreeing to medication.

Beware of medication for disabilities which do not have a clear medical cause.

I am not anti-medication. If a diagnosed disability is causing chaos in a child's life, medication might propel him up out of a self-destructive rut into a better path.

But recognize that very little research has been done on the long-term effects of dosing a still-developing mind with stimulants (commonly prescribed for ADHD) and psychotropic drugs (given for anxiety, depression, and obsessive behavior).

Psychotropic drugs, less commonly used, should only be prescribed by a qualified psychiatrist, *after* significant time spent with the child *and* the family, and should always be accompanied by ongoing talk therapy. (Antidepressants, in particular, should not be prescribed by a family physician or general practitioner. This happens too often.)

ADHD medications are a much bigger problem. It's already known that these stimulants frequently slow or delay physical growth. "Children who remain on medication may be late to attain full growth, but they do catch up eventually," remarks one standard guide to learning disabilities, blithely, and then adds, "Some experts advise 'drug holidays' during vacation periods to allow children's growth to catch up." This alone seems like a major red flag to me; these medications are messing with natural patterns in a major way, and we simply do not know what effect this will have in the future.[15]

In addition, they can be frighteningly addictive—even for adults. In March 2013, playwright Kate Miller wrote in *The New York Times* about beginning Adderall in college and then escalating her dosage over the next years until she was finally forced to admit that the drug had become a dangerous addiction:

> I was an emotional wreck, angry, disconnected and unglued. . . . I ignored red flags that in college I had kept a stern eye on, having had a history of alcoholism in my family. But because my drugs came from a doctor's notepad in an office two blocks from the Metropolitan Museum of Art, I felt safe.[16]

Recreational use of ADHD drugs has become a major problem, because the stimulants provide a sense of euphoria. Yet these powerful, brain-altering drugs are routinely prescribed—many times, *before* or in the *absence* of actual behavioral therapy. In 2011, a staggering *11 percent* of children aged four to seventeen years (that's 6.4 million children) had been diagnosed with ADHD. The CDC reports that only *one third* of those children were receiving both medication *and* therapy.[17]

Other statistics suggest that ADHD medications are too often used to drug children into compliance—rather than working to adjust their settings to fit them. Among *preschoolers* diagnosed with ADHD, *half* were on medication (which is not recommended by the CDC, or any

15 Corinne Smith and Lisa Strick, *Learning Disabilities: A to Z: A Parent's Complete Guide to Learning Disabilities from Preschool to Adulthood* (New York: Simon & Schuster, 1999), p. 168.

16 Kate Miller, "The Last All-Nighter," *The New York Times* (March 4, 2013), http://opinionator.blogs.nytimes.com/2013/03/04/the-last-all-nighter/ (accessed November 26, 2016).

17 "Attention-Deficit/Hyperactivity Disorder: Data & Statistics," Centers for Disease Control and Prevention, http://www.cdc.gov/ncbddd/adhd/data.html (accessed November 26, 2017).

responsible agency, for preschoolers), and of those, one in four were receiving *only* drugs—no other services. The CDC also found that children in foster care were three times more likely to be diagnosed with ADHD and prescribed medication. These are children who show all sorts of behavioral problems that require long, complicated intervention; drugs may certainly help, but can also be a convenient shortcut for overworked therapists and can replace other interventions.[18]

In my opinion, the ADHD diagnosis itself is often problematic. The huge rise in cases reveals a system desperate to fit children to itself, rather than the other way around; the vast number of different symptoms folded into the disease (for girls, being withdrawn, low self-esteem, trouble focusing, anxiety; for boys, inability to sit still, talking excessively, impulsive behavior) have far too much overlap with immaturity and many other causes.

Since I'm not a mental health professional, let me offer you this statement, jointly written by two clinical psychologists, two neuropsychologists, one counseling psychologist, and one pediatrician:

> Children are usually suspected of having ADD/ADHD because they have attention problems or because they are hyperactive. The child who truly suffers from ADD/ADHD has attention deficits associated with a range of specific neurological injuries and mild developmental delays.
>
> However, the diagnosis of ADD/ADHD is supposed to be a diagnosis of last resort, to be made by exclusion only after ruling out other possible disorders or problems such as depression, anxiety, learning disabilities, preoccupation with personal problems, unrealistic expectations, situational difficulties, boredom due to a mismatch of abilities and expectations, auditory processing deficits, concussion or mild traumatic brain injury, ill health, substance abuse, fatigue from sleep disorders, lack of energy because of poor eating habits or an eating disorder, and even cognitive slowing caused by current medications. Because a clinician must take the time to rule out many other possibilities including all those listed

18 Jeremy Loudenbuck, "ADHD Diagnosis Three Times More Likely for Children in Foster Care," *The Chronicle for Social Change* (November 3, 2015).

above, ADD is a difficult diagnosis to make. The diagnosis of ADD should not be given following a 10-minute appointment with a family doctor who has looked at a questionnaire filled out by the parent and the school personnel.[19]

If ADHD *is* diagnosed, medication should be a last resort for a child who cannot function across most of his or her life, not just in the classroom. "We all want that magic bullet to take care of learning problems," says board-certified clinical neuropsychologist Cheryl Weinstein. "Unfortunately, the belief that medication alone will work is too readily embraced."[20]

Flex the system, not just the child.

Don't be rushed, frightened, talked, or bullied into medicating or labeling your child before you're ready.

Teachers can be amazing resources, but they also only see your child in *one* environment. You see them in the rest of their lives. Trust your gut instincts about what your child needs. She *may* need medication and an IEP. She may not. She may, instead, need a completely different environment with more freedom to learn in her own way.

Remember that the problem is a mismatch between the system and the student, not a deficiency in your child. Diagnose it. But then use the strategies I'll outline in Parts III, IV, and even V to work the system so that it fits your child—not just the other way around.

No particular curriculum will "fix" your child. There is no such thing and your child isn't broken. She just processes differently. Your child will need scaffolding for some things, remediation for some things, opportunity to run with her strengths, and a lot of love and patience while you navigate these waters.

19 F. Richard Olenchak, Jean Goerss, Paul Beljan, James T. Webb, Nadia E. Webb, and Edward R. Amend, Preface, *Misdiagnosis and Dual Diagnoses of Gifted Children and Adults: ADHD, Bipolar, OCD, Asperger's, Depression, and Other Disorders* (Tucson, AZ: Great Potential Press, 2005).

20 "Treatment for Learning Disabilities," PBS Parents, http://www.pbs.org/parents/education/learning-disabilities/basics/treatment-for-learning-disabilities (accessed November 26, 2016).

Be prepared for a lot of trial and error as you try to find specific materials and ways of providing instruction. Every child is different because of different balances of strengths, weaknesses and personality. Please be patient with yourself and your children as you travel this path. There is no quick fix, but the journey can be wonderful if you take time to focus on the positives and your time as a family. Don't let the stresses and worries rule you.   —ALEX

CHAPTER FIVE

The Perils of the Gifted and the Good

Good students and gifted learners can be misfits too.

My older brother was one. My mother, a certified elementary-school teacher, taught him to read before sending him to kindergarten; she'd seen far too many struggling readers in fourth- and fifth-grade classrooms to put all her trust in the system. By the time he got into first grade, he was reading on a seventh-grade level. (My mother is a very good reading teacher.)

He was bored out of his skull by a first-grade curriculum that had him identifying letters of the alphabet. And he was a typically twitchy and energetic six-year-old boy. So he talked too much, distracted his classmates, fidgeted, and developed an annoying habit of reading ahead of the teacher and then correcting her, out loud, in front of the rest of the class.

After a few weeks of this, his teacher suggested he might be better off in another grade.

The school skipped him forward into second grade. The second-grade work wasn't much more interesting. Plus, the second-graders resented the presence of this upstart, and refused to play with him at recess.

He begged to go back to first grade where his friends were. The school complied—but this didn't work either. He was still bored; and now, his classmates resented the fact that he'd been identified as "special," and turned a cold shoulder.

"By this point," my mother says, "every time he got off the bus, he was either fighting or crying, and I was spending all my time undoing what was happening at school." His intellectual ability was so out of step with his physical and social development that she couldn't find a place for him at school—which is what led her, back in 1972, to venture into homeschooling.

WHAT IS GIFTEDNESS?

American education has no accepted definition of what giftedness is. The National Association for Gifted Children has proposed this:

> Gifted individuals are those who demonstrate outstanding levels of aptitude (defined as an exceptional ability to reason and learn) or competence (documented performance or achievement in top 10% or rarer) in one or more domains. Domains include any structured area of activity with its own symbol system (e.g., mathematics, music, language) and/or set of sensorimotor skills (e.g., painting, dance, sports).[1]

But the NAGC is an independent nonprofit with no authority to influence education departments.

Among the states, definitions range from the extremely vague (Indiana says that gifted students either have, or show potential for, an "outstanding level of accomplishment") to the bewilderingly bureaucratic: In Connecticut, a "planning and placement team" identifies a pool of children who either score well on standardized tests or show some sort of (undefined) "potential" for achievement, and then the "top five percent of children so identified" qualify for "differentiated instruction or

---

1 National Association for Gifted Children, "Redefining Giftedness for a New Century: Shifting the Paradigm" (March 2010), http://www.nagc.org/sites/default/files/Position%20Statement/Redefining%20Giftedness%20for%20a%20New%20Century.pdf (accessed November 28, 2016).

services." And many school systems simply rely on an IQ score: Anything over 130 is gifted.[2]

Among teachers and parents, an ongoing argument over the word "gifted" bubbles along: Should it be applied to children who are quick learners, or are these children "merely bright" (a dismissive term that pops up dismayingly often)? Should it be reserved for those children with such unusually quick or acute mental processes that they don't fit *any* classroom well? Or are these children "profoundly gifted"? And what about "talented"—where does this word fit?

Given how fuzzy the label is, you might wonder why it's important to figure out if *your* child is "gifted." There are two good reasons:

1. Meeting your state's standards for "giftedness" can give your child access to tutoring, more challenging curricula options, and other helpful services.
2. Giftedness can create enormous learning problems.

Let me propose a barebones, working definition of "gifted," for the sake of helping you evaluate whether this is a useful puzzle piece to fit

---

2 Here's the very weird Connecticut statute:

[T]he following words shall have the following meanings:

(1) "Extraordinary learning ability" means a child identified by the planning and placement team as gifted and talented on the basis of either performance on relevant standardized measuring instruments, or demonstrated or potential achievement or intellectual creativity, or both. The term shall refer to the top five per cent of children so identified.

(2) "Gifted and talented" means a child identified by the planning and placement team as (1) possessing demonstrated or potential abilities that give evidence of very superior intellectual, creative or specific academic capability and (2) needing differentiated instruction or services beyond those being provided in the regular school program in order to realize their intellectual, creative or specific academic potential. The term shall include children with extraordinary learning ability and children with outstanding talent in the creative arts as defined by these regulations.

(3) "Outstanding talent in the creative arts" means a child identified by the planning and placement team as gifted and talented on the basis of demonstrated or potential achievement in music, the visual arts or the performing arts. The term shall refer to the top five per cent of children so identified.

(4) "Pregnancy" shall be deemed a condition which grants eligibility for special education and related services.

No, I don't know why pregnancy is in there either.

into your child's experience: Gifted kids have the ability to work at least two grade levels ahead of their peers in any given subject.

FOUR CHALLENGES OF GIFTEDNESS

If you can avoid getting hung up on the definition, "gifted" can be a useful label; it can help you think realistically about your child's strengths, and weaknesses, and point you toward a plan for dealing with both.

As you consider whether "gifted" might describe your child, keep the following in mind.

Giftedness is always asynchronous.

Asynchronous development, as I noted in Chapter 3, simply means that the child is developing different abilities at different rates.

Children who are globally gifted or profoundly gifted—working at a high intellectual or creative level across the board—suffer from asynchronicity because their minds are developing in an accelerated timeframe, and their bodies are not. Other children experience giftedness itself as asynchronous: they find mathematics, for example, to be a place of delight and ease but struggle with written language.

Asynchronicity makes grade placement a knotty problem. It can also bring gifted children to the point of despair. "It is important to realize," write the authors of *Misdiagnosis and Dual Diagnoses of Gifted Children and Adults,*

> that brilliance in one area apparently can sit side by side with normal, or even below average, performance in other areas. Gifted children are often keenly aware of their internal asynchrony. They frequently experience frustration because they are able to do some things very well but cannot manage other things nearly as well.[3]

Motor skills can get in the way of a soaring intellect; a gifted child who can design a suspension bridge may melt down over efforts to build a model of it. And a child who reads at an amazingly high level while in elementary school will be that much more aware of her average (or

3 Olenchak et al., *Misdiagnosis and Dual Diagnoses*, Chapter 1.

struggling) place in mathematics; she knows how it feels to work easily, so she may interpret her difficulties with math as impossible to overcome and give up.

Giftedness can mimic a learning disability.

Gifted children are too frequently misdiagnosed with disabilities or even actual disorders *because* of their giftedness.

Children who are bored with too-easy work often lack the maturity to say so; instead, they are restless, fidget, don't pay attention, and can end up diagnosed with ADHD. In fact, one type of ADHD is actually *defined* as "inability to pay attention when the subject is uninteresting or boring":

> [P]eople with ADHD . . . struggle, sometimes mightily, to sustain their attention to activities that are longer than usual, especially those that are boring, repetitious, or tedious. Uninteresting school assignments . . . and long lectures are troublesome, as are reading lengthy uninteresting works, [and] paying attention to explanations of uninteresting subjects . . . [4]

Life, of course, requires us to develop the ability to finish tasks that we're not particularly interested in. But for a gifted child, the entire school day may be one long exercise in paying attention to boring and uninteresting subjects. ADHD-like behavior is a natural consequence. "I am convinced," says education psychologist Richard Olenchak, "that many students who have Attention Deficit Hyperactivity Disorder are, in fact, not students with ADHD at all but are gifted students. . . . They are often highly creative, highly inventive, highly analytical and insightful young people who have trouble with a worksheet-driven, textbook-driven, state high-stakes tests-driven curriculum."[5]

Olenchak, along with several colleagues who are clinical and neuropsychologists, has done extensive work on the misdiagnosis of gifted children. Their intensity of focus and perfectionism is sometimes

---

4 Russell A. Barkley, *Taking Charge of ADHD: The Complete, Authoritative Guide for Parents* (New York: Guilford Press, 2013), p. 37.

5 F. Richard Olenchak, speech given at the McKay School of Education, Brigham Young University, May 2001.

labeled as obsessive-compulsive disorder; when intellect outstrips judgement, executive function disorder can be diagnosed; because their minds go so much faster than their hands, they may be told that they are dysgraphic (especially if they've been accelerated out of their age grade).[6]

Giftedness can *mask* a learning disability.

Some children disguise real learning difficulties by using other, high-level skills to cover; for example, a mathematically gifted student who has trouble reading can employ a phenomenal memory and good listening skills to fake reading.

> *My son seemed to be reading. He got 100s on his Accelerated Reader comprehension tests. He also got 100s on his spelling tests in school.*
>
> *He wasn't actually reading. He had phenomenal auditory memory and would have others read him his stories before he "read" them back. He could repeat, verbatim, seventy or eighty pages (granted, they were books with a lot of pictures) and have full comprehension. He wasn't actually decoding the words. He didn't even know he wasn't reading.*
>
> *Knowing this meant that we were able to tap into that strength for certain types of learning but we also recognized that we had to take a different approach for certain things, like learning to decode words. His strength was masking his weaknesses and his weaknesses were masking his strength.*　　　　　—ABBY

Gifted students with learning problems can sail through the early grades, but as the material that they're struggling with grows more difficult, their performance begins to suffer. And because they are so clearly bright and capable, this decline is too often chalked up to a behavior problem, lack of motivation, lack of effort, or laziness—rather than properly treated as a difference in learning.

The term "twice exceptional," or "2E," first used in the mid-1990s, has become more common as more and more students have been diagnosed with learning disabilities. A twice-exceptional child is a "gifted

6 Olenchak et al., *Misdiagnosis and Dual Diagnoses*, Chapter 6.

learner" with "significant cognitive discrepancies"—either an actual diagnosed learning disability, or simply an unusually sharp difference in achievement.

Giftedness lends itself to perfectionism, which can stall learning.

Because gifted children can do some things so easily and so well, they see their failures—the areas in which they *cannot* perform at a high level—with unusual clarity. As Olenchak et al. write:

> It seems to be part of their nature to regard tasks that come easily to them as trivial and to value only those that are challenging. Their self-worth, in their eyes, is focused more on the difficult tasks than on the easy ones. When we add to this their intensity and perfectionist, all-or-none thinking, we end up with a very bright child who feels like he "cannot do anything right."[7]

Perfectionism can lead to tantrums, enormous frustration, and an actual inability to learn; unwilling to put up with less-than-perfect results, they simply refuse to try.

> *My son learned his letters and sounds on his own by the time he was two and began begging to do "school" like his big sisters. But if he doesn't write his letters exactly the way they are in the book, he gets really upset and hard on himself. His mind is so advanced in the way he thinks about things, that he gets so frustrated when his little body isn't capable of all the things his mind wants to do.* —EVA

This perfectionism is often unwittingly amplified by teachers, schools, and even parents. Parents praise gifted kids for their high achievements; gifted and talented programs separate them out, tell them that they're smart, and then reward their accomplishments with grades, certificates, trophies, and recognition. The message comes across with perfect clarity: Success is proof of intelligence. Failure is the opposite. So our reward system for gifted kids teaches them, over

---

7 Ibid.

time, that failure is shameful; by extension, that repeated failure can invalidate their giftedness.

When failure is not treated as an inevitable and valuable part of learning, children learn to avoid failure—which means avoiding experimentation, and steering away from tasks that they know are a little beyond their reach.

If "gifted" seems to fit the bill, the specific strategies in Part III can help you tweak your child's education to make it a better fit. But before you start choosing strategies, take the time to go through the following four steps.

ACTION PLAN

Do your research.

Before you pursue the label for your child, do some initial research about what giftedness is, and what the label can offer.

First, spend some time reading about giftedness. You will find helpful titles listed under "Acceleration" and "Learning Differences and Disabilities" in Appendix C. In addition, visit three websites:

> The organization SENG, Supporting Emotional Needs of the Gifted (sengifted.org), provides many parent resources along with guides to diagnostic and testing materials.
> The nonprofit Hoagies' Gifted (http://www.hoagiesgifted.org) has proved invaluable for many parents of gifted and twice-exceptional kids.
> The Accelerated Learners forum at forums.welltrainedmind.com contains thousands of discussion threads on gifted, advanced, and accelerated learning.

As you read, try to ignore all the nitpicking, score-parsing, and line-drawing. You'll find far, *far* too many parents bickering about the difference between gifted and garden-variety bright (whatever that means).

Remember that giftedness, like learning difficulties, lies on a continuum that simply doesn't have clear lines of demarcation. If your child is finding his/her grade level confining, you're dealing with a mismatch, and "gifted" may be the best label to help you correct that mismatch. Don't be obnoxious and throw the word "gifted" around on the playground (or whatever chat board you frequent) to intimidate the other parents and their garden-variety-bright toddlers; that's just good manners. But also, don't feel defensive about claiming the term, in a discreet and polite way, for your kid. What I said about labels in the last chapter applies in this one as well:

> Labels point to solutions. Labels cannot become part of who the child is. And a label should never play a major part in deciding what not to do (where to not bother applying to school, what subject not to tackle, what sport not to try out for). A label should only provide a way forward.

Second, investigate whether your local school district offers any resources labeled "gifted and talented." If so, could they be useful for you? In many areas, these enrichment programs are available to all children of school age, whether they're enrolled full-time in the public school system or not.

If there *are* resources available, how do children qualify for them? Find out whether test scores (the most common screening tool) or some other standard is used. And then, decide whether it's worth your while to go through the screening.

Test, but test privately, and avoid the IQ test as long as possible.

Ability tests are deeply flawed—particularly when used as a gatekeeping device that admits some students and keeps others out.

In a minute, I'm going to recommend that your child take them anyway. But first, let me give you some context in which to evaluate the results.

- Most ability tests measure the same thing: how well students solve problems, read, and draw conclusions from written material. So they tend to identify propositional thinkers—students comfortable with fact-based information (see Chapter 14 for a fuller discussion), who read and write with ease, and who find sitting still and concentrating second nature. Other areas of giftedness get missed.

- Ability tests are often given in a written format, disadvantaging children whose fine motor skills lag behind their thinking abilities.
- Perfectionists, a category that includes *many* gifted kids, don't tend to do well because they can see ambiguities in the answers. In fact, statistics suggest that the more gifted a child is—using this term to mean *very* highly inclined to understand abstractions, solve problems, and make connections—the more likely he is to pull an inaccurately low score on the standard ability tests.[8]
- The tests are usually timed, which rattles many students, particularly younger ones.

With that said: Giving your child a couple of ability tests, if used as one method of getting a clearer view of her strengths and weaknesses, can help you decide what strategies will help your child. The results can also improve your knowledge of how your child processes information, what she enjoys, and where she might need some extra help. Use these tests as Binet intended his IQ test to be used: as a starting point *only*.

My suggestions:

- Test privately, outside of the school system, if you can afford it. Once scores are an official part of a child's school record, they can dictate placement and participation in a way that might not be helpful. Some tests need to be administered by a psychologist, but others (such as the Iowa Basic and the Otis Lennon School Ability Test) require no training—just someone to read the instructions from the manual and to proctor. Some tests you can even give at home, and then send away for scoring. See Chapter 8 for *much* more

8 See, among others, Anna H. Avant and Marica R. O'Neal, "Investigation of the Otis-Lennon School Ability Test to Predict WISC-R Full Scale IQ for Referred Children," paper presented at the Fifteenth Annual Meeting of the Mid-South Educational Association, http://files.eric.ed.gov/fulltext/ED286883.pdf (accessed November 28, 2016); "Testing and Assessment: What Do the Tests Tell Us?", Hoagies' Gifted Education, http://www.hoagiesgifted.org/tests_tell_us.htm (accessed November 28, 2016).

information on currently available tests, the skills tested, administration, and scoring.

- As I wrote in the last chapter: Avoid the IQ (Stanford-Binet) test. It's too closely identified with a static "measure of intelligence." If you're testing through a school or psychologist, you might come under some pressure to agree to this test. You can *always* say no.
- The first time you test, try to administer at least two different tests on two different days (widely spaced . . . by weeks, if the testing was hard work). No one test will give you a completely accurate picture, and (no matter what a test administrator might tell you), kids test differently at different times of day, and their results are affected by the amount of sleep they've had, what they ate for breakfast, whether it's Monday or Friday, and how preoccupied they are with the latest Marvel superhero movie/most recent online multiplayer game tournament/most recent crush. Don't ever test when a child is upset about something (or while a teen is recovering from a broken heart).
- If you have the option and the child suffers from test anxiety, don't time the test. Often, children with anxiety will finish within the allotted time anyway; it's the ticking clock that panics them. (And if the child is paralyzed by the timer, you've already identified a weakness that needs addressing, probably by a therapist or specialist.)

You may find out that the student is working at a similar level across the board, in which case it's useful to have some idea of where that level is in relationship to her age-grade. Or you may discover asynchronous development—a wide gap between skills (verbal and mathematical, oral and written language, mathematical concepts and mathematical computation).

This will help you, as you move through Part III, to decide whether to advance the child forward across the board, or supplement in particular areas. It will also let you know whether you need to go back to the previous chapter and go through the steps of evaluating the child for a disorder or disability. *Very* wide gaps are a pointer to true twice exceptionalism, in which a gifted child is struggling hard with a problem that needs intervention.

Testing several years in a row will also clue you in as to whether the child is, in fact, progressing. If learning stalls, test results will decline, and you know that there's an issue to be addressed.

> *My son was not learning at evenly spaced intervals and was calling himself all kinds of awful names because he was reading at a high level, and could multiply three digit numbers, but couldn't remember from one day to the next what 1 + 2 was.*
>
> *He took the WISC IV and Woodcock Johnson[9] from two different psychologists. His math sub-score was in 46 percent (somewhere around there), and the rest of his scores were in the 96–99 percent range. That really surprised us. But his psychologist pointed out to us that even though he was underachieving in math, overall, he was testing as highly gifted. We learned that we could push him a little more than we were—and, in fact, that was what he wanted and needed.*
>
> —NITA

> *Honestly, I thought my son was just not that bright. He always refused to do his work, and I thought he had learning disabilities.*
>
> *I had him take the ITBS and CogAT[10]. He scored in the 70s percentile on the ITBS, which is not gifted. But on the CogAT, he was 99th percentile across the board!*
>
> *After that, I changed up everything we do completely. I had to sit with him and catch him up on the basic skills, but he literally passed over an entire grade level. I no longer assume that he simply isn't bright, or just needs more and more and more review, or to go slower.*
>
> —JANE

Be aware that you may be conveying "You're smart" to your child. And then stop.

We want to be good parents. We want to praise our children. But it's very easy, as we try to express our pride and approval, to reinforce that message of *You are valuable to me because you are smart.*

9 These are common achievement and intelligence tests: WISC IV is the Wechsler Intelligence Scale for Children test, 5th ed. (see p. 108) and the Woodcock-Johnson test measures cognitive ability (reasoning and problem solving; see p. 112).

10 ITBS is the Iowa Test of Basic Skills (see p. 109). The CogAT is the Cognitive Abilities Test (see p. 106).

In our current system of education, both gifted and good students are taught to rise to expectations. This may seem like sound educational practice; but not only does it train them to avoid failure at all costs (even when failure is the very best way forward into new ways of thinking and doing), but it traps them in an anxiety-inducing cycle in which one poor grade, one bad test, one semester where hormones or illness or just plain immaturity keeps them from excelling, seems like the end of the world.

It's not just because they're afraid that they won't get into college (although that can certainly play into the panic). It's that their *identity* is wrapped up in being *smart*, and failure means they're not smart.

I understand this struggle. I was a good kid, a gifted student. I had almost perfect grades and test scores. I was self-motivated, self-disciplined. I never submitted a poor assignment; I was responsible, and conscientious, and the universe paid me back with applause and scholarship money and recognition.

In college, I had a stomach ulcer. In graduate school, I had panic attacks. And in my thirties, I had a serious bout of depression that took years to deal with. I had a photo of Sam and Frodo trudging through Mordor on the bulletin board in my office, because continuing to achieve felt like walking through the wilderness, with nothing waiting for me on the other side but Mount Doom.

I'm happy to report that what lay on the other side wasn't Mount Doom; it was the realization that, for the first time, I needed to truly understand why I was a high achiever. And it was for me, as it is for so many of the gifted and good, *fear.*

Kids who struggle, who have differences and disabilities that make them feel like misfits in our K–12 system, find their school years to be a trial; but if they're given good scaffolding and support, they find their place. The beginning of their journey is, in many ways, the hardest part. But the gifted and the good often hit their wilderness in the middle, at the point when they have to come face-to-face with the motivation for their goodness and achievement.

And that motivation, often, is: They're terrified.

They are afraid that they will fail. They are afraid that, when they fail, everyone will realize that they're *not* actually all that smart. They are afraid that they are not worthy of love. *That* is the peril of the gifted and the good.

A few suggestions, as you parent your gifted child:

- Don't say, "You're a good kid," or "You're so smart." Say, "I love you," and "I enjoy your company," and "I love the person you're becoming."
- Don't say, "I'm proud of your grades" (or SAT scores, or musical performance, or whatever the achievement is). Say, "I am so proud of how hard you've worked." Or, "I'm amazed at how your hard work has improved your skills." Or, "I'm so excited to watch you progress." Or "I'm so interested in what you're doing" (specifics are good), "I can't wait to see what you do next."
- Don't praise the child's *accomplishments* in front of others. Praise her perseverance, her dedication, her effort, her courage in trying something new, her willingness to work toward a result.

Put your child in a position to fail.

I have perfectionist leanings; I am the mother of perfectionists. And I've realized that it is immensely important to help our gifted, good kids fall on their faces. The only way to reassure kids that the world won't end if they fail is for them to fail, and see that the world goes on.

Let them take a too-difficult course, and get a C or D, and then tell them how great it is that they learned new and fascinating stuff.

If they want to sign up for an activity that you *know* won't go well, let them sign up, and then allow them to drop out, without saying "I told you so," when they've had enough.

When they set completely unreasonable goals for themselves, offer counsel—but if they don't listen, back away and wait.

And then, when the failure happens, don't offer an explanation or solution; just empathize.

It feels horrible when something goes badly, doesn't it?

Then, move on. Don't harp on, refer back to, or use the failure as an object lesson. A child—particularly a teenager—can only learn from the failure if you're not rubbing his nose in it.

Don't discourage the child from trying the same thing again. Trying once more gives her the chance to put what she's learned into action, to see whether it's made a difference or not.

This is hard for parents. We so desperately want to protect our children from pain that we do our best to steer them away from painful situations (as we should) and try to assure their happiness (which we can't). And when we predict disaster and it happens, it is a huge exercise in self-discipline to *not* say, "I told you so. See, if you'd just have done this instead . . ."

But our children need to learn that failure is just a section of the path, not the end of the line. They can only learn that if we keep our moralizing to a minimum.

And *when* gifted learners finally realize that failure is not the end of the world, they will be protected from one of the most damaging kinds of pain: the oppressive dread that we must keep working, because if achievement flags, we've lost our identity.

Like my daughter, I was also a gifted child who did not like challenges. I suspect it was related to the fact that everyone always bragged to me about how smart I was, based on how quickly and easily I solved ordinary problems, instead of pointing out to me how interesting the various subjects were. So I got the idea that my self-esteem rested on always getting everything correct instead of learning the fun of exploring new things. When things were not immediately clear to me it threatened my self-concept as a smart kid. —MOIRA

First of all, I always told my kids that, if they ever get to the point at which they aren't making mistakes, especially in schoolwork, that would be bad, because it would mean they aren't stretching and growing. Making mistakes and then correcting them means they are learning.

Second, I let them see me making mistakes and handling it well.

Third, we've done a lot of visualizing and role play. When one of my kids freezes up or gets stressed because of worry about making a mistake, I sit down with the child in question and ask him/her to tell me exactly what was the worst thing that might happen if he/she made a mistake. Sometimes, I prime the pump with humor, coming up with the most exaggerated, ridiculous outcome I could imagine and delivering it in hysterical, panicky tones. Usually, that would get the kiddo laughing, which would help him/her relax, and then we could talk about the real, underlying fears.

And I never, ever let them walk away from something because they were afraid of failing. Every time either of them survived a "failure," it proved my point: Failure isn't fatal. And they get stronger with every experience. —JENNY

CHAPTER SIX

The Toxic Classroom

So far, we've assumed that teachers, administrators, and class-rooms are essentially benign. They might not fit your child, or his learning style, or his needs; they might be overwhelmed and under-staffed; but they're not out to cause harm.

Unfortunately, that's not always the case.

My fifth-grader attended one of the excellent private schools in our area. The kids are so polite there, never any commotion, so I did not have any clue that my son was having problems until I realized his birthday/xmas gift money was missing. He had started giving it to some kids in school.

Turns out that a few kids very quietly controlled the social dynam-ics of his grade. They picked the teams that played at recess, picked each other to pair for team projects, did not attend his parties, and told the other kids who to talk to. Basically, they locked arms to bar him from entering their chosen circle. My son was giving money to the kids on the fringe of this group—"the ones closest to liking him."

—HARRY

*The teacher pulled books out of my daughter's hand while stating
they were too hard for her to read. After six weeks in first grade, my
daughter informed me that she was dumb and that she was unable
to learn.* —GRETCHEN

*Third grade — wasted year. Brand-new teacher! Very nice guy, but he
was new to the classroom, and had at least five very disruptive kids
in the class. He missed a lot of days because of a very ill child, and
was trying to rebuild his house to deal with mold issue that caused the
illness. I sympathized with his issues, but I could see my son falling
farther and farther behind.* —P.J.

Classmates can be bullies. Teachers can be incompetent (for a number of reasons) or overwhelmed. A teacher can even be hostile; teachers are human, and sometimes take a dislike to a child. Administration can be disorganized or clueless.

These things can make school a misery for any child. And miserable children cannot learn.

In some ways, these are much simpler problems to deal with than learning differences. Even though solutions may be hard to find, the difficulties themselves are external to the child. They won't always be with her. They are not *part* of her.

The most direct solution is to remove the child from the classroom completely (that would take you straight to Part V). That's not always an option, so you may need to work with some of the suggested strategies in Part III instead.

But your first task is to find out what's really going on.

UNCOVERING THE PROBLEM

The younger a child is, the less developed his frame of reference will be. It may not occur to him that he *shouldn't* put up with name calling, or that being shamed by the teacher is *not* normal. He may not be able to put what's happening into words. He may be embarrassed.

He may even think that you already know what's happening. You're the parent. Small children think that parents are omnipotent and omniscient. Sometimes, they don't realize parents are human and limited until they're into their teens.

> *I never, ever, ever told my parents about how awful school was for me. I still haven't told them. I don't know if they could sense it or not. I was ashamed.* —GLORIA

> *I always assumed my parents knew I was being bullied. I mean, how could they not? But when I finally told them years later how utterly depressed I had been, my dad just sat in stunned silence. He truly didn't know.* —RHONDA

Your child may tell you straight out that another kid is harassing him, or that the teacher is picking on him. But you may need to be alert for signs that all is not well.

The anti-bullying website NoBullying.com suggests looking out for the following signs that peer bullying is happening: your child

- Refuses to talk to you about the day.
- Suddenly begins to show behavior problems.
- Has constant stomach-aches or head-aches.
- Often claims to be sick in order to skip school.
- Becomes increasingly withdrawn.
- Refuses to take part in school-based social activities.
- Comes home angry and hostile.
- Doesn't want to ride the bus.
- Is often in the nurse's office.
- Misses personal items and won't tell you where they've gone.
- Asks for additional money.
- Doesn't use the bathroom at school (waits until home and races to the bathroom as soon as he comes in the door).

When the problem is the teacher, the child may show some of the same behaviors; she may also say "My teacher is mean," or "The teacher doesn't like me," or "My teacher never calls on me."

Of course, "My teacher is mean" might just mean, "She makes me do all of my work." Your job is to follow up with additional questions to find out—which sounds simple, but often isn't. It's not always easy to get a kid to verbalize what's going on during the day. "How was school today?" often elicits a detail-free answer like, "It was okay."

So you'll have to be a bit craftier. Try a few of the following instead:

- "What was the best thing that happened today?" (If the child says "Nothing," that's a clue that things are not good.) Or, "What was the worst thing that happened today?" Listen for repeated mentions of other students, or of something the teacher did.
- "If you could send anyone in the whole school to live in a colony on Mars, who would it be?" (Whoever gets exiled to Mars might be causing a problem.)
- "When were you the happiest today?"
- "If you and your teacher switched places tomorrow, what would you do?" Listen for what the child would do *differently*.
- "If you and your teacher switched places tomorrow, what would your teacher like about being a student in your classroom? What would she hate?"
- "What word did you hear the most often today?"
- "What was the hardest thing you did today?"
- "When were you bored today?"
- "If you could read one person's mind, whose would it be?"
- "If you could get rid of one subject (or class), what would it be?"
- "What do you think your teacher might say about you today in the teacher's break room?"
- "Who did you sit with on the bus?"
- "When did you get annoyed or frustrated today?"
- "How many times did you speak up in class today?" "Never" is a sign of withdrawal and discomfort in the classroom.
- "Which one of your classmates is most likely to survive a zombie apocalypse?" Listen for whether the survivor is smart and wily—or violent and strong. Try not to get sidetracked into the plot of the latest zombie series.
- "Does anyone in your class have a hard time following the rules?"
- "What was your favorite thing in your lunch?" (If someone's commandeering the child's cookies, that's bullying.)
- "If your teacher suddenly turned into an animal, what animal would it be?" Lions and boa constrictors suggest that the child doesn't feel safe.

• "What was one game that you played at recess?" If the child played nothing, she may have spent recess staying out of the way of an overbearing classmate.

If you start to see an unhealthy pattern in the child's day (a particular classmate who always pops up in a bad light, a certain class or situation that's causing stress, a place—bathroom, lunchroom, playground— that seems to be associated with negative answers), you can begin to zero in with more specific questions.

Don't pepper your child with questions; ask one or two at a time. Don't tackle the child the minute she walks in the door; give her a snack and a chance to quietly unwind first. Children need space and time to process their day.

Follow your instincts. We second-guess our parental instincts far too often. If you sense something is wrong, push for answers. If you think the child needs to be left alone, back off for a time.

But if you become aware of an unhealthy situation, intervene. And the younger the child, the more prompt your intervention should be.

You may hear the opposite advice: It's important for children to work out their own problems. School is a place where they should figure out how to act independently. Teach your child to talk back to the bully/avoid the bully/understand the bully/defuse the bully. Learning how to deal with a bad teacher is an important step in maturity—it will help your child later in life when he has to deal with a bad boss.

I disagree. Vehemently.

Children in school are powerless. They have been placed in a situation where they have no freedom of movement, no option to walk away or quit or leave. They've probably been taught that being a tattletale is a bad thing, yet they have no legitimate weapons of their own to use against bullies and shamers. Dealing with a bully or a hostile teacher requires a sophistication and clarity that adults have a hard time achieving—let alone eighth-graders.

Or third-graders. Or kindergarteners.

Intervene and protect.

School is not the real world. It is a purely artificial construct. In the real world, if you hit me, I need to know no more than how to dial the constabulary to come and deal with you. When adults fight, it is a criminal act, dealt with by proper authorities.

In school (not the real world) children are not afforded the real world solution of complaining to the authorities. No child should ever have to "learn to deal" with criminality upon their person. In the real world, that simply is not tolerated. Why should it be whitewashed in schools? —AUDREY

I was bullied as a kid. Imagine your absolute most embarrassing moment ever—something that still makes you blush and cringe. That sense of humiliation and mortification was with me every single day, all day long in school, while the kids made fun of me.

It's really hard to get over that. In fact, I always thought I'd forgiven the children who bullied me, but just last week I caught myself fantasizing that I met up with one of them and gave her a big slap across the face. I'm thirty-five and I've never hit anyone in my life! I realized that I hadn't forgiven her. And I'm not really sure how to do so at this point.

I never breathed a word of it to my parents. I was so ashamed and humiliated. I loved them and they loved me and I knew they would be so hurt to realize people were treating me so badly. —GINA

My son was suspended in first grade for hitting a child who was holding him against a brick wall and banging my son's head on it! My son punched him to get free, and, apparently, some adult saw this happen and both boys were taken to the principal's office. Both were suspended until the following Monday.

We asked the principal what our son should have done and were told that he should have gotten an adult. When we asked how he should have done that since he was being held against a wall, we got no answer.

In this country, we have the right to defend ourselves. We realized that at school, our son did not have this right. We realized that dropping him off at school was like dropping him off in a foreign country. Shortly after this incident we decided to homeschool. —CATH

ACTION PLAN

Document, document, document.

Nothing is more frustrating for teachers and administrators than vague complaints. When you realize there's a problem, your first impulse may be to descend on the school to resolve the situation before your child has to live through even one more day. That's natural, but it's also likely to be counterproductive. You say the teacher is shaming your child; the teacher denies it. You say that another child is bullying your first-grader; the child denies it. The school has no way to know who's telling the truth.

Ask to visit the school. Sit in on classes. Observe the lunch room. Nothing is going to happen in front of your eyes, but you may get a whole new take on the child's situation once you've spent some time inside it.

If the school refuses to allow you to visit, I would take that as a warning sign that this is not a healthy environment. Object to the policy and ask them to make an exception. If one isn't granted, consider how you might bring some pressure to bear; perhaps, talking to local media about the policy, in an attempt to force more transparency.

Write down every incident with as much detail as possible: times, dates, places, exact words used. This is still a self-report, but a careful log kept over time is much more convincing to administrators than a laundry list of complaints without accompanying details.

Ask your child who else witnessed the incidents. If possible, talk to the witnesses and write down their take on what happened.

For a student who's old enough to discreetly manage a tape recorder, many anti-bullying advocates suggest purchasing a small digital voice recorder for the student to keep in her pocket. This might give you very direct proof of inappropriate teacher behavior or peer bullying. Depending on the state you live in, you may or may not be able to use this when you address the issue with the school, but it will certainly provide you with more clarity on what's happening. Be aware that the taping itself is not legal in a few U.S. states, but be sure to check your state laws; bullying is wrong, but I don't recommend breaking the law to combat it.

There's little that a school can do on a verbal accusation—especially when that accusation comes from a third party (parents). Every incident reported at our school (by anyone) gets investigated, but if admin ends up with a "he said, she said" situation, how is the school supposed to know who is telling the truth? Are those of us who work in schools supposed to have magical powers?

If there's enough to go on, the school acts—sometimes even involving legal authorities. But otherwise, if there just isn't evidence, the school can't do anything. We'd get in trouble legally. And we might indeed be wrong if we believe a story that just isn't true.

To any parent or kid involved, report it with specific details. Then report again and again. Honestly, this is the only way the school can act. Telling friends, neighbors, or Facebook does absolutely nothing.

—CORY

Go buy a small digital voice recorder from OfficeMax or Staples—even Walmart probably carries them—and send it to school with your child. Have him practice discreetly turning it on in his pocket or somewhere it won't be seen. Have him record at least a week's worth of classes. That will let you hear exactly what's happening. Then you can decide if the teacher has it out for your child, or if the teacher is simply strict.

If the teacher really is bullying, schedule a meeting with the teacher, counselor, and principal and let them hear the recording for the first time at the same time. I think kids do need to learn how to deal with unreasonable people, but not like that, in a school setting where the teacher has all the power. Fight for your son and don't stop until you get the resolution you want.

—ROBERT

A problem child with violence issues began bullying and hitting my son, unprovoked. The private school turned a blind eye.

I took names, I gathered witness accounts. I wrote precisely one concise and itemized letter describing each event, specifying dates, times, and detailed eyewitness accounts, and handed it to the principal in person with very little discussion. My letter was something that could easily be handed to police or social workers, or superintendents of non-public education.

My unspoken mantra was something like: You now know. I know you know. There is no way you can deny that you know. Either refute each and every bullet point on this letter or make this problem go away. Like, right now!

The problem went away.

—SAMANTHA

Go up the chain of command properly.

When you're ready with your documentation, *always* start with the teacher.

In a case of bullying by other students, the teacher probably doesn't know what's happening—or the scope of it. Bullies aren't stupid; they act out of the presence of authorities who could punish them. You're doing the teacher a huge favor by helping him find out what's going on.

If the teacher is the problem, plan how to bring up the issue in a firm, accurate, but respectful and kind manner. Don't accuse. Share your observations and concerns, and ask what changes might be possible. And take notes on what is said during the meeting on both sides.

When bad teacher behavior is the problem, you'll very likely end up dealing with administration to resolve it. But it's unfair to the teacher to go directly to the school without first addressing the problem with the person involved.

I'm a parent, but also a former teacher. Always begin by talking to the teacher in person. You don't necessarily know the whole story.

Teachers are professionals. Treat them that way, at least to start the conversation. You will learn a lot about how the teacher operates, what is important to her, and what are the keys to success in her class. If the teacher is unprofessional or incompetent and cannot address your concerns, then you can go up the chain of command. —ALI

If the teacher can't, or won't, resolve the problem, take your notes to the administration. If you feel that the situation is fraught or escalating, take an advocate or friend with you to witness the administration's response.

And if the situation involves any sort of physical threat or criminal behavior, then go to the police.

School administrators are not law enforcement. They may prefer to deal with theft, assault, or other illegal acts privately, but they're not actually qualified to do so. If your child is injured, or property is stolen, professional resolution is necessary.

> When my youngest daughter entered eighth grade, she became a target for a couple of mean girls. They picked on her for a few months and then finally stole her cellphone. They used her cellphone to text boys pretending to be her and then made sexual advances toward these boys. It was a mess.
>
> Stealing her cellphone went way over the line, and we decided to press charges because they stole our property. —DAPHNE

Persistence, documentation, and the (politely phrased) threat of legal action and publicity can resolve many situations. But if the problems continue, you may be faced with the choice of removing your child from the classroom.

> After managing stomachaches and tears and missed school days for nearly six months, we met with the principal and counselor. The school counselor stated outright she did not believe us and that she would not be addressing the behavioral issues and bullying, because she just knew the named children could not be acting out how we described. Long story short, we withdrew our daughter a week later.
> —PENELOPE

PART III

Taking Control

CHAPTER SEVEN

Basic Principles
(Or, How Not to Be "That" Parent)

Once you've identified the mismatch between your child and the system, you have two choices:

Stay within the system, and try to flex it so that it's a better fit for your child.

Or step completely out (an eventuality dealt with in Parts IV and V of this book).

If you're going to stay in, you will need to constantly negotiate with teachers and administrators. This can be difficult—particularly if you find yourself dealing with an inflexible teacher, or a principal who tends toward the autocratic side.

Your challenge is to speak up for your child, without becoming one of "those" parents.

Just to develop some empathy for the teacher's point of view, do a Web search for "parents teachers hate" or "teachers dealing with difficult parents." You'll come up with all sorts of lists. (They used to be along the lines of "Five Types of Parents Teachers Hate" or "Ten Types of Difficult Parents," but recently the lists have been more like "Twenty-one Parents Teachers Loathe," which doesn't seem like a healthy trend.)

You'll find that teachers aren't crazy about Ghost Parents (who never appear or answer simple requests), Drama Kings and Queens (who blow tiny incidents up into enormous crises), Scapegoaters (always blaming problems, from low grades to playground fights, on anyone other than their own child), and Helicopters (you already know what a helicopter parent is).

But the most hated on most lists: the Special Snowflake Parent, who believes his or her child should be treated differently.

Which is going to be tricky for you, since most of the chapters that follow recommend asking for special treatment of one kind or another.

Here's a basic principle of human relationships: It's all in how you ask.

LAYING THE FOUNDATION

Before you start requesting changes, make sure that you're standing on solid ground. I would recommend two specific strategies.

First: Assume goodwill on the part of all, and hold on to this assumption for as long as possible. (This is pretty good relationship advice generally, so please feel free to apply it across the whole of your interpersonal conflicts, not just when dealing with your child's teachers.)

You should *always* start out with the premise that the teacher, the administration, and the staff have your child's best interests in mind and want your child to flourish. Sure, it's possible that this belief will be dented over time. If you go through all of the steps recommended at the end of this chapter, and are continually confronted with anger and/ or apathy, you might have to revise your position.

But don't *start* with suspicion and hostility.

A teacher's brusque demeanor can cover an intense commitment to help students achieve. A laidback deportment can signal a nurturing style, rather than a lack of interest. Believing the best can help you understand the teacher's approach; presuming the worst can torpedo discussions before they even start.

Second: Get involved before you start negotiating.

Where there is already a relationship in place, negotiations are easier. If you've made the effort to understand and help the teacher, the teacher is much more likely to make efforts on your behalf as well.

If you've never participated in the classroom, put in any work to support the teacher's goals, or attempted to identify yourself with what the teacher is doing, descending on her with special requests is going to seem presumptuous. And obnoxious.

So before you approach the teacher and ask for a change, show that you're in sympathy with the teacher's goals. Try to *help* and *understand*. Spend some time visiting.

And then, if it is at *all possible*, volunteer for some task or responsibility.

> *Work hard on the relationship, to start off with. If your timetable allows (and the school is willing), volunteer in class, try to work out how you can help the teacher, be someone whom she knows and trusts. Be a solution, not a problem. You can also see what actually happens in class that way—it was eye-opening when I did this with my son, as his behavior in class was not at all what I had assumed.* —LAURA

Regular volunteering is the best way to a teacher's heart, but if your schedule doesn't make that possible, consider the following:

Chaperone a school trip.

Always attend back-to-school celebrations and parent-teacher conferences.

Always answer teacher emails or notes sent home.

At the same time, don't email the teacher to ask questions that are answered on the school's website (which you should acquaint yourself with) or in the parent handbook (which you should read, even if you don't want to).

Are there supplies that you could purchase and donate to the classroom? Many parents aren't aware that teachers, in both private and public classrooms, spend an average of $500 per year of *their own money* to stock pencils, paper, and other materials.[1] If you can help, you'll not only be easing the burden on an underpaid teacher, but you'll be demonstrating that you understand school dynamics.

Offer to clean out, sort, and organize the supply closet.

Ask if you can help sharpen pencils. This sounds minor—but most elementary teachers spend valuable after-school time sharpening all the pencils for their students. (Nothing wastes more time than having second-graders sharpen their own.)

---

1 Sarah Ruiz-Grossman, "How to Help Teachers Forced to Buy Supplies with Their Own Money," http://www.huffingtonpost.com/entry/teacher-appreciation-week_ us_5728d095e4b0bc9cb044a767 (accessed March 7, 2017).

Offer to design, or help design, a new bulletin board for the classroom. That's a time-consuming task, and even the most dedicated teacher eventually runs out of fresh ideas.

The class might also have a Pinterest board (or another social media presence) that could benefit from parent input. Offer to help, or even manage, a classroom social media channel.

Once you're involved in the classroom, in whatever way is possible for you, you'll have a much more credible voice in which to speak your concerns.

THE WAY FORWARD

Strategy 1: Do your research to demonstrate your own dedication—not to educate the teacher.

Nothing is more annoying to a professional (in any sphere) than to be informed about your work by a layperson.

If your gifted, or different, or learning disabled child needs additional support, you're likely to have done a fair amount of research before you approach the school. But if you begin by explaining educational theory to a teacher, you're likely to scuttle any possible cooperation within the first five minutes. If the teacher had decent training, he already knows about different learning styles, disabilities, best classroom practices, etc. And if not, he's likely to go on the defensive.

Bring your research, but use it to show that you're not just complaining without understanding the issues—you've taken the time to be thoughtful, to educate yourself, and to think carefully about how your child learns best.

"I'm not a teacher, of course, but I've really enjoyed learning more about gifted math students," or "I know teachers have training in dealing with dyslexia, but reading more about it has been eye-opening to me" is likely to go over better than "Here's what you need to understand about my child's problem."

Strategy 2: Always observe the chain of command.

I addressed this in the last chapter, but it's worth repeating: Even if the accommodation you're asking for will have to be arranged by the principal or administration, *always begin with the teacher.* Going over his or her head reveals a lack of respect. And whatever accommodation is made will require the teacher's cooperation and help.

Addressing the teacher first acknowledges her importance and authority. Heading straight for administration diminishes and marginalizes her.

Strategy 3: Always be specific.

Never come in with a vague complaint, whether it's "My child is bored" or "My child doesn't understand what's going on in the classroom." Document specific *times* when the child was bored:

> Nov. 11, she finished her math worksheet in five minutes and then had nothing to do for the remaining 35 minutes of the class.

> Dec. 5, the in-class reading assignment was from a book he's already read several times, so he spent most of the time doodling.

or confused:

> Mar. 7, she came home not understanding the pictorial representation of math problems. We worked together on it that evening but over the next week she still didn't seem to be following the explanations given in class (the problem was with the work on pp. 72–78 of the text).

You need to establish a pattern of specific events or problems connected to the larger issue you intend to address.

This reassures the teacher that you have been working to identify a real problem, rather than venting general discontent with the classroom or method. (The teacher has some control over *how* she teaches; she probably has very little say in the material assigned to be covered or the overall pace of the class.)

Strategy 4: Always come armed with a workable alternative.

Simply complaining is *never* productive.

A workable alternative (I'll offer a number of these over the next few chapters) has three characteristics:

It doesn't cause more work for the teacher—just for you and the child.

It doesn't disrupt the classroom or cause problems with the student's classmates.

It won't cost the school money or cause a blip in the school's adequate yearly progress.

Adequate yearly progress is an accountability measure (set by the No Child Left Behind Act) that many public schools participate in. To show adequate yearly progress (or AYP), schools have to demonstrate that (1) 95 percent of all students took part in yearly reading and mathematics testing; (2) these tests were also taken by 95 percent of each of the following subgroups: white, black, Hispanic, disabled, ESL, and "economically disadvantaged" students; and (3) overall *and* in each subgroup, the test scores average out to be either above a set mark, *or* show 10 percent improvement over previous test scores. (Other factors are counted as well, but the test scores carry the most weight in showing AYP.)

As we'll see in Chapter 8, this doesn't mean that your child *has* to participate in yearly standardized testing; just be aware that holding a child out of testing is going to create a lot more pushback from the school than a proposal that your child accelerate or switch classrooms for certain subjects. Test scores and money (these two things are usually related) tend to be more on the minds of administrators than the daily progress of one individual child.

> *Make a list for yourself of accommodations that you want to ask for. Prioritize them and decide which ones you are willing to bend or let go of, and which are hard limits. Realize that the principal is most likely concerned about money, test scores, and data-driven AYP and keeping the number of parental exceptions to a minimum. All of those things keep the school culture intact. You want to make it clear that you are not trying to threaten them.*
> —ELLEN

Individual teachers need to know that you are *not* asking them to develop material for your child alone (they're probably already working at full capacity), and that you are *not* aiming to create a situation in which other students resent or envy your child.

In the elementary grades, what worked best was for us to send in supplemental material for him to work on, which we did not expect the teacher to teach or grade. —M.B.

Let the teacher know that you realize her job is very difficult, dealing with all the different levels in her class (even dealing with high achievers). Carry on being a solution by saying, "It must be so difficult to keep the quick finishers busy while you work with those who need more help. I was in the book shop the other day and I noticed this math text. Would it be okay if I slipped one of these into X's bag for him to work on in odd moments? Are there any other children who might benefit? The text comes with photocopying rights." Then work from there. —LAURA

CHAPTER EIGHT

Control the Tests

Standards tests are inevitable—but not mandatory.

Let's start with *inevitable*.

American education is a patchwork. Not a pretty one, like a State Fair–winning quilt, but an ugly clashing mélange of public and charter schools, administered by states and districts with widely varying standards and treasuries; private schools (religious, secular, accredited, non-accredited); distance education; and homeschoolers.

Standardized test scores are the only way for outsiders to gauge how the quilt pieces measure up against each other.

If you're a homeschool parent, you probably already realize that when your high-school student applies to college, a Mom-and-Dad-graded transcript is going to carry less weight than the student's standardized test grades. But if your child is in a regular classroom, you may not realize that this is true for *every* student.

If (for example) two students with a 3.7 are applying to the same college admissions office, but one student attended a well-off suburban private prep school and the other an undersourced rural public school, the college (by necessity) has to use standardized test results to figure out how equivalent those 3.7s are.

You also may not realize that it doesn't particularly matter which school is "accredited" and which isn't. Accreditation is an extremely fuzzy qualification. (See Chapter 2.) In most states, private schools (particularly religious ones) don't actually have to be accredited. Online schools that *are* accredited are still viewed with reservations. And public schools can lose their accreditation for low performance, though in most cases, they keep on running without appreciable effect.

Given this complete lack of any meaningful national standard, tests are the only leveler that outside observers can use. So standardized tests are not going to go away anytime soon.

Knowing how to take those tests can actually be a valuable life skill, even though they're arbitrary and unreliable. However, up until SAT/ACT time, test results are probably going to be more useful to the school system than to you and your child.

In fact, testing before college admissions exams has almost *nothing* to do with your child—and everything to do with the system.

WHAT THE TESTS MEASURE

There are two kinds of tests given in most school systems: learning ability tests and achievement tests.

Learning ability tests are essentially intelligence tests: IQ-test alternatives intended to measure intellectual ability (of various kinds).

Achievement tests measure *how much* students have learned in any given academic area.

Within schools, learning ability tests are used to funnel students into gifted and talented programs or to identify learning disabilities. Achievement tests are used to show whether or not the school is meeting minimum academic standards and showing adequate yearly progress. Ability tests have to do with the student; achievement tests, by and large, have to do with the school.

If your child tests well, doesn't suffer from anxiety, and is deft at filling in tiny bubbles, she may actually enjoy taking standardized tests— or, at least, view them as just one of those mundane tasks to check off the list so that she can get back to something more interesting, like recess or lunch.

But for other students, testing can be incredibly fraught: stressful, burdensome, and even damaging.

Children who miss a gifted-and-talented cut-off, thanks to an ability test score, know that they have been ranked and found wanting. And children with unusually low ability test scores are given the clear message that they are below average—even though the test scores may have been seriously affected by reading or writing disabilities, comprehension differences, or just childishness.

My daughter knew the right answers, but if there was an animal (or something else she liked) in any of the other answers, she would pick the wrong choice because "I like animals." —ELIZABETH

When my son took his first tests in first grade, he scored very highly. I hadn't talked to him about the tests at all. We didn't do anything to call attention to it, because I knew he always got stressed about tests that were "important."

In third grade, the teacher did nothing but talk about how critical it was they take the test seriously, and how they better do well or they might not even make it to fourth grade, etc. My son was so stressed before he even got to school that he didn't sleep at all the night before, and then threw up that morning. He froze and didn't even finish the test. And when he got home he burst into tears and told me he was afraid he would never finish third grade. —ANNA

Achievement tests (those are the ones schools use to show that they're doing a good job) can cause even more chaos. Because the test results affect some kinds of school funding, or can bump a school's reputation up or down, or can lead to additional state oversight, school administrators *need* those scores to be high.

So days and weeks are lost to the testing itself. Weeks and months are often dedicated to preparing directly for the tests, rather than to real learning and teaching.

When I taught kindergarten, I was amazed at all the worksheets they started running off in January, to prep the kids for the test taking that would begin in first grade. Worksheets on filling in the bubbles all the way! They spent every afternoon test prepping, for months, with tons of extra worksheets, and the kids were just zombies by the end of the day. —MOIRA

I sometimes felt that due to the Texas state achievement tests, all the kids were learning was how to bubble in Scantrons. My last year teaching, some friends and I sat down after the last day of school and counted out the days we'd lost to testing. It was more than seventy days that we didn't get to teach because we were giving benchmarks, or practice tests. That doesn't even count the classroom testing. —KATE

THE RIGHT TO REFUSE

In 2014, in Tulsa, Oklahoma, first-grade teachers Karen Hendren and Nikki Jones, faced with the job of giving a new and lengthy battery of Common Core–aligned standardized tests, simply refused. In an official protest to their school board and in letters to the parents of their six-year-old students, Hendren and Jones described the damage the lengthy testing process was doing to learning. A local reporter chronicled the circumstances that led to their protest:

They wrote of one conscientious first-grader, "We watched his eyes well up with tears. We watched the student nervously pull at his hair. Eventually, the student scratched red marks down his face in distress over the test."

A special education student "looked around the room and noticed everyone clicking away even though he was still on question 6. The child raised his hand and said 'Why am I counting apples and he has math with lots of numbers?' He then stood up and threw his chair."

Adaptive tests are supposed to be more "personalized" but Hendren and Jones describe another result of those sort of tests that ask more or less difficult questions, based on the student's answers, until he reaches the zone of proximal development (ZPD). This is the result for a student who is a "pleaser," tried to do his best: "This particular student quickly noticed that each question he answered correctly generated a more challenging question. Once out of his ZPD, the student laid his/her head down in tears and clicked through the test randomly selecting an answer, then clicking the arrow to proceed. We are talking about a student that is funny and happy. He can tell us jokes all day long. He takes care of the classroom and is in tune with people's feelings. This student knows when he is respected and when he is not."

As a result of their testing boycott, Hendren and Jones lost their jobs (both are now in private education). But the public outcry that followed their whistleblowing led the Tulsa public school system to cut mandated in-class testing hours by 54 percent—from (an unbelievable) *138* annual hours, back to 66 hours (which is still, by the way, around ten full school days of testing, not counting prep time).[1]

It also brought new attention to the basic rights of parents to keep their children out of standardized testing.

After Hendren and Jones expressed their concerns, the Tulsa superintendent of schools responded in a public statement "We cannot afford to wait until third grade to determine whether students are on track for success," adding that opting out of standardized testing "is **not an option**" (emphasis his, not mine).[2]

Actually, as Tulsa parents who empathized with Hendren and Jones soon found, testing *is* optional.

The organization FairTest: The National Center for Fair and Open Testing (www.fairtest.org), which is dedicated to helping parents and children opt out of standardized testing when appropriate, points out that most states have regulations that allow parents to pull children

1 Andrea Eger, "Two Teachers' Refusal to Give Tests Puts Their Jobs at Risk, but They Say It's Worth It," *Tulsa World,* November 24, 2014, http://www.tulsaworld.com/homepagelatest/two-teachers-refusal-to-give-tests-puts-their-jobs-at/article_a3b100 5b-09c2-555f-9a5d-39eaeb497205.html (accessed December 6, 2016); Andrea Eger, "Teachers Who Instigated Over-testing Examination in TPS No Longer Work There," *Tulsa World,* August 4, 2015, http://www.tulsaworld.com/news/education/teachers-who-instigated-over-testing-examination-in-tps-no-longer/article_157a6031-9da2-57 94-840a-40d194c750fc.html (accessed December 6, 2016); John Thompson, "Tulsa Cuts Testing Time Fifty-Four Percent!" *Administr@tor Magazine,* August 25, 2015, http://scholasticadministrator.typepad.com/thisweekineducation/2015/08/thompson-tulsa-cuts-testing-time-by-54.html (accessed December 6, 2016); John Thompson, "Why Tulsa Teachers Risk Their Jobs to Opt Out of the Testing Madness," *The Huffington Post,* January 25, 2015, http://www.huffingtonpost.com/john-thompson/why-tulsa-teachers-risk-t_b_6218080.html (accessed December 6, 2016).

2 "Read a Letter from TPS Superintendent Keith Ballard Issued Tuesday Evening," *Tulsa World,* November 18, 2014, http://www.tulsaworld.com/read-a-letter-from-tps-superintendent-keith-ballard-issued-tuesday/pdf_81dde15f-0261-5a3c-a964-4ed418 9889cf.html (accessed December 6, 2016).

from standardized testing. And states that don't allow opting out only mandate assessment testing, which does *not* legally equate to standardized achievement testing. FairTest provides a template for an opt-out letter that specifies how the child will be assessed *without* standardized testing, along with many other state-specific resources.

So if testing is making your child miserable, or if you have reason to think that scores will be artificially low or otherwise damaging, remember this: Tests are *not* mandatory. *You have the authority to excuse your child from yearly testing.*

Because standardized test results matter to schools (if more than 5 percent of the student body opts out, the school may be subject to additional state oversight), you may find yourself pressured to participate. Parents of high-achieving students report encouragement (and sometimes guilting) to put their opted-out kids back into the classroom so that their scores can be counted.

> *When I notified the school that we would not be testing, the principal called me personally and told me he needed as many kids in the school as possible to participate, particularly "those of [my daughter's] caliber."* —AMY

> *When we opted out, a teacher told my eight-year-old, "We're having an ice cream party to celebrate CSAP completion, but you won't be going to that unless your parents let you take the test like the rest of the class."* —ROBERT

> *It is legal here to opt out, but parents are not informed of this very often, so few know. One mother asked about the opt-out policy and was told by the school that her children did not qualify to opt out. This woman already knew the law and eventually got the school to admit that she could opt out, but they asked her not to tell other parents they could opt out. They told her that they needed her child in the testing because he would score high: "Won't she feel bad if the school scores low because she opted her child out? How about the teacher? Don't you want the teacher to be rewarded for her hard work?"*
> *Another mother was told that if she wanted to, she could keep her child home sick from school on test days. Her daughter was expected to score poorly on the tests.* —PENNY

While I understand the desire of an institution (particularly one doing a vital and important job) to put its best foot forward, I also believe, very strongly, that schools rely far too much on standardized testing to measure progress.

Our current standardized exams encourage schools to teach test preparation instead of history, science, music, art, and foreign languages, none of which are typically tested. They are unfair to students with immature fine-motor skills. And they have repeatedly been shown to unfairly lowball poor and minority students who don't share the same cultural references as their white middle-class classmates, as well as gifted students—who can always think of reasons why more than one multiple-choice answer might be considered correct.

Opting out of school-based testing can be not only a protection for your child, but also a protest against the vastly overblown role that standardized tests play in contemporary American education—and against the amount of valuable classroom time squandered on preparing for them.[3]

I also believe, as a friend of mine eloquently puts it, that young children suffer when their own needs and mental health are subordinated to the good of the collective. Children who will be stressed, discouraged, or pigeonholed by school-administered testing should be opted out, even if this is not ideal for the school.

Schools exist to serve children, not the other way around.

TYPES OF TESTS: WHAT THEY ARE
AND HOW TO USE THEM

Here's the other side: Tests, both ability and achievement, can be useful.

They can be useful when they're given in a non-pressured individualized setting, tailored to the student's learning and expression styles, and treated as only one of many ways to find out how to meet the child's educational needs.

---

3 Daniel Koretz's study *The Testing Charade: Pretending to Make Schools Better* (Chicago: University of Chicago Press, 2017) provides an eye-opening examination of the unreliability of our standardized tests, the distortions to learning that happen when those tests are made the center of education reform, and the amount of instructional time wasted in preparing for them.

There are *many* different, highly regarded standardized tests out there, both for analyzing learning ability and for measuring achievement. Some are more visual; some are more verbal. Some are oral; others use paper and pencil; others are computer-based. Some make use of patterns and abstract designs; others measure skill in symbol use. Some gauge standard language use and mathematical computation, while others test knowledge in history, geography, literature, logic.

While you don't have to line up for school-administered tests without question, you also don't need to abandon testing entirely.

As I've already pointed out, tests can help determine learning styles, possible disabilities, and areas of difference and giftedness. A combination of achievement and ability tests can clue you in to instruction that's missing the mark; high ability scores and low achievement scores signal a troubling disconnect. Achievement testing can give you a sense of where your child is in comparison to others in his or her age-grade. And when you talk to teachers and administrators about necessary changes for your child, having test scores in hand gives weight to your own assessment of your child's ability.

The following three charts list the most commonly used ability and achievement tests. There are others (particularly if you're able to consult a clinical psychologist, who can give tests that are only provided to medical personnel), but these will give you a sense of your options.

Notice that a number can be given by a parent and sent away for scoring. For others, you'll have to visit a psychologist and ask for testing.

One further note: These are all used nationally. Some states have their own state-developed achievement tests. I have not tried to summarize these, but the categories below will give you a sense of what information to look for when researching tests.

Searching for additional information on any of these tests will lead you to sample questions; add your locality and you may find private test administrators and psychologists who specialize in testing.

LEARNING ABILITY TESTS

Content	Grades	Time	Administration Options
Cognitive Abilities Test (CogAT)			
Tests reasoning and problem-solving in three areas: Verbal (verbal classification, sentence completion, verbal analogies); quantitative (quantitative relations, number series, equation building); nonverbal (figure classification, figure analogies, figure analysis)	3–12	2 ½ hours. Each of the three batteries may be given individually, if desired.	Can be administered by any parent with a BA or BS degree and sent away to private scoring service (setontesting.com). Paper and pencil.
Das-Naglieri Cognitive Assessment System (CAS)			
Measures "cognitive processing abilities"—the capacity to plan, pay attention, and process information simultaneously and sequentially. Designed as an IQ-test alternative. Used to predict achievement and diagnose learning disabilities.	K–12	40 minutes for the Basic Battery (8 sections), 60 minutes for the Standard Battery (12 sections)	Must be given by an accredited school, licensed psychologist, or medical facility/clinic/practice. Paper and pencil.
InView InView also provides a four-section cognitive skills test for K–1 known as the Primary Test of Cognitive Skills (PTCS)			
Cognitive skills test with five sections: Verbal reasoning (words), verbal reasoning (context), sequences, analogies, and quantitative reasoning.	2–12	2 hours (may vary slightly by level). The PTCS test is untimed.	Must be given by an accredited school, licensed psychologist, or medical facility/clinic/practice. Paper and pencil (both).
Kaufman Assessment Battery for Children, Second Edition (KABC-II)			
Processing and cognitive ability test with multiple subtests: face recognition, conceptual thinking, pattern reasoning, story completion, number recall, word order, riddles, verbal knowledge, use of expressive vocabulary. Designed as an alternative IQ test; higher emphasis on nonverbal skills than some other tests.	Preschool–12 (ages 3 to 18)	25–70 minutes depending on level.	Must be given by an accredited school, licensed psychologist, or medical facility/clinic/practice. Paper and pencil.
Leiter International Performance Scale, Third Edition (Leiter-3)			
Intelligence test that offers a completely nonverbal measure. Designed to measure cognitive, attentional, and neuropsychological abilities in students who are nonnative speakers, hearing or speech impaired, on the autism spectrum, or cognitively delayed.	Ages 3 through adult	20–45 minutes	Must be given by an accredited school, licensed psychologist, or medical facility/clinic/practice. Uses games and manipulatives rather than paper and pencil.

Content	Grades	Time	Administration Options
Naglieri Nonverbal Ability Test—Third Edition (NNAT3)			
Nonverbal assessment of cognitive ability. 48 multiple-choice items, making use of abstract shapes and designs; questions in pattern completion, reasoning by analogy, serial reasoning, and spatial visualization.	K–12	30 minutes	Can only be given by an accredited or approved school or school district. Online, tablet, or paper and pencil.
Otis Lennon School Ability Test, Eighth Edition (OLSAT-8) and Ninth Edition (OLSAT-9)			
Cognitive ability assessment measuring verbal, nonverbal, and quantitative thinking. Multiple choice questions in verbal comprehension (following directions, antonyms, sentence completion and arrangement), verbal reasoning (aural reasoning, arithmetical reasoning, logical selection, verbal analogies and classifications, inference), pictorial reasoning (picture classification, analogies, and series), figural reasoning (figural classification, analogies, and series, pattern matrices), and quantitative reasoning (number series, numeric inference, number matrix).	K–12	40–75 minutes, depending on level	Can only be given by an accredited or approved school or school district. Paper and pencil.
Raven's Standard Progressive Matrices (SPM) and Raven's Standard Progressive Matrices Plus (SPM Plus)			
Assesses nonverbal cognitive ability: ability to make sense and meaning out of complex or confusing data; ability to perceive new patterns and relationships; ability to create nonverbal constructs of understanding. Makes use of abstract designs and patterns rather than verbal and written questions.	1–12	Untimed; 20–45 minutes to administer, depending on level.	Can be administered by anyone with a master's degree in psychology, education, social work, occupational therapy, or a related field; anyone with a degree or license in a healthcare field; or anyone who has had specialized, formal training in related educational therapies. Paper and pencil.

Content	Grades	Time	Administration Options
Universal Nonverbal Intelligence Test, Second Edition (UNIT2)			
Alternative "intelligence assessment" for "individuals who have speech, language, or hearing impairments; have different cultural or language backgrounds; or are verbally uncommunicative." Six subtests in Symbolic Memory, Nonsymbolic Quantity, Analogic Reasoning, Spatial Memory, Numerical Series, and Cube Design.	K–12	10–15 minutes for Abbreviated Battery 30 minutes for Standard Battery 45–60 minutes for Full-Scale Battery	Must be given by an accredited school, licensed psychologist, or medical facility/clinic/ practice. Nonverbal format, making use of charts and manipulatives.
Wechsler Intelligence Scale for Children, Fifth Edition (WISC-V) (Achievement test equivalent: the WIAT in the following chart, p. 111)			
Cognitive ability test. Assesses fluid reasoning, working memory, processing speed, verbal comprehension, and visual/spatial ability; sections on word reasoning, matrix reasoning, picture concepts, letter-number sequencing, vocabulary, math reasoning. An alternative IQ test. Previous versions of this test, the WISC-III and WISC-IV, are sometimes still given.	1–10	60 minutes	Must be given by an accredited school, licensed psychologist, or medical facility/clinic/ practice. Paper and pencil or online.

ACHIEVEMENT TESTS

Subjects Covered	Grades	Time	Administration Options
California Achievement Test (CAT) (Some updated levels are known as TerraNova—the newest edition of the CAT; see p. 110.)			
Language and math achievement: vocabulary; reading comprehension; language mechanics and expression; math computation; math concepts and applications.	4–12	2½ hours	Can be given at home by any parent and sent away to private scoring service (setontesting.com). Paper and pencil.
Iowa Tests, Form A *The K–8 test is the Iowa Test of Basic Skills (ITBS)* *The 9–12 test is the Iowa Test of Educational Development (ITED)*			
Language, math, science, social studies, and study skills: language skills (vocabulary, reading, language, spelling; word analysis and listening for K–3 only); math concepts, computation, and problem solving; social studies, science materials, and sources of information.	K–12	The core areas of reading, language, and math can be given alone. Time for the full batteries are approximately: • K–3, tests are untimed but will take approximately 2.5 hours for the core, 5 for the full battery, over 3 days. • 4–8, tests are timed and take 3.5 hours for the core, 6 for the full battery, over 3 days. • 9–12, tests are timed and take approximately 3.5 hours for the core, 4.5 hours for the full battery, over 2 days.	Can be administered by any parent with a BA or BS degree and sent away to private scoring service (setontesting.com). Paper and pencil.
Peabody Individual Achievement Test, Revised/Normative Update (PIAT-R/NU)			
General academic achievement test with six measures: General Information (science, history, humanities, social studies), Reading Recognition, Reading Comprehension, Mathematics, Spelling, and Written Expression. Useful for measuring achievement in students who may struggle with written and verbal processing and/or test anxiety.	K–12	Untimed; administration takes approximately 1 hour	Usually administered by a trained counselor or professional (independent) test administrator. Although the publisher (Pearson) now considers the test "retired," it is still widely available through independent testing services. Test format is oral but makes use of printed reading materials and allows scratch paper for computation. Written Expression subtest requires writing.

Subjects Covered	Grades	Time	Administration Options
Stanford Achievement Test Series, 10th Edition (Stanford 10)			
General academic achievement test, multiple choice, with sections on reading skills and comprehension (includes word study skills for grades 3–5 only), vocabulary use and listening comprehension; mathematics (concepts, computation, estimation, connections, reasoning and problem solving); language use (mechanics, usage, sentence structure, written expression); spelling (locating misspellings); social studies (basic understanding of U.S. government and history, Western civilization, non-Western societies, and geography); and science (using reasoning skills to answer questions in life, physical, and earth sciences)	3–12	Untimed but usually given over 2 full days.	Sold directly only to accredited/approved schools and school districts, but can be taken online by individual students through independent services such as setontesting.com. Pencil and paper or online.
TerraNova/CAT 6 (Updated version of the CAT; see p. 109. Both versions are currently in use.)			
Science, social studies, and language and math achievement: vocabulary and word analysis; reading comprehension; language mechanics and expression; math computation; math concepts and applications.	K–12 (Complete Battery) 2, 3, 4, 6–12 (Survey: a shortened version of the Complete Battery)	Complete Battery: 2–5½ hours depending on level, generally spread over 3 days. Survey: 2½–4½ hours over 2 days.	Can be given at home by any parent and sent away to private scoring service (setontesting.com). Paper and pencil. NOTE: Unavailable in Georgia. Upper levels unavailable in North Dakota, Wisconsin, and Washington, DC.

Subjects Covered	Grades	Time	Administration Options
Wechsler Individual Achievement Test, Third Edition (WIAT-III) (Learning ability equivalent: the WISC in the previous chart, p. 108)			
Tests the student's level of skill in reading, mathematics, written language, and oral language. Sections include: Listening Comprehension, Oral Expression, Early Reading Skills, Word Reading, Pseudo-Word Decoding (sounding out imaginary words to test phonetic principles), Reading Comprehension, Oral Reading Fluency, Alphabet Writing Fluency, Spelling, Sentence Composition, Essay Composition, Math Problem Solving, Numerical Operations, Math Fluency in Addition, Subtraction, and Multiplication	Preschool–adult	35–104 minutes, depending on level	Can be administered by anyone with a master's degree in psychology, education, social work, occupational therapy, or a related field; anyone with a degree or license in a healthcare field; or anyone who has had specialized, formal training in related educational therapies. Paper and pencil or online.

COMBINED LEARNING ABILITY/ACHIEVEMENT TESTS

Content	Grades	Time	Administration Options
Differential Ability Scales® II (DAS-II)			
17 of the 20 sections measure cognitive ability; three measure verbal and mathematical achievement (for comparison with ability measure). Cognitive subtests measure mental processing: conceptual and reasoning ability, verbal ability, nonverbal reasoning ability; spatial ability; verbal and visual working memory; immediate and delayed recall; visual recognition and matching; processing and naming speed; phonological processing.	Preschool–12 (ages 2 years 6 months through 17 years 11 months)	25–65 minutes for preschool 40–65 minutes for K–12 cognitive tests 15–25 minutes for K–12 achievement tests	Must be given by a licensed psychologist or psychiatrist, or by someone with a doctorate in education and training in test administration. Paper and pencil.
Woodcock-Johnson IV (WJ IV)			
The test has three separate batteries: WJ IV Tests of Cognitive Abilities, WJ IV Tests of Achievement, and WJ IV Tests of Oral Language. The first two batteries can be used independently as pure cognitive ability or achievement tests. The Oral Language battery tests both cognitive ability and academic achievement. The Cognitive and Achievement batteries come in Standard and Extended versions. The cognitive batteries test mathematical and verbal thinking, as well as visual pattern recognition. The achievement batteries test skills in reading, spelling, writing, computation, science, humanities, and social studies. The oral language batteries test verbal skills and listening comprehension/decoding. The previous version of this test, the Woodcock-Johnson III, is sometimes still given.	Preschool–adult	3 sections (Reading Fluency, Math Fluency, Writing Fluency) are timed; the rest are untimed. The entire test takes between 60 minutes and 3 hours to administer, depending on how many Extended versions are used.	Can be given by an accredited or approved school or school district, by a licensed psychologist, or by a trained private examiner. Paper and pencil or online.

THE WAY FORWARD

Strategy 1: Decide whether or not to take part in school-administered tests.

Find out what tests the school is administering, and when they'll be given. With the charts on pages 106–12 as your starting point, do a little bit of fact-gathering.

What areas does the test emphasize? Are they areas in which your child soars or struggles?

Does the style of the test match your child's style of processing? Children who read slowly, suffer from any degree of dyslexia, or otherwise process information more easily aurally and by means of patterns (rather than words) are disadvantaged by many of the standard tests.

How does your child feel about taking the test? Some nervousness is normal, and older children (say, twelve and up) do need to learn how to deal with test-taking jitters. But there is absolutely no reason to stress younger children. If the prospect of the test brings on stomachaches or headaches, seriously consider opting out.

Does timed work panic your child? This is very common. Some students cannot think straight when there's a ticking clock in the background. Often, this problem is resolved with maturity. Sometimes it persists into adulthood. It isn't a failure or flaw, simply a reflection of learning style. But standardized tests with time limits do not accurately evaluate these children.

If you decide to opt out, talk directly and personally to the teacher first. Express your appreciation for the teacher's hard work, and explain that you're not opting out because of anything the teacher has done. You're simply making the best choice for your particular child.

Then write an opt-out letter to the school administration. FairTest (fairtest.org) provides invaluable guidance in how do this.

Most states also now have an Opt Out Facebook page with state-specific tips; I just searched Facebook for Opt Out Virginia and immediately found two separate groups. Both link to the most recent Department of Education pronouncement on opting out. I'll quote, and then analyze this, as a model of how you might approach your own state's regulations:

All students enrolled in the Virginia public schools are expected to take the applicable state tests. The *Virginia Board of Education Regulations Establishing Standards for Accrediting Public Schools in Virginia,* available online, state:

> "In kindergarten through eighth grade, where the administration of Virginia assessment program tests are required by the Board of Education, each student shall be expected to take the tests" and "each student in middle and secondary schools shall take all applicable end-of-course SOL tests following course instruction" (p. 9).

The regulations do not provide for what is sometimes referred to as an "opt out policy" for students regarding the Virginia assessments. If, however, parents refuse to have their student participate in one or more of the required Virginia assessments, the following procedures should be followed within the school division:

- The parents should be informed that their student's score report will reflect a score of "0" for any test that is refused.
- The school is strongly encouraged to request a written statement from parents indicating the specific test(s) the parents refuse to have their student complete. The document should be maintained in the student's file as a record of the decision.
- To account for the student, a test record for the refused test(s) is to be submitted for scoring with a Testing Status 5 coded to indicate the refusal to take the test.[4]

Notice that although the language says the test is "required," *this is not true.*

There is no consequence to the child if the test is declined. That "0"

4 Patricia I. Wright, Superintendent of Public Instruction, "Student Participation in Virginia Standards of Learning Assessments," http://www.doe.virginia.gov/administrators/superintendents_memos/2013/142-13.shtml (accessed December 7, 2016).

score is meant to be disturbing (the Department of Education *wants* your child to take the test), but it *means nothing to the student.*

K–12 standardized test scores don't affect college applications. (Colleges never see them.) The scores don't affect transfer from one public school to another, either. Students who apply to transfer from a public to a private school *may* be asked, by the private school, to provide test scores—but this requirement can be satisfied through private testing if necessary.

The 0 score only affects the school and its relationship with the State Board of Education, not the student.

Remember: Schools should serve students, not the other way around. Make the decision that is right for your child.

If you do opt out, some schools will allow you to keep the child home; others may require children to come in even if they're not being tested. If that happens, send books, coloring books, and worksheets in for the child to do while they're waiting.

■ ■ ■

If standardized testing is used to determine promotion into particular grades (in Georgia, for example, fifth and eighth grade graduations are tied to standardized test scores), you will find opting out to be more complicated. However, it's still possible.

In a 2016 interview with the *Atlanta Journal-Constitution,* Knox Phillips, director of research, assessments, and grants for the DeKalb County School District, stated, "The State of Georgia's legislation does not permit opt-outs from state mandated assessments (Georgia Law O.C.G.A. §20-2-281). . . . [Third], 5th, and 8th grade students must score proficiently on the Reading and Vocabulary components of the ELA End-of-Grade assessment to be considered for promotion."

Later in the interview, when asked directly "If students in 3rd, 5th, or 8th grade opt out, can you use other data points for promotion?" Phillips answers, "Other data points will be considered by the local school promotion/retention committees, and students of parents who refused participation in the Milestones will have to participate in a complementary assessment to measure the skills readiness and provide additional insight into the student's readiness for the next grade level."

In other words: Yes, you can opt out, and the school can use other benchmarks for promotion. (The Opt Out Georgia Facebook group, which currently has more than five thousand members, provides additional information on this particular situation.)[5]

Strategy 2: Choose private testing that suits your child and your family.

Use the charts above to pick two tests and make your own arrangements for testing.

Both learning ability and achievement tests can be given by parents, at home, and sent away to Seton Testing for scoring. (This is what I did for my four home-educated children, all the way through twelfth grade; the scores met the Commonwealth of Virginia testing requirement for homeschoolers. I chose tests that suited my children and gave them in a non-pressurized environment.)

They can also be given by private testing services and psychologists; you'll probably want to go this route if you intend to use the test scores to access a gifted and talented program (such as the Davidson Young Scholars or the Johns Hopkins Center for Talented Youth program).

If you suspect a learning problem (see Chapter 4), it's useful to have the test given by an experienced psychologist who will pick up on test-taking problems.

5 Maureen Downey, "Can Parents Opt Their Kids Out of State Testing? Not Without Consequences," *The Atlanta Journal-Constitution*, April 19, 2016, http://getschooled .blog.myajc.com/2016/04/19/can-parents-opt-their-kids-out-of-state-testing-not-with out-consequences/ (accessed December 7, 2016).

CHAPTER NINE

Challenge the Homework Monster

In the United States, it's not uncommon for a child to spend seven hours at school, and then do another three or more hours of follow-up work at home.

Seriously, people. That's a *ten-hour day*.

Even those of us who are adults struggle when we regularly spend more than eight hours per day at work. Yes, we can do it, but it leaves us feeling overwhelmed, exhausted, and frazzled, like important things are constantly slipping away from us.

Sadly, your own experience with a full school day followed by homework has probably preconditioned you to find this way of life acceptable. It may even have preconditioned you to accept a fifty- or sixty-hour workweek as an inevitable part of human life.

But ten-hour workdays are neither healthy nor necessary.

WHEN HOMEWORK DOESN'T WORK

A ten-hour day would be unreasonable even if homework filled a vital educational need.

This is far from certain.

Repeatedly, homework has been shown to be ineffective for elementary students. That's right: *all* homework given to young children fails to reach its goal.

Homework is helpful for middle-school students *only* in much smaller amounts than is usually assigned.

And the most recent study of high-school homework assignments shows that productivity plateaus at two hours per night. Past that, students are learning nothing, while stressing themselves unnecessarily and losing the chance to spend time doing other important things (visiting friends, interacting with family, pursuing creative interests, exercising).[1]

What about homework's role in developing other important non-academic skills—self-discipline, for example, the willingness to work hard, and the ability to handle pressure?

As Etta Kralovec and John Buell point out in *The End of Homework* (a 2000 study that fired the first salvo in the war against homework), homework only teaches self-discipline and the willingness to work hard if *parents* (not teachers) "systematically structure and supervise homework with that goal in mind"—a pattern that many families, particularly those with two working parents, simply can't follow.

In fact, the value of self-discipline and hard work can be (and is) taught to children in many different parts of life. It doesn't take homework to develop these qualities.

What about handling pressure?

Kralovec and Buell sum up this widely heard argument: Since "schoolwork is to the child what paid work is to the adult," children who "learn to handle the pressure" of homework are "also developing sound work habits." But they then object, strongly: "[D]o we really believe that learning how to handle work pressure is an appropriate goal for a fourth-grader?"

I agree. Children are not miniature adults. Requiring them to learn how to deal with adult levels of pressure is not good teaching—or parenting.[2]

Yet that's what we're doing.

---

1 Clifton B. Parker, "Stanford Research Shows Pitfalls of Homework," *Stanford News*, March 10, 2014, http://news.stanford.edu/2014/03/10/too-much-homework-031014/ (accessed December 7, 2016).

2 Etta Kralovec and John Buell, *The End of Homework: How Homework Disrupts Families, Overburdens Children, and Limits Learning* (Boston: Beacon Press, 2000), p. 13.

Ten years ago, surveys found that elementary students were doing an average of seventy-eight minutes of homework every night, middle-school students ninety-nine minutes, and high-school students between three and five hours—despite standing recommendations from the National Education Association (NEA) and National Parent Teacher Association (NPTA) that homework assignments be shorter than twenty minutes per night in grades K–2 and thirty to sixty minutes per night in grades 3–6.

And even the NEA guidelines are out of line with studies showing that homework does not benefit younger students *at all*.[3]

Parents who find the amount of homework assigned to their children to be a massive burden often second-guess their reactions. Homework seems to be a natural part of school, it's in the child's best interest, and the teachers must know what they're doing.

But there's no solid evidence that homework improves learning. Little attention in teacher training is given to how, why, or when to assign it (homework's pretty much invented by the teacher on the spot). And there are very shaky historical precedents for its use (homework was rarely assigned early in this century; schools then cycled through anti- and pro-homework phases, more or less in tune with national anxieties about America's economic status, despite studies showing *no* correlation in any developed nation between homework assigned and national economic wellbeing).[4]

Homework researcher Cathy Vatterott, professor of education at the University of Missouri–St. Louis, identifies five assumptions behind homework assignments:

1. Schools have the responsibility to care for and occupy students outside of school hours.
2. Intellectual activity is intrinsically more valuable than other kinds of activity, and should take precedence over them.
3. Completing homework is the primary way that students learn responsibility.

3 Sara Bennett and Nancy Kalish, *The Case Against Homework: How Homework Is Hurting Our Children and What We Should Do About It* (New York: Crown, 2006), pp. 10–11, 38.
4 Cathy Vatterott, *Rethinking Homework: Best Practices That Support Diverse Needs* (Alexandria, VA: ASCD Publishing, 2009), pp. 6–12.

4. The more homework, the better the school (curriculum, teaching).

5. Good (i.e., rigorous) teachers give lots of homework; good (i.e., high achieving) students *do* lots of homework.[5]

Simple common sense should make you skeptical about 1 and 2 (for more about why the custodial role of schools should be questioned, see Chapter 15). Numbers 3, 4, and 5 have been repeatedly contradicted by research. In fact, a 2012 study done at the Indiana University School of Education finds *no* relationship between homework and mastery in math and science—even for high-school students.

There was, however, a correlation between homework time and "performance on standardized tests."

Professor Adam Maltese, coauthor of the study, found that students who spend "more time on homework" are "getting exposed to the types of questions and the procedures for answering questions" that are common on standardized tests.[6] That might benefit the school system as a whole, but it certainly isn't preparing the child for real life.

More and more voices are challenging the value of homework, particularly for the lower grades.

In 2015, PS 116 in New York City did away with mandatory homework for pre-K through fifth-grade students.

A few months later, Harris Cooper, professor of psychology and neuroscience at Duke, stated unequivocally, "There is no evidence that any amount of homework improves the academic performance of elementary students."

Second-grade teacher (and mother) Brandy Young went viral, in the summer of 2016, with her announcement to parents that she would no longer assign homework: "Research has been unable to prove that homework improves student performance," she wrote in her note home. "I ask that you spend your evenings doing things that are proven to correlate with student success. Eat dinner as a family, read together, play outside, and get your child to bed early."

5 Ibid., pp. 10–14.

6 "When Is Homework Worth the Time?" *IU Bloomington Research*, January 8, 2013, http://research.indiana.edu/2013/01/when-is-homework-worth-the-time/ (accessed December 7, 2016).

Schools in Nevada, Washington, California, and elsewhere have recently joined the no-homework for elementary students bandwagon and are reevaluating the amount given in middle and high schools as well.[7]

You can climb on the bandwagon too.

Don't assume that the amount of homework sent home is inevitable, or even well-thought-out. Don't resign yourself (and your child) to evenings of drudgery. There are better things to do with that time.

"It's not just that homework itself has no academic benefits for little kids, and may even be harmful," writes teacher Jessica Smock. "It's also that homework is replacing other fun, developmentally appropriate, and valuable activities—activities that help them grow into healthy, happy adults." Smock lists thirty-one alternatives to homework, including: sleep, reading or listening to audiobooks, doing puzzles, playing outside, helping with dinner, walking the dog, practicing an instrument, hanging out with a grandparent, drawing, playing dress-up, helping with household chores ("University of Minnesota researcher Marty Rossman found that one of the best predictors of a kid's future success is whether they contributed to household chores as a young child"), listening to music, riding a bike, and just plain zoning out.[8]

If your child is overwhelmed with hours of homework, help her reclaim her evenings so she can enjoy some of those alternatives.

---

7 Lee Igel, "What Happens When an Elementary School Abolishes Homework," *Forbes*, March 12, 2015, http://www.forbes.com/sites/leeigel/2015/03/12/what-happens-when-an-elementary-school-abolishes-homework/#1207686b3fad (accessed December 7, 2016); Heather Shumaker, "Homework Is Wrecking Our Kids: The Research Is Clear, Let's Ban Elementary Homework," *Salon*, March 5, 2016, http://www.salon.com/2016/03/05/homework_is_wrecking_our_kids_the_research_is_clear_lets_ban_elementary_homework (accessed December 7, 2016); Brandy Young, "Why I Did It: The 'No Homework' Letter," *The Huffington Post*, August 30, 2016, http://www.huffingtonpost.com/entry/why-i-did-it-the-no-homework-letter_us_57c5b5bfe4b004ff0420daf3 (accessed December 7, 2016); "What Research Says about the Value of Homework: Research Review," Center for Public Education, February 5, 2007, http://www.centerforpubliceducation.org/Main-Menu/Instruction/What-research-says-about-the-value-of-homework-At-a-glance/What-research-says-about-the-value-of-homework-Research-review.html (accessed December 7, 2016).

8 Jessica Smock, "31 Things Your Kid Should Be Doing Instead of Homework," parent.co, October 27, 2016, http://www.parent.co/31-things-your-kids-should-be-doing-instead-of-homework/ (accessed December 8, 2016).

THE WAY FORWARD

Strategy 1: Keep an accurate account of time spent on homework over the course of two or more weeks.

Most teachers don't have a good sense of how long an assignment takes.

High-school teacher Stacey Goodman points out that teachers usually guesstimate, and often get it wrong: "Do [teachers] do it themselves first—not factoring in that they already understand the content?" he asks. (That's a rhetorical question; they don't.) "How on earth do you measure the length of time it takes for a student to think through a problem or a question, and not just write the answer down on a piece of paper?"[9]

If you don't let the teacher know that assignments are taking far too long, he'll continue to assume the workload is manageable.

So document, accurately, how much time the homework is actually requiring. As you do so, make sure that the time spent on homework actually *is* spent on homework. Middle and high-school students can fritter away an awful lot of time sitting in front of books while actually entertaining themselves on social media. While you're documenting, you'll need to keep a closer eye on older students than usual; if you're going to approach a teacher about homework assignments, you'll need to verify that your eighth-grader *did* actually spend three hours on that problem set.

Now, average out the homework time. Is it unreasonable?

In my opinion, *any* homework in grades K–2 is unreasonable, but if it's under fifteen minutes a day, it's probably not worth challenging. More than that, though, should be addressed—especially if your child is exhausted and frustrated every evening.

Ideally, third- and fourth-graders shouldn't be doing any homework either, but up to thirty minutes is probably not unreasonable.

Middle-school students should *not* do more than an hour per night, and if they're doing an hour every *single* night, that's too much.

9 Stacey Goodman, "The Risks of Guesstimating Homework," Edutopia.org, October 18, 2016, https://www.edutopia.org/blog/risks-guesstimating-homework-time-stacey-goodman (accessed December 8, 2016).

High-school students hit a documented achievement plateau at two hours. Some highly academic kids in eleventh or twelfth grade might be comfortable with two and a half, but no more.

Don't forget that, according to the Mayo Clinic, teens need a minimum of nine hours of sleep per night. If the student is taking so many AP classes that she can't get enough sleep, she's taking too many AP classes. (And if she's taking those AP classes to get into Stanford, give her permission to back off; see my Postscript.)[10]

Strategy 2: Address the teacher, then the administration.

So what if your kid is spending too much time on homework?

As always, address the teacher first.

"Call teachers," says a former Ivy League college admissions officer. "Bug the school . . . You may be surprised what happens when you call a teacher and say 'my son worked on this for two hours and still couldn't finish, so I sent him to bed.' Oftentimes, it's a reality check the teacher needs and welcomes."[11]

Show that you've done your research. Take your homework logs and a couple of the studies that have found excessive homework to be counterproductive. (Use the books in Appendix C as sources.) Ask for a reduction in take-home work, and more time spent on the assignments in class.

If appropriate, offer an alternative. Sometimes students are spending all their time on unnecessary busywork, when real learning could be happening in that time instead. You may be able to replace inappropriate assignments with self-designed work that can actually be done in less time.

> *I got my son's entire first-grade reading send-home curriculum replaced with an at-home program I did. His teacher was extremely nice and gracious about it. I just needed to go and talk to her and explain what was going on and what I would like to do.* —LECKA

---

10 "Teen Sleep: Why Is Your Teen So Tired?" MayoClinic.org, http://www.mayoclinic.org/healthy-lifestyle/tween-and-teen-health/in-depth/art-20046157 (accessed December 8, 2016).

11 "Parents: Let Harvard Go," roxandroll.com, November 5, 2014, http://www.roxandroll.com/2014/11/parents-let-harvard-go.html (accessed December 8, 2016).

My younger son got a "needs improvement" grade on his homework at the end of the year. That was really the only consequence of not doing homework.
                                                                    —*NAN*

If the teacher is unresponsive, it's completely reasonable to then address the principal.

Take your concerns, along with detailed notes on your failed teacher meeting, to the principal's office. Ask what school policy is.

If the policy doesn't align with the guidelines I outlined in Strategy 1—which are entirely compatible with NEA recommendations—politely point this out. And if there isn't a school policy, ask for one to be formulated.

Strategy 3: Accept the consequences (when reasonable). Or adjust the child's schedule.

What happens if the teacher, and/or administration, doesn't respond?

If the alternative is an exhausted kid who hates school, cut down on the homework yourself, and take the consequences.

"Send your kid to bed anyway," says that same Ivy League admissions officer, "and tell him you'll love him even when his teacher marks him down for unfinished work." You *do* have the authority to tell your child to stop doing homework and go play outside. And then, don't worry about points off. In grades 1–8, it really doesn't matter if the student gets marked down for unfinished homework. (See Chapter 2. Those grades simply don't matter.)

Parents are ultimately responsible for the mental and physical health of children. So protect them.

One exception: If the consequence visited on your child is losing recess in order to do the homework, do *not* accept that. Go to the principal and ask for a schoolwide policy change.

I work as a school psychologist, and teachers making kids miss recess is one of my pet peeves. I have to stop myself from rolling my eyes when a student who has been diagnosed with ADHD has recess taken away and then the teacher complains to me how fidgety and inattentive the student is after recess. At Individualized Education Program meetings, I almost always insist that no missing recess for missing/

late/incomplete homework is written into the IEP. All kids need a break to move around, talk to friends, play a game, etc. —NAN

My kids attended two different public schools. In one, the principal was adamant: zero recess time was ever lost for any child through sixth grade, unless steps had been taken first, up through parent conferences, with no resolution to the problem, and the team agreed that losing recess time would somehow be effective in deterring future problems, that it somehow helped address the specific problem. This was an urban school, and it had fewer behavior problems than any elementary school I have ever seen.

The other school my kids attended was a wealthy suburban school with smaller class sizes, and a big banner across the front proclaiming (in Orwellian fashion), "We are a superior school!" (because of test results). For every single infraction, real or imagined, kids were instantly kept indoors from recess. Sometimes entire classrooms stayed in for an entire recess because of the actions of a single kid. The kids were going nuts. The school spent more time on discipline than on teaching. —JEN

In grades 9–12, grades do matter, and if students lose significant points on unfinished homework, this could affect their transcripts.

But the truth is that high-school students who regularly spend more than two hours per night on homework are taking too many classes, or too difficult classes, and should cut back.

Cramming a high-school student's schedule full of AP classes to make them more competitive in college admissions is a mistake, if that means the student has no life apart from school.

Getting a kid into any particular college is a complete spin of the roulette wheel. Selective colleges see, literally, *thousands* of applications from students with all-AP schedules and GPAs of over 4.0. (The titles listed under "College" in Appendix C provide plenty of documentation for this.) If your high-school student is doing three to four hours of homework every night, she is leading an unbalanced life *and* not particularly raising her chances of college admission.

Give her permission to breathe.

Strategy 4: If the school remains inflexible, realize that you may be moving toward a more drastic solution.

Depending on the teacher, homework can be the most difficult part of a classroom to negotiate, and leads many parents, ultimately, toward some form of homeschooling.

> *I was fighting with my first-grader son about his homework starting in November. In February/March, I called it quits. I told his teachers (reading, math, and "homeroom") that we weren't doing it anymore.*
>
> *The teachers reacted differently.*
>
> *The math teacher sympathized.*
>
> *The reading teacher, whose homework was what sent us over the edge, told me I was violating the Parent Handbook agreement. Her homework was two pages of reading comprehension worksheets, five reading comprehension questions, plus a writing assignment every night (and a weekly spelling assignment). The writing assignment went from "write a paragraph" daily in the first half of the year to "write an essay" daily for the second (with the occasional "write a newspaper article" or "write a poem"). In first grade. It was ridiculous.*
>
> *My son continued to score above 80 percent on all tests after not doing homework. But the whole thing spiraled when the reading teacher was unwilling to work with us, saying she didn't want to lower the standards of the class. We were able to make it through a few months, but I don't think I can send him back to that school and continue the defiance for another year. We're considering homeschooling.*
>
> —DEBI

> *Homework is what finally forced me into homeschooling.*
>
> *After a year of full-day kindergarten with my twins, during which we spent several hours each evening doing homework while we were all exhausted, and spent no time playing outside, I decided homeschooling couldn't be any harder and might actually be easier.*
>
> *It was, because we were finished after a few hours each day. Then they played outside the rest of the day. What a relief it was!*
>
> —JENNIFER

CHAPTER TEN

Accelerate
(But Don't Necessarily Skip)

W hat if your child is working on a higher grade level than others his age?

My advice: As long as you're still within a school system, try not to skip a grade.

This doesn't necessarily apply to profoundly gifted students, who may indeed be so bored that they need to skip two or more grades. Profoundly gifted students are poorly served by classrooms and need customized curricula. (In fact, if you're the parent of a profoundly gifted child, I'd seriously recommend going straight to Part IV now.)

My take on grade-skipping for all but the profoundly gifted is based on the nature of maturation. It's a tricky and uneven process. (See Chapter 4.) A fourth-grader who's unusually advanced, both emotionally and intellectually, can be easily bounced up several grade levels—until suddenly she finds herself, at age twelve, in learning situations with seventeen- and eighteen-year-olds. She may be their emotional and intellectual equal, but they will be light-years ahead physically and sexually, detaching from parental guidance and moving toward independent living. No matter how extraordinary your twelve-year-old, she doesn't belong in that company.

Given the unnatural and arbitrary way that our K–12 system

matches ages and grades, if a child needs to remain in the classroom, it's usually better to match grade placement to *social* maturity rather than to intellectual maturity. Children spend the majority of the day in *company* with their classmates. Their learning can be adjusted, but usually, their social development cannot.

I tend to think this is true for home-educated students as well, at least when we're discussing college admissions.

Even though age-grade placement is less complicated for home-schooled kids, who can usually advance at their own pace in each subject without taking the time to worry about what grade they're in, at the point where home-educated kids reenter our age-graded system by going into university, it's usually better for them to be college aged. To benefit fully from the college experience, students need emotional and social maturity as well as intellectual ability; those things only come with time.[1]

Rather than skipping or repeating a grade, consider asking for single-subject acceleration.

SINGLE-SUBJECT ACCELERATION

The two-volume study *A Nation Empowered: Evidence Trumps the Excuses Holding Back America's Brightest Students* (see Appendix C) lists *twenty* possible forms of acceleration, only five of which involve moving younger children into higher grades.

Most of these, such as mentoring, and compacting or telescoping curricula, require substantial investment and development on the part of the school (the point of the study is that schools do *not* do a good job serving gifted and talented kids).

---

1 Far too often, parents explain to me that their sixteen-year-olds have finished high school and need to go on to college because there's nothing left for them to do. I always roll my eyes at this, although I try to do it internally: They've read *all* the Great Books? Traveled, studied foreign languages? Volunteered to help the homeless or poverty-stricken? Worked a job? Learned to program? Mastered plumbing, carpentering, electrical work, car repair, or the other things that they'll end up paying huge amounts of money for someone else to do for them? I seriously doubt it. Give the kid a few more challenges and the chance to mature before you launch her into her freshman year.

Single-subject acceleration, however, requires no huge action on the part of the school.

Single-subject acceleration is a relatively new development in many districts. The Portland public school system offers a standard definition: "Single Subject Acceleration (SSA) occurs when a student meeting the District's criteria is allowed to study the curriculum of a single subject (e.g. Mathematics or English Language Arts) from a grade ahead of where s/he would be according to his/her chronological age. The student continues to study other subjects in his or her original grade level class."[2]

If your child needs a greater challenge, identify her strongest area and ask your school whether it is possible to single subject accelerate her.

In some cases, the school already has an SSA program but doesn't broadcast its existence widely to parents. ("We have lots of helicopter parents in our system," one mother told me, "so getting into accelerated subjects is done very hush-hush. Otherwise everyone would apply.") In other cases, no such program exists.

But you can ask for one to be created. Test scores showing high achievement (Chapter 8) can help you make your case; a portfolio of work done independently on a higher level than the child's current grade can also be convincing. Also ask whether the child can take a year-end exam in the subject to show she's ready for the next level.

If the school refuses, pursue the subject after school for a time and then provide still more examples of the student's achievement.

Even though single-subject acceleration is a simple, no-cost way for a school to meet the needs of a child who's developing asynchronously (which, frankly, is *most* children), you may meet with pointless resistance. Professional educators are often so entrenched in the age-grade system that they will only agree to advance children globally in an entire grade. But this isn't always in the child's best interests. Thousands and thousands of children need to keep working at grade level in all but one subject—and in that subject, they desperately need to be challenged.

2 Quoted from the Portland Public School TAG Communities website, http://www.ppstag.org/Bh2393ndt/showthread.php?tid=27 (accessed May 6, 2017).

My daughter is strongest mathematically. She's going into second grade this year and has just started reading with fluency. But she's working at the fourth- to fifth-grade math level. Subject acceleration in math has kept her engaged, and she fits into her grade level in everything else.
—BERNICE

Our first grader needed more of a challenge in math. Even though we were just asking for math acceleration, the school administration recommended acceleration to second grade. We agreed.

Unfortunately, the result has not been what we had hoped. He is struggling with writing, which is the one area that he tested average in and we knew he would need support in. He is having a hard time completing assignments and then has to stay in for recess because of it. He had to type a paragraph out the other day in order to make grammatical corrections to it for an assignment. This was not easy for him—as a six-year-old he is not a skilled typist.

When we had a meeting after the first two weeks, we were asked to back off and put ownership on him to figure things out. But he's six. He comes home exhausted and unable to engage in homework until it's bedtime. He is too tired to complete assignments, but is afraid to not have them done. He is sad about school and asking to come home . . . and we are considering it.
—LORILORI

THE WAY FORWARD

Strategy 1: Search your district's official website for any existing policy on acceleration.

Strategy 2: Identify the class you'd like your student to accelerate into.

Remember: Approaching the administration with specifics is *always* more likely to succeed.

Strategy 3: Assemble test scores and portfolio work.

A combination of achievement and learning ability scores (see Chapter 8) is more convincing than a single score. Consider using private or home testing to supplement any scores from school-based testing.

Keep any samples of advanced or independent work that the student has done.

If possible, find and administer a test covering the material in the student's present course.

Strategy 4: Persist. Keep asking. Persist politely. But persist.

CHAPTER ELEVEN

Shift the Method

Back in 1983, developmental psychologist Howard Gardner published *Frames of Mind: The Theory of Multiple Intelligences.*

The book, which became a massive international bestseller, proposed that the type of intelligence measured by standard IQ tests (which happens to be the type of intelligence best suited to classroom learning) is only *one* kind of capability. Gardner argued that there were, in fact, eight different kinds of intelligence: linguistic/verbal, musical/rhythmic, logical/mathematical, spatial/visual, bodily/kinesthetic, interpersonal, intrapersonal, and naturalistic. The theory of multiple intelligences gave educators a way to think about how different kinds of "smarts" showed themselves in the classroom, and before long, the need to teach to multiple intelligences became an educational byword. Thomas Armstrong's now-standard *Multiple Intelligences in the Classroom* (third edition) offers forty teaching strategies for multiple intelligences (five for each of the eight kinds); *Multiple Intelligences in the Elementary Classroom: A Teacher's Toolkit* offers teachers five "pathways" into "MI teaching," including "storyboarding" and "establishing exploration centers"; *Multiple Intelligences and Student Achievement* recommends integrating art into daily lessons, and offers suggestions for incorporating music, dance, and creative writing into assignments.[1]

Yet despite the past thirty years of multiple-intelligence exploration, many classrooms still lean heavily on one type of assignment: reading- and writing-based, a great fit for linguistic-verbal learners who are comfortable with propositional knowledge (see Chapter 14), but less effective for many others.

If your child's classroom consistently assigns *one* type of work, you can propose alternative projects.

SAMPLE PROJECTS DESIGNED FOR MULTIPLE INTELLIGENCES

Consider the following; use or alter to suit your child.

For literature

Find and listen to unabridged audiobook versions of the assigned literature. Evaluate the narrator. Does he or she add to, or detract from, the story?

Find five items that represent five different key moments in the story, arrange them in order, and then explain to the class what each one symbolizes.

Create and film a newscast about the book.

Make a chart (like a football play chart) of the book's action.

Watch a film version of the book and compare the book and film. Which works better?

Make a résumé for one or more of the book's major characters (as if the character were applying for a job).

Choose a celebrity to play each character in the book, and explain why the celebrity and the character are a match.

---

1 Thomas Armstrong, *Multiple Intelligences in the Classroom,* 3rd ed. (Alexandria, VA: ASCD Publishing, 2009), pp. 72–99; Susan Baum, Julie Viens, and Barbara Slatin, *Multiple Intelligences in the Elementary Classroom: A Teacher's Toolkit* (New York: Teachers College Press, 2005), pp. 40–46; Linda Campbell and Bruce Campbell, *Multiple Intelligences and Student Achievement: Success Stories from Six Schools* (ASCD Publishing, 1999), pp. 14–20.

For upper-level students: Imagine that you're ordering for your library. What ten titles *about* the piece of literature should be in the library?

For writing

Choose twenty words. The student should use these words in every possible interaction for the next week.

Draw a comic strip that develops an argument.

Produce a storyboard that would turn your writing assignment into a movie.

Develop and write out a policy governing some kind of behavior (at movie theaters, in the cafeteria at lunch, changing classes) that accounts for every possible deviation from what's acceptable.

Create a regular podcast (at least five brief episodes). The podcast series should have a title, theme, and different but related episodes.

For more advanced students: Create and film an infomercial that uses techniques of persuasion.

Prepare a lecture for students several grades below you, on any topic.

For math

Work out problems with objects: pencils, chocolate chips, erasers, paper clips.

Find three different websites that explain a concept or procedure in three different ways.

Design a game that teaches the math concept or procedure.

Build exact miniatures of houses, playgrounds, parks, or any other physical area, keeping the proportions of the measurements absolutely accurate.

Design and fold mathematically complex origami shapes (for example, https://mathigon.org/downloads/origami.pdf).

Create and administer a survey, and then evaluate its accuracy based on the sample.

Invent a fictional company. Calculate how much investment would be needed to get the company off the ground and how much return the investors would need.

For older students: Teach the math concept or procedure to a
　younger student.

For science

Create a calendar showing the timeframe for a particular scientific
　event.
Write a journal entry about a scientific discovery, in the persona of
　the scientist who made the discovery.
Prepare an "Ignorance Report": Summarize everything that is *not*
　known and *not* understood about a scientific principle.
Design a toy that makes use of the scientific principle under study.
Create an itinerary for a traveler who's investigating the place
　where the scientific principle or discovery works itself out.
For more advanced students: Find two different peer-reviewed
　articles on the same scientific question and compare them. Or,
　compare a popular science article to a scholarly article on the
　same topic.
Design and model a submolecular process as though it were a size
　that could be easily seen and grasped.

For history

Memorize and deliver a famous speech; be ready to explain its
　place in history.
Sketch or make a piece of clothing from the era. Explain where
　each part of the material came from, plus how and why the
　clothing functions as it does.
Research and create a family tree for a historical figure.
Make an audio CD or MP3 that describes a historical event,
　period, or figure; include quotations from speeches, a
　narration, music, etc.
Make a timeline.
Create a museum display, complete with explanatory captions.
Design a Web page to inform visitors about a historical event,
　person, or situation.
Put a historical figure on trial for a controversial action. Locate
　witnesses and testimony. Decide on conviction or acquittal.
Create an accurate scale model of a historical place (building,
　battle site, mountain range, ship, etc.).

For older students: Invent a primary source. Come up with a
persona, that persona's background and history, and the type
of primary source he or she would write. Then, create the
primary source itself.
Create and film a documentary about a historical event.

These are just starting places. In Strategy 2, below, I've listed some reference guides with many more ideas.

You can also hunt around the Internet for inspiration. Try searching for "projects in [subject]," "alternative assessment in [subject]," or
"teaching [subject] for multiple intelligences."

And remember this: You never have to insist that an assignment
be completed *simply* because the teacher assigns it (or the curriculum
guide lists it). Always think about the *purpose* of a task—and if you can
find an alternative and better path toward the same goal, take it.

THE WAY FORWARD

Strategy 1: Decide which subject would most benefit from an alternative arrangement.

Don't appeal across the board (at least not to start)—instead, focus your
efforts in on one particular class.

And don't ask for the student to be exempted from *all* assignments. Students who learn best through kinetic or auditory means
still need to know how to write persuasive essays and complete
research papers. It's just that this shouldn't be the *only* kind of assignment they're given.

Strategy 2: Meet with the teacher.

Come armed with:

(a) Research showing that many students do *not* learn best simply
through traditional word- and symbol-focused assignments. Feel free
to use one of the following:

Carol A. Corcoran, Elizabeth L. Dershimer, and Mercedes S.
Tichenor, "A Teacher's Guide to Alternative Assessment: Taking

the First Steps," *The Clearing House* 77, no. 5 (2004), 213–16 (http://www.jstor.org/stable/30189900).

Thomas R. Hoerr, *Becoming a Multiple Intelligence School* (ASCD, 2000), particularly chapters 1 and 4.

Kenneth D. Moore, *Effective Instructional Strategies: From Theory to Practice,* 2nd ed. (SAGE, 2009), particularly pp. 46–49.

Ken Robinson, Ph.D., and Lou Aronica, *Creative Schools: The Grassroots Revolution That's Transforming Education* (Viking, 2015), pp. 74–95.

Daniel T. Willingham, *Why Don't Students Like School? A Cognitive Scientist Answers Questions About How the Mind Works and What It Means for the Classroom* (Jossey-Bass, 2009), pp. 151–66.

This is vitally important: You are *not* familiarizing yourself with this research in order to educate the teacher. Nothing is more annoying to a professional (in any sphere) than to be informed about your work by a layperson. If you explain educational theory to a teacher, you're likely to scuttle any possible cooperation within the first five minutes. In any case, if the teacher has had decent training, he already knows about different learning styles.

No: Your goal is to demonstrate that you're not *just* complaining— you've taken the time to be thoughtful, to educate yourself, and to think carefully about how your child learns best.

(b) Specific suggestions as to what the alternative assignment should be.

Teachers are already working full-time to teach subjects in the traditional way; never ask them to create new individual assignments that depart from the pattern. Instead, bring a brief (less than one page) written description of the proposed assignment, specifying:

- what the student will do
- what the goal of the new assignment is
- how it should be evaluated (on originality? clarity and persuasiveness? functionality? demonstration of a particular skill?)

If the assignment will bring value to the classroom (for example, the student's model can be used to demonstrate principles to other students; the alternative project can be entered in a fair or contest, or displayed at open houses; the project involves, or can be presented to, the rest of the class), be sure to highlight this.

For elementary students, you should take the lead, but if your student is middle- or high-school aged, involve him or her in both the planning *and* the presentation to the teacher.

CHAPTER TWELVE

Teach, Yourself

The most straightforward way to flex your school to fit your child: Become a part-time home educator. Pick the subject that most needs changing, and teach it yourself.

Thanks to the last three decades (or so) of legalized home education, hundreds of new curricula and resources have been developed that are designed for parents to use with children, one on one, without the need for specialized teacher training. Use the strategies in Part V to locate and teach a single course to your child.

The homeschooling guides in Appendix C are a wonderful starting point for finding parent-friendly books and programs; you can find many more resources and links at welltrainedmind.com.

Homeschool resources, techniques, and lingo gave me the confidence I needed to articulate my goals for my children during parent-teacher conferences. This allowed me to spot learning issues early on, and make course corrections before minor issues became major problems. Both of their teachers came to respect/value my insight and my willingness to work with them as partners. —ADRIENNE

From my experience of home educating, then schooling, then back to home educating, I would say that the major impact of my homeschool-

ing on the school situation was in my attitude and increased level of confidence. Instead of viewing education as something I should leave to the teachers, I felt that the teachers and other school staff were all members of my education team.   —ISABEL

THE WAY FORWARD

Strategy 1: Preteach

Before your child ever heads off to school, *make sure that she can read.*

Not only can reading difficulties disrupt an entire educational experience, but learning how to read often requires a very individualized approach. Children can easily be diagnosed with a learning disability when, in fact, they simply need a different method of teaching.

Here's a quick-start: Begin with a simple one-volume primer that only requires you to sit together on the sofa for ten minutes at a time, sounding out letters. Try:

> Jessie Wise and Sara Buffington, *The Ordinary Parent's Guide to Teaching Reading* (Well-Trained Mind Press, 2004)

or

> Dolores G. Hiskes, *Phonics Pathways: Clear Steps to Easy Reading and Perfect Spelling,* 10th ed. (Jossey-Bass, 2011).

If the primer approach doesn't catch the child's attention, investigate the series *All About Reading,* which is more expensive and complicated, but also teaches reading in a multisensory way that's much clearer to brains that process differently:

> *All About Reading.* All About Learning Press (allaboutlearningpress .com).

Developed by dyslexia researcher Marie Rippel, *All About Reading* is a four-level series that uses flash cards, flip charts, cutting and pasting, and other nonwriting activities to reinforce phonics learning—which makes it appropriate for preschool and kindergarten children.

If you don't see progress with *All About Reading,* I would suspect some degree of dyslexia that needs therapeutic treatment; have your child assessed by a clinical psychologist or neuropsychologist (see Chapter 4).

By preteaching reading, you'll have discovered this difficulty early on, before it can short-circuit your child's progress. Both of these programs assume *no* expertise (or English as a first language) on the part of the instructor—so any parent can make use of them.

Strategy 2: Afterschool

Thousands and thousands of parents "afterschool": pursue the independent study of one or more subjects at the end of the school day, over the summer, or on Saturdays.

You can join other parents who are supplementing, swap recommendations, and find out what's working on the afterschooling message board at forums.welltrainedmind.com.

The challenge with afterschooling is to find a time when the student is still fresh enough to benefit. If she's being assigned too much pointless busywork as homework, use the strategies in Chapter 9 to free up study time for more productive, parent-directed study.

Then, aim to use a program or curriculum that teaches in a way *significantly* different from what the child is doing in school. Online tutorials and games, computer-based programs, and activity-centered learning can be a welcome change from the day's work.

I do thirty minutes of second-grade math with my daughter, along with one page of a vocabulary workbook, and then piano practice. They write a lot at her school, and do a lot of science and art and foreign language, so I don't push that at home. —PAT

My girls, aged five and eight, are at school till 3 p.m. every day and then spend two days a week at gymnastics for two hours, so afterschooling is difficult. I stopped my eldest doing any mathematics homework that was coming from the school, and we do our own math program with her instead. I read out loud to them from the Story of the World

while they eat breakfast, and leave books in the car that they read to
themselves on the way to gymnastics or on the way to school.

—TANYA

We afterschool for about an hour in the evenings, because their home-
work load is pretty light. It's still a balancing act. I insist on having the
kids do something physical most days, but we can still work through
selected books, and do some independent reading every day.

—SEAN

We spend about an hour and a half each night reading. She reads to
me and I read to her. We read poetry, Aesop's Fables, the Bible, and
children's literature. My goal is to expand her vocabulary and expose
her to good writing. We spend a lot of time talking about the language
in what we read. We talk about what words mean. When we read
poetry, we discuss how changing a word changes the meaning of the
poem. The key for us is doing as much as possible orally. After a long
day at school or camp, she's resistant to writing and workbooks.

—AMELIA

Strategy 3: Pull out

If the biology, or math, or literature class your child is enrolled in is completely missing the mark, you can ask for a pull-out: request that the student use that class time to do independent work sent from home.

The key here is to be part of the solution, not just the one who points out the problem. You need to find the work, administer it, grade it yourself, and keep good records. A math teacher who's dealing with students who still count on their fingers isn't going to be able to give your advanced student personal attention on the level he needs, but he might be grateful for your help. He might even allow your child to work on a computer-based math program that doesn't require intensive teacher interaction during math time.

Test results showing advanced learning ability or achievement (see Chapter 8) will lend your request weight and make administration approval much more likely.

I would suggest first asking to test out of the grade level in order to sub-ject accelerate. There are logistical difficulties with subject accelera-tion because most elementary schools don't have all classrooms doing math at the same time. If your child can test out, but subject accelera-tion isn't an option, ask the teacher about sending in your own math materials for your child to work on during math time. If needed, you can give instruction in the evenings and then send in "homework" for her to do at school. With this sort of arrangement, you are more likely to get what you want if you ask for less effort from the teacher (make this as easy as possible on the teacher).

Alternatively, you can let her do the school math as a form of easy review and afterschool math on your own as time allows. —WREN

It's been my experience that district administrators will write you off as a "pushy parent" unless you already have private testing results in hand. That's objective evidence that kids are out-of-the-mainstream in terms of their academic needs. —CINNA

Our school was pretty open to moms, and I got permission to go in every Tuesday and Thursday to do math with my son. Then he did homework at home which his teacher just stamped the next day with everyone else's. —SAM

PART IV

Rethinking the System

CHAPTER THIRTEEN

The End Result

My son is way ahead of his classmates, so he spends his days doing worksheets.

My daughter comes home crying because she doesn't understand what's going on and she feels stupid.

My child already knows the material and is bored.

My child is behind and failing.

This is where we tend to start when we're trying to solve the problem of school: in emergency mode, trying to figure out how to patch a broken part of the system, so that it will work just a little better for our kids.

But if you find yourself spending the K–12 years in constant triage, you may need to take an entirely different approach.

Rethinking the entire system, looking for alternatives, is no easy task. As I pointed out back in Chapter 1, the system is so powerful that it presents itself as the *natural* choice, an inevitable reality.

But that's an illusion. Over the last millennia of human existence, many different educational systems have proved useful, helpful, *human*. The one we have is *not* the one we're stuck with.

The next four chapters are designed to help you step away from the paradigm, reevaluate the system, swallow the red pill.

You may or may not end up moving from Part IV (Rethinking) to Part V (Opting Out). But if you take some time to rethink now, you may find that you have a whole new way to think about taking control, as well; a more powerful way to flex school to fit your child.

THINKING BACKWARD

Most schools are designed to pop out eighteen-year-olds who look essentially the same.

Educational reformer Sam Sherratt calls this a mold system, one that's designed to channel students either into employment or into college. It is a "factory model," in the words of William Tolley, designed to "calibrate" students "to factory standards for the college admissions process or the workplace."[1]

Tinkering with the mold itself isn't going to break this factory model. Instead, stop and think about what's coming out the other end.

Who do you want this child to *become*?

A caution here: Please don't first ask, "What do I want this child to be able to *do*?"

It's our natural impulse, because we know that launching our kids into adulthood is going to require them to find work, and do it well enough to support themselves. But the "What will my child do?" question is a fruitless one—largely because the world keeps changing.

And it's been changing more and more rapidly.

For most of human existence, "making a living" was *not* about preparation to go and get a job. If you were a parent, you gave birth to or sired children, did your very best to keep them alive, and then assimilated them into the family trade or apprenticed them to a relative. (Or,

---

1 Sam Sherratt, "Breaking Traditional Moulds," https://www.youtube.com/watch?v=V_UWHIOYrsE&feature=youtu.be; William J. Tolley, "Why the Factory Model of Schools Persists, and How We Can Change It," http://www.edweek.org/tm/articles/2015/10/30/why-the-factory-model-of-schools-persists.html (accessed October 24, 2016).

possibly, waited for someone else to die so that they could become king, but that was a much smaller segment of society.)

With the advent of the Industrial Revolution, work began to move out of homes and villages, into factories and eventually offices—and became increasingly severed from family life. Getting a job was no longer a matter of learning the traditional family skill; getting a job required you to master specific skills (reading and arithmetic chief among them) and to get comfortable with a particular type of regimented day (divided into segments, controlled by others) so that you could fit into a factory or office.

And then, as the workplace became increasingly complex, a college degree was added to those twelve years of regimented training as the best possible preparation to enter the workforce. Just thirty years ago, a college degree almost guaranteed you a job.

And now? A bachelor's degree can land you in tens of thousands of dollars' worth of debt, and promises you much, much less.

College grads still have lower unemployment rates, but the job landscape is shifting so quickly that figuring out what skills you'll need in even four or five years' time is aiming into the dark:

> "The jobs that are hot don't stay hot for very long," said Peter Cappelli, a management professor at Wharton and director of the Center for Human Resources. In other words, a student choosing a major at age 17 or 18, who may or may not graduate in four years, is making a long-term bet on opportunities that may change before they get their degree.[2]

If the span between the freshman year and graduation is a "long term," how useful is it to speculate on the exact skills your fourth-grader is going to need when she joins the workforce? "The top 10 in-demand jobs projected for 2010 did not exist in 2004," wrote Linda Darling-Hammond, in the long-ago year 2009. "Thus, the new mission of schools is to prepare students to work at jobs that do not yet exist, creating ideas and solutions for products and problems that

2 Kelley Holland, "Can Your College Major Guarantee a Job?" http://www.cnbc.com/2014/11/05/can-your-college-major-guarantee-a-job.html (accessed October 25, 2016).

have not yet been identified, using technologies that have not yet been invented."[3]

So, for the moment, forget about teaching subjects. Quite apart from the impracticality of projecting work-related skills fifteen years into the future, it's dehumanizing to approach your child's years of education by asking: What kind of *student* do I want my child to be? It reduces that small human being to a single aspect of herself—an aspect that may not even reflect her greatest strengths and talents.

Instead, think about your hopes for the *whole* person your child will become.

I wish I'd done more of this when my children were school-aged. I spent far too much time fretting about specific academic challenges—and allowing *those* to shape our years of education.

Now, as a parent of grown children (and a grandmother), I can tell you that almost every massive educational roadblock we encountered appears, in the rearview mirror, minuscule.

He still isn't ready for algebra and he's already in high school. That was a big one. The child is now a charming, witty, thoughtful, persistent young man, a university graduate working hard to make it in his dream career. The fact that he didn't hit algebra until tenth grade has had exactly zero consequences in his life.

I sure did waste a lot of valuable parenting energy on it, though.

THOUGHT EXPERIMENT 1

What qualities, not accomplishments, are important to you?
What qualities would make your adult child a good dinner companion?

Curious. Book-loving. Imaginative. Confident. Thoughtful. Responsible. Gentle. Those are a few of mine. (Your answers to this probably will have something to do with the person *you* want to be. That's called "passing on family values.")

Before you go on, write down six to ten descriptive words that have *nothing* to do with skills or earning ability, and everything to do with the person you want your child to become.

3 Linda Darling-Hammond, *The Flat World and Education: How America's Commitment to Equity Will Determine Our Future* (New York: Teachers College Press, 2015), p. 2 (quoting her own 2009 speech at the University of Alicante).

CHAPTER FOURTEEN

The Child's Vision

Your vision for your child is only one part of the equation.

The second part is: Who does the *child* want to be?

"What do you want to be when you grow up?" is almost always the wrong question, for a number of reasons. The younger the child, the less realistic the answer (among the elementary-aged students I know, vet and superstar singer are trending high). The older the student becomes, the more fraught the answer. Teenagers feel expectation, keenly; they conform to it, or buckle under it, or angrily reject it. (Even those of us who are much farther along life's road have difficulty envisioning our lives as they could be without the judging gaze of others upon us.)

The grammarian in me also needs to point out that "what" and "to be" are an unequal pairing. None of us *are* what we do. And most of us are more than one "what" in our lives. We do a number of different things, in many different contexts, at different times.

"Who do you want to be?" (the question highlighted in the last chapter, from a different point of view) is a much more honest question—but one that we spend most of our lives trying to answer. It's not reasonable to ask a fourteen-year-old to give a well-thought-out answer to that query. At nearly fifty, I'm only now beginning to comprehend it.

THE CHALLENGE OF SELF-AWARENESS

Most of us do not even remember what it was like to think about our lives outside of the K–12 educational system.

It's the reason that so many people plug away at jobs they hate. During the most formative years of their lives, they hated their daily routine, but learned that they couldn't escape it. Is it any wonder that they've continued to live by those same rules?

> [There are] millions of people all over the world who hate their jobs, who go to work and count the hours until the end of the day, and count the days until the end of the week. They're wishing their lives away. We put them there.[1]

Marianne Cantwell had a dream job—a director-level position in a top London firm. "People kept telling me I was lucky to have such a 'great job,'" she writes, "while I secretly felt I was dying inside."

> *The worst part was the attitude.* Everyone around me seemed to think this was normal—they seemed resigned to this career-cage fate. "I had such adventures when I was younger," reminisced an older colleague. "I wish I could do that sort of thing now. Of course you have to get it out of your system before reality strikes."
>
> What? *Reality?* This man thought that this life—in an artificially built, over-air-conditioned building in the middle of a screaming roundabout, hardly seeing daylight three months of the year, with the only hope of escape being winning the lottery—he thought that was *reality*?[2]

It's not reality. It's just what school prepares us for.

Years spent in our artificially constructed educational system can detach students from reality, and instead accustom them to a mode of

1 Sherratt, "Breaking Traditional Moulds."
2 Marianne Cantwell, *Be a Free Range Human: Escape the 9–5, Create a Life You Love and Still Pay the Bills* (Philadelphia: Kogan, 2013), p. 2.

life which has nothing to do with their actual learning styles, joys, talents, and passions.

As parents, we have to take on the task of helping our children connect—or reconnect—with these vital pieces of self-knowledge. And the longer our students have been in school, the more help and encouragement they may need—particularly if they've already received a message of failure and inadequacy.

I'm going to suggest three different challenges—activities that can move your child toward greater self-awareness. Your child can't just do them once and forget them; he or she will need to return to them again and again as he or she grows, matures, and changes.

But they will help both of you begin to figure out how to adjust education to fit personality and passions.

In fact, all of them are echoed again and again in scores of books designed to help adults escape from the trap of a job they hate. *Making a Living Without a Job: Winning Ways for Creating Work That You Love; I Could Do Anything: If I Only Knew What It Was; Be a Free-Range Human: Escape the 9–5, Create a Life You Love and Still Pay the Bills; Un-Jobbing: The Adult Liberation Handbook.* Teaching your child these strategies of self-awareness now won't just help you to improve her present experience; it might also short-circuit the chances that she'll get funneled into a job she hates, accept this as a normal part of real life, and then buy all of those books when she's thirty-five.

CHALLENGES FOR YOUR CHILD

Challenge 1: Pay attention to your emotions and feelings; look for patterns.

Start simply: Give younger students *two* emotions to focus on, one positive and one negative. Say to the student, "I want you to pay special attention today to when you're bored, and when you're having fun." Or *confused* and *interested*. Or *frustrated* and *happy*. Pick feelings that your child has expressed to you on previous occasions.

And then give the child permission simply to feel (particularly the negative emotions) without apologizing—just noting *when* those feelings occur.

Students who struggle are often given the impression that feeling frustrated, or confused, or bored, is a bad thing: a symptom of their inadequacy. (It's a rare teacher, or homeschooling parent, who will say, "If you're confused, that's probably my fault.") Children learn to be ashamed of those feelings, and push them down; this doesn't improve learning, just confuses the mental landscape.

It also means that the negative emotions may be manifesting themselves as physical sensations—stomachaches are the most common—so you might want to include aches and pains as something to be aware of. These can also point to allergies or other problems (see Chapter 4), but when it isn't safe to express feelings, pain can stand in for the unacceptable emotion.

Then, begin a series of conversations after each day of learning. *When did you feel confused today? When did you feel happy?* Or, *When were you angry? When did you laugh?*

Look for the patterns. Are the negative emotions attached to certain subjects, particular teachers, times of day, environments? You may find that a student always is confused when the entire class meets together, but feels happy when working alone or in a small group; this points to a learning style that needs to be accommodated for the student to thrive. You may discover personal hostility between a teacher and child, an emotion that's making learning impossible. Or frustration whenever faced with an open text, or with writing on the board, may indicate vision problems or learning differences.

Home educators are not exempt from this exercise.

It's far too easy for homeschoolers to slip into a curricular rut, or a pattern of teaching that's producing poor results, and simply push forward with gritted teeth even if students are not flourishing.

I speak here from personal experience; I have fallen into this trap myself. And at scores of home education conferences, I've heard questions like this one: "My child cries every time I pull out the math program. What should I do?"

I ask, "How long has this been going on?"

"For the whole year."

That's far too long.

The answers? *Listen to the emotion. Ditch the program and try something else. Get a tutor. Get an evaluation. Don't just push forward.*

Older students can pay attention to more than two emotions at once. This is called *metacognition*—awareness of your own thought process—and it develops most fully in adolescents between the ages of twelve and fifteen.[3] Teens who improve their metacognition tend to perform at a higher intellectual level; self-awareness, in other words, is good for the brain.

Some adolescents may find it useful to keep a learning journal in which they record their stronger emotional reactions, and note when they occur. Others, particularly if they are not natural verbal processors, will find this overwhelming. If your child likes to write things down, a journal might be a good idea; otherwise, keep on talking to them about their emotions during the day.

Challenge 2: Be aware of the things you love.

We're all wired to find joy in some activities and stress in others; to prefer some settings and types of company; to be refreshed and rejuvenated in some situations, while others exhaust and deplete us.

The best learning happens when students are working with, not against, their natural wiring. But education too often becomes a long struggle *against* those inborn inclinations. An extroverted child who loves to be physically active is not going to thrive if he has to learn sitting still and listening to a lecture; an introvert who enjoys abstractions will not learn well if she is in a large noisy crowd doing hands-on activities.

This may seem like a very basic principle, but it's easy to lose track of it.

Children often begin school at a time when their essential wiring isn't easy to discern; they're adaptable, anxious to please, accustomed to doing what they're told. And then, once slipstreamed into the system,

---

3 If you're interested and don't mind professional jargon, two recent studies worth consulting are Leonora G. Weil, Stephen M. Fleming, et al., "The Development of Metacognitive Ability in Adolescence," *Consciousness and Cognition* 22, no. 1 (March 2013), pp. 264–71, http://www.sciencedirect.com/science/article/pii/S10538100130 00068 (accessed October 26, 2016), and M. van der Stel and M. V. J. Veenman, "Metacognitive Skills and Intellectual Ability of Young Adolescents: A Longitudinal Study from a Developmental Perspective," *European Journal of Psychology of Education* 29, no. 117 (2014), http://link.springer.com/article/10.1007/s10212-013-0190-5 (accessed October 26, 2016).

they often go on doing what they're told, while the mismatch between their natural gifts and the way in which they're taught becomes more and more severe.

So encourage your child to be constantly aware of *what he loves*. List-keeping is the simplest way to do this: a running account kept on a piece of paper that says

Things I Love.   *Places I Love.*

This will begin to give you some sense of whether your child has a bent toward propositional knowledge or procedural knowledge: what Ken Robinson defines as the difference between *knowing that* and *knowing how.*[4]

Propositional knowledge, "knowing that," is most at home in the traditional classroom; it is theoretical, abstract, reading-and-writing focused:

> There are three principal elements in academic work. The first is a focus on what philosophers call propositional knowledge—facts about what is the case, for example, that the Declaration of Independence was signed in 1776. Second, there is a focus in academic work on theoretical analysis—of concepts, procedures, assumptions, and hypotheses, for example, the nature of democracy and liberty, the laws of motion, the structures of sonnets. The third element follows from these. It is an emphasis on desk studies that mainly involve reading, writing, and mathematics rather than on technical, practical, and applied work that involves manual dexterity, physical skills, hand-eye coordination, and the use of tools.[5]

4 These two categories were first introduced into teacher education by Benjamin Bloom and four collaborators in 1956. Bloom proposed that education involved six categories of capability, the six being sorted into the two governing categories of knowledge (propositional) and intellectual skills (procedural). The six levels, known as Bloom's taxonomy, are universally taught in teacher training. If you want to explore this further, Vanderbilt hosts a useful site with many links: https://cft.vanderbilt.edu/guides-sub-pages/blooms-taxonomy/.

5 Ken Robinson, *Creative Schools: The Grassroots Revolution That's Transforming Education* (New York: Penguin, 2016), pp. 76–77.

Propositional knowledge, also called "conceptual" or "declarative" knowledge, comes most naturally to children who read early and easily, are comfortable with memorization, and process information verbally. It is, in the words of one teacher-training manual, "knowledge that can be recited . . . facts that can be remembered and expressed. . . . The student must demonstrate the ability to repeat or regenerate it, to report it, to answer tests with it, and in general to present it verbally."[6]

Procedural knowledge, on the other hand, is information put to use: painting, dancing, cooking, sewing, making, *doing*. Obviously, procedural knowledge requires some propositional knowledge (you have to comprehend something about the theory of drawing in order to actually draw), but that knowledge is primarily expressed through action, rather than through symbols (words or figures).

Yes, all students need to be comfortable with reading and writing; all students need practice in verbal expression. But the child whose "I Love" list is filled with acting, showing, moving, *doing*, probably has major strengths in procedural knowledge—and *won't* be served well by teaching that relies almost exclusively on reading and writing, memorizing and testing.

I'm a propositional learner. Two of my children are propositional learners. The other two are procedural thinkers. I didn't realize how important it was for me to flex my own teaching style for my older hands-on learner; how vital projects and demonstrations were, how much the child needed to create and invent and manipulate in order to understand. It's one of my great regrets as a parent-educator—and I think I'm doing a much better job with the younger one. (Yes, older siblings; as you always suspected, you *are* the practice children.)

There is much more you can begin to glean from the list. Does the child like to be alone or in a crowd, quiet or noisy, surrounded by activity and color or in a clean and sparse environment? Does he prefer to create or absorb? Invent or analyze? Argue or contemplate?

Don't forget that this is a self-awareness exercise, not a diagnostic tool. ("There may be said to be two classes of people in the world," Robert Benchley remarked in 1920, "those who constantly divide the peo-

6 Suzanne Wegener Soled, *Assessment, Testing, and Evaluation in Teacher Education* (Westport, CT: Praeger, 1995), p. 48.

ple of the world into two classes, and those who do not. Both classes are extremely unpleasant to meet socially.")[7] Most people are not pure procedural or pure propositional learners (in fact, that would shade over into an actual disability). We may lean toward being extroverts or introverts, but most of us are a mix. Use the list to help identify patterns in what makes the child open, receptive, and happy—not to find labels.

One last note: Don't worry too much if your child can't think of anything she loves.

Kids who've been in a mismatched environment for a long time have often lost sight of their natural tendencies; they're spending so much time struggling through the day and thinking how hard it is that they never practice paying attention to good feelings. Switch the exercise around; tell her to list things she *most* hates to do and the places she *loathes,* and then help her figure out what the opposite would be.

Challenge 3: Take self-knowledge tests (and apply salt).

Self-awareness is a rough gig. It's hard to chase, hard to grasp, hard to frame in your own mind.

I was home educated from first grade by my mother, a trained teacher from a poor farming community who was the only girl in her high-school class to go to college; I was ferried to weekly sports lessons and weekend competitions by my physician father, also a first-generation college grad, child of a blue-collar New Orleans family. Somehow (I'm still unclear on this), they had evolved unlikely enthusiasms for British mysteries from the Golden Age of Murder, Gilbert and Sullivan operettas, classical music, and J. R. R. Tolkien (before he was big-screen cool); this, side by side with family-transmitted skills in pig butchering, chicken raising, construction, plumbing, wiring, and self-educating.

The motto of my growing years: "Well, we could go find a book and figure out how to do that." (Which is why we ended up having to jack up the center of our three-story house, which was originally designed as a single story, but that's another tale.)

---

7 Robert Benchley, "The Most Popular Book of the Month: An Extremely Literary Review of the Latest Edition of the New York City Telephone Directory," *Vanity Fair* (February 1920), p. 69.

Another constant: We took every self-knowledge questionnaire that came across our paths. Personality tests, learning-style surveys, aptitude quizzes, "Your Perfect Career"—we did them all.

This has turned out to be immensely valuable.

A lot of those tests were silly, or badly designed, or just puzzling. But the simple act of *taking* them put us into an objective, self-evaluative mode that isn't necessarily natural.

And if you do enough of those tests, you start to see patterns.

Taken all together, those tests told me that I wasn't a misfit in my college dorm: I just needed private space (in very short supply during my college years) to function well. I wasn't unfriendly; I was introverted. I could solve analytical puzzles; I worked best on my own; I was impatient with repetition, flourished when given creative freedom, had difficulty with arbitrary tasks that had no clear payoff.

This was self-knowledge. And it gave me the power to shape my adult life into a style that fitted me.

There are many fun, insightful, well-designed tests available to anyone with an Internet connection; I maintain an up-to-date list with links at welltrainedmind.com. Among them are the widely used Myers-Briggs, the RHETI test, the Keirsey Temperament Sorter, and the Princeton Review Career Quiz. The *Psychology Today* website hosts dozens of tests to identify introversion/extroversion, analytical reasoning capabilities, creative problem solving skills, and much more. That old standby, *What Color Is Your Parachute?*, has a teen edition that contains useful exercises as well.

One caution: As I've mentioned before, I don't recommend IQ tests, online or otherwise. Like most tests, IQ tests only measure *one* type of ability. But our culture has put such outsized weight onto IQ that the tests tend to have an inflated influence on how we think about ourselves and each other. (See pp. 55–56.)

Do these tests for *fun*.

If the results ring true to you and your child, you've gained useful knowledge.

If the outcomes sound puzzling, shrug and forget about it. No personality quiz is going to measure the human psyche with complete accuracy.

But taken together, they can point you toward recognizing patterns that might otherwise have gone unnoticed.

THOUGHT EXPERIMENT 2

Once your child has had some practice with self-evaluation and self-awareness, and has gained a little maturity (I'd pitch this thought experiment at grades five and above), ask this question:

If you could have a *perfect* day, what would it look like? Describe it—in writing, or orally, or by drawing pictures.

You may need to lend a hand. We're so used to restrictions and conditions that it is almost impossible to think outside · them, and mental fences erect themselves at a very early age.

So, if the child has a hard time, ask leading questions about that perfect day . . .

- When do you wake up?
- What's the first thing you do when you wake up?
- What do you eat for breakfast?
- After breakfast, do you go somewhere (where), or stay home (what do you do there)?
- What do you have for lunch? Where do you eat it?
- How do you spend the afternoon?
- What about dinner?
- What do you do after dinner?
- When do you go to bed?

This is an exercise that's often done in find-your-way self-help books, where it often begins with: *Where do you live? What kind of house? What country? Whom do you spend time with?*

My experience has been that children get stymied by these questions, because they can't imagine a world in which they have the power to choose their house or companions.

Instead, let the child stay within the familiar framework and tell you how the hours would be spent.

Take an absolutely neutral stance. Do *not* point out that it is impossible to actually live with wolves, or unlikely that the president will agree to a meaningful conversation over coffee.

Do *not* suggest that sleeping for the entire day shows a lack of imagination (or energy). Do *not* show approval or disappointment over *any* elements of the day.

Help, and listen.

That "perfect" day has a message for you.

If it's crammed with activities and accomplishments, that might tell you that your child is an energetic, possibly bored doer. If it's stuffed with fantastic creatures, imagination might be the engine that drives the child forward. If it's filled with long slow hours, you could be dealing with a contemplative, meditative loner.

If the child wants to sleep all day, take that seriously as well. Complete retreat is a signal that something's wrong: He may need to be saved from something, or may need a medical diagnosis, or could benefit from a qualified therapist, or is begging you for a much less crammed schedule.

CHAPTER FIFTEEN

All the Other Things School Does

To properly rethink school, you've got to look beyond education.

Take a moment to look backward: In 1950, *Life* magazine offered "average citizens" with "no special knowledge" about education a sixty-three-question quiz to help them rate their local schools. "How Good Is Your School? 'Life' Test Will Tell You," the article headline trumpeted. "This list of simple questions, the first of its kind, gives parents a practical way to measure the education their children are getting."

Of the sixty-three questions that followed, *four* dealt directly with academic instruction (including "Science courses include at least one hour of laboratory work for every four hours of classroom instruction" and "The school makes use of a remedial reading specialist").

Six had, indirectly, to do with the quality of teaching (for example, "At least 50% of the classroom teachers have master's degrees" and "The school board contributes financial aid for in-service training of teachers").

The remaining *fifty-three* questions had nothing whatsoever to do with learning.

Among them:

There are citizens present at all open school-board meetings.
High school has vocational or industrial arts courses.

All students study community, including techniques of local
    government, through visits and participation.
There is a psychologist or psychiatrist available for consultation.
Students can obtain hot food at the school.
The school provides inspection and cleaning of teeth by a dental
    hygienist at least once a year.
There is an organized intramural athletic program in the high
    school.
At least 65% of the pupils participate in voluntary club or hobby
    programs.[1]

These quiz items could still be answered with a yes in scores of school systems today (including the "inspection and cleaning of teeth," often provided through school-based healthcare clinics).

None of this has to do with education.

Here's the point: Since 1647—more than a century before the United States took shape as a nation—American education has claimed a much broader role for itself than academic instruction. On November 11 of that year, the tiny Massachusetts Bay Colony passed a resolution that every township with more than fifty families in it should pay a teacher to instruct children in reading and writing, and that every town of more than one hundred families should establish a formal grammar school. This wasn't for the love of letters; it was so that the "old deluder, Satan" would be unable to make the "true sense and meaning" of the Scriptures to be "clouded and corrupted." The law, known afterward as the Old Deluder Satan Act, was a religious provision, meant to keep Puritan children safe within the fold of the faith.[2]

Since then, American education has been assigned an increasingly overstuffed grab-bag of tasks to accomplish. And those tasks are a huge part of what keeps us trapped inside the K–12 mold.

The list below does not speculate on whether schools *should* be doing these things. That would be an entire book in itself; in fact, it has been. But getting a clear view of the nonacademic functions that

1 "How Good Is Your School?" *Life* (October 16, 1950), pp. 54–55.
2 "The Old Deluder Act (1647)," *Records of the Governor and Company of the Massachusetts Bay in New England*, Vol. II (1642–1649), ed. Nathaniel B. Shurtleff (Boston: William White, 1853), p. 203.

schools serve is an important step toward asking yourself: Do schools *have* to be the path toward these goals? And are there other ways that these tasks could be carried out?

THE NONEDUCATIONAL TASKS

Let's start with the most basic: Schools are now custodial.

Those 1950 schools served hot meals and provided dental care because they were child-minders—taking on the parental role of overseeing the whereabouts, activities, and basic physical needs of children. Since the United States has no national childcare network, schools continue to fulfill this role: "Schooling," in the words of educational researcher John Goodlad, "is the most comprehensive, least expensive system of childcare ever devised."[3]

The need for affordable, reliable childcare, particularly in homes where both parents work, drives the length of the school day, the increasing push to begin formal education at age three or four, and the development of truancy laws: Students are compelled to go to school, because the school is responsible for their safety and wellbeing.

Schools are also the American funnel into the job market. In 1950, those vocational and industrial arts courses prepared non-college-bound students for blue-collar jobs; today, schools also push students en masse toward college, with a two- or four-year degree the bare minimum qualification for a large percentage of entry-level jobs.

Schools offer physical training: children learn how to exercise, and play sports, have the opportunity to join teams (like those intramural programs), and are taught basics of nutrition and good health habits.

Schools monitor mental and emotional health. The psychiatrist or psychologist on staff has been joined by mental health classes, emotional awareness courses, counseling centers, school support groups, and drug and alcohol education.

Schools provide access to recreation. Hobbies and clubs aren't primarily academic resources; they're ways to draw students into

---

3 Robert A. Roth, ed., *The Role of the University in the Preparation of Teachers* (Philadelphia: Taylor & Francis, 1999), p. 3.

activities and associations that can turn into adult pastimes and grown-up relaxation.

Schools are agents of socialization. This is a huge aspect of American education, and one with several faces.

"Socialization" most commonly seems to mean "getting along with others" and "fitting in with peers"; most homeschool parents will tell you that "How will they be socialized?" is the first question most new acquaintances ask, and that what they really mean is, "Will they be social misfits who don't know how to carry on a conversation or relate to others outside of spelling bees?" (As one standard handbook to educational law puts it, "Social interaction with other students . . . is an essential ingredient of school.")[4]

But, in a larger sense, "socialization" means "becoming accustomed to social norms"—absorbing the essential characteristics and qualities of our national character, the elements that make us a country, the habits and beliefs of our larger society. In that same 1950 issue of *Life*, historian and civil rights activist Henry Steele Commager wrote an accompanying essay laying out the part that schools play in making Americans American—an essay that begins by dismissing academics. "It is not because education advances scholarship that it has been so prized in America," Commager explains, "but rather because it promised to bring to real life the American dream of the good society."[5]

How do schools do this? They're supposed to teach students what democracy is and how it functions (that's why "all students study community" and citizens have the opportunity to influence school board meetings); they're supposed to supply a diverse population that has little else to hold them together with a shared set of stories, images, and values, a "common language" and a way to understand a "common heritage"; and they're supposed to demonstrate the core American value of equality. As Commager puts it, in flowery but quite clear prose:

> This most heterogeneous of modern societies—profoundly varied in racial background, religious faith, social and economic interest—has

4 Kern Alexander and M. David Alexander, *The Law of Schools, Students and Teachers in a Nutshell*, 5th ed. (St. Paul, MN: West Academic Publishing, 2015), p. 30.
5 Henry Steele Commager, "Our Schools Have Kept Us Free," *Life* (October 16, 1950), p. 46.

ever seemed the most easy prey to forces of riotous privilege and ruinous division. These forces have not prevailed. . . . In the classroom, the nation's children have lived and learned equality—all subject to the same educational processes and the same disciplines.[6]

That is the broader meaning of socialization: to become what academics call "enculturated," assimilated into "the full array of expectations and responsibilities a democratic society requires."[7]

QUESTIONING THE AGENT

I am not denying that all of these nonacademic roles are important to a civilization, but we should seriously question why we've relinquished them all to a single institution.

None are essentially connected to the project of *learning.*

Let's start with socialization, which is not only the broadest but the most problematic and complicated of all these functions, and work our way backward to the custodial job schools do, which is simultaneously the simplest, and the most difficult for many families to arrange without the help of the local public school.

Of course children need time with peers and the opportunity to learn how to relate to them. But there's absolutely no compelling reason to tie this to academic learning. T-ball teams and Little League, dance classes and gymnastics, youth choirs and music groups, art lessons and community theater, Lego clubs, young writers clubs, YMCA and community center programs—there are so many out-of-the-classroom opportunities for young people to be with peers and friends that it's often more challenging to limit them than to find them.

And don't forget that personal relationships go far beyond peer groups. Our current model of classroom socialization, where students primarily spend their days with others born within a twelve-month period, does nothing to prepare students for real life. Once out of the classroom, they've got to spend their days dealing with a multigenerational world—not the single-age culture they've been conformed to.

6 Ibid.
7 Roth, *The Role of the University in the Preparation of Teachers,* p. 49.

And as many, many critics of our system have pointed out, single-age peer groups are more likely to devolve into Lord-of-the-Flies nastiness than to evolve standards of conduct that will waft students into productive adult behavior.

Arranging peer socialization that takes place outside the classroom isn't particularly difficult or complex. But grappling with the larger aspect of socialization—assimilation to common cultural habits and beliefs—is both.

Anyone who lived through the 2016 election will immediately realize that we don't really seem to *have* "common habits and beliefs" anymore, or at least not a set that's agreed-upon enough for schools to be able to impart it. That element of school-based socialization has pretty much entirely broken down.

In fact, even Commager had his doubts about it, all the way back in 1950. The twentieth century, he worried, was throwing three challenges at schools that they weren't yet able to meet.

First, no one could agree on whether schools were supposed to be preparing students to be good Americans, or to be good global citizens ("whether . . . education should reinforce nationalism—or inspire internationalism"), and the two seemed to clash at important points.

Second, new demands of industry and the workplace made it necessary for schools to take a bigger part in training students for specific kinds of jobs, and this seemed likely to push the time needed for proper socialization into a smaller and smaller chunk of the school's time. ("In a day of specialization schools are called on more and more to prepare not so much for life, citizenship or democracy as for particular tasks and competence.")

And third, the students who were supposed to be assimilated into the ideals of democracy were becoming increasingly distracted by conflicting messages from other media. "Schools no longer have anything like the monopoly . . . they [once] exercised," he laments. "Today they share responsibility with the movies, and radio and television and, to a far larger extent than before, with the newspaper and the magazine." (He's particularly concerned with the influence of *Reader's Digest,* the YouTube of the 1950s.)[8]

Defining what "ideals of democracy" *should* be socialized into chil-

8 Commager, "Our Schools Have Kept Us Free," p. 47.

dren is far beyond the scope of this book; I merely want to point out that not only are schools not the only place where this can happen, but they have *not* been the only—or even primary—place for it, for at least the last seventy-five years.

And as far as demonstrating equality goes, schools are as likely to destroy a sense of equal opportunity as to promote it.

Canadian educator Mark Holmes points out that schools tend to operate as "allocative" filters, determining who gets what in life:

> In the U.S.A. and Canada, the division is quite crude. One group of students, high school dropouts, is channeled to either unskilled, blue collar work or to the underclass of unemployables, temporary and seasonal employees, low income family homemakers, and nonunionized workers. . . . A second group (of high school graduates) forms a nucleus of the "respectable" working class and the lower middle class. A third group (of college and university graduates) forms the burgeoning and influential middle and upper class and a pool from which society's various elites can be drawn. . . . [S]chool . . . serves as the allocative mechanism.[9]

Rather than being instruments of equality, classrooms tend to shove students into pigeonholes that can confine them for the rest of their lives. "Schools classify people," writes educational philosopher Robin Barrow. "They classify them in general as good and bad students." This is a problem, because "good student" tends to translate into "poised for success," while "bad student" means that you're doomed to a second-class life:

> [E]ven the more specific kinds of judgement (e.g., "not very good at French") tend to be seen as general judgements on character and ability. . . . [But a] bad student is not necessarily a bad citizen. This tendency of society to interpret judgements made in the context of schooling as of permanent global significance is a most unfortunate by-product of schooling.[10]

9 Mark Holmes, "The Secondary School in Contemporary Western Society: Constraints, Imperatives, and Prospects," *Curriculum Inquiry* 15, no. 1 (1985), pp. 17–18.
10 Robin Barrow, *The Philosophy of Schooling* (New York: Routledge, 2015), p. 66.

In short, classrooms have not taught the ideals of democracy well.

Rather, Americans have always been socialized through a whole array of institutions; family, media, religious and civic organizations have as much influence on socialization as our schools.

What about access to recreation and physical training?

See the above agents of socialization: Youth sports programs, clubs, hobby groups, dance and music organizations, and many more provide opportunities for recreation and exercise, and those hosted by community centers and other community organizations are often free or nominal in cost.

Monitoring mental and emotional health?

An important job, but one equally well performed by family doctors, licensed counselors, and community mental-health clinics. Like socialization, preserving mental and emotional wholeness is something schools often don't do well anyway. Having a psychologist on staff does not necessarily make up for placing a young psyche into a situation where bullying often occurs; where low grades become the child's measure of his worth as a person; where increasing numbers of young minds are drugged with Ritalin or Adderall to fit them into the classroom's confines; and where students are taught that physical exercise and creativity are secondary to the carrying out of regimented tasks.

Funnel into the job market?

See Mark Holmes's analysis on the previous page; students who master technical skills easily, but are less comfortable with abstract thought and written expression are often shunted into low-paying jobs solely based on academic grades.

Alternatives to this highly broken system: internships, apprenticeships, hands-on training in an actual job environment where students are rewarded for their actual performance, not their grades in unrelated subjects. The nonprofit organization Year Up, in recognition that schools are failing drastically in their job-funneling function, identifies young adults who've been relegated to the underclasses, spends a year providing training and internship, and places 85 percent of them in jobs or university classes.

And that custodial function?

In the absence of national childcare, this continues to be the most difficult nonacademic role to replace, and it is often the sole factor that keeps parents from stepping out of the system entirely (see Part V).

I have no easy answers, but as I suggest alternatives, at least keep in mind the difference between schools as places of learning and schools as child-minder.

THOUGHT EXPERIMENT 3

On a piece of paper, jot down two or three alternatives that would work for your family, and your children, to replace the school's role in each of the following:

- child-minding
- recreation and exercise
- job preparation
- developing mental and emotional health
- person-to-person socialization
- cultural socialization

Here is the most basic rule of a thought experiment: Don't allow yourself to think, "Oh, that's impossible" when an idea comes into your head.

Impossibility is often an illusion. It's very easy for us to get into a rut and believe that the limits of the rut are reality, when in fact we're perfectly capable of pulling ourselves up out of them and over into a new way of doing things.

Don't think about academics yet (we'll do that in the final chapter of this section). Just imagine how these specific classroom functions could be met in another way.

Take some time; return to this as you read, whenever new ideas come to you.

And then move on to the final part of your new vision.

CHAPTER SIXTEEN

Solving for *X*

W hat we all want, as parents, is to find the educational situation that matches our child's particular blend of passions,
abilities, and talents; meshes with our vision for our kids; and teaches
to our child's strengths while gently improving on weaknesses.

That is *X*: The place where the best possible learning happens.

X is unobtainable, of course. You'll never find it, any more than
you'll find the perfect job, the perfect house, or the perfect spouse.
(Or the perfect children, come to that.) *X* is ideal, so it always eludes
our clutches.

But you can *imagine X*.

WHY IMAGINE?

Imagining perfection is a time-honored strategy for finding an escape
route from the status quo—as scores of self-help books will tell you:

> Imagine you could wave a magic wand and make your life perfect
> sometime in the future. What would your perfect life look like?
> How would it be different from today?

Imagine that you have been handed a dream free range life. In this fantasy, there are no constraints in terms of money, responsibilities, skills or experience. You can do anything at all. The only rule is that everything you include has to fill you with a buzz and make you think "yes!"

Let your imagination run free, and give yourself the gift of designing the world's most perfect job. Create your own hours, your own activities, your most desirable environment. Don't limit yourself with reality or practicality. . . . The only limitation is this: It must be a job, not a life. That is, it has to have tasks in it, hours to keep, and some kind of remuneration. After that you can run wild.[1]

I picked these at random from three of a large assortment of books about career change; I could have quoted twenty or thirty similar assignments.

This is the most wide-ranging of the four thought experiments in this section, so let me spend a little more time explaining why it's important.

Imagining the perfect situation isn't a silly game; it's a serious philosophical exercise (even if you *are* being instructed to "wave a magic wand" and feel the "buzz"). Its classical ancestor is the Escape from Plato's Cave.

In the *Republic,* Plato explains that the universe first came into being, uncorrupted and perfect, in the mind of its creator. But as that ideal universe came into *physical* existence, it slipped slightly away from its original conception, and so the physical universe that resulted was not quite what it should have been, but rather a visible but inferior Copy of the original Ideal.

We now live in the Copy, and since we have never seen anything *but* the Copy, we think the Copy is all there is. We are, Plato writes, like prisoners chained in a cave who have never seen the sun; we have only ever seen the shadows of the reality outside, reflected indirectly

---

1 In order, these quotes are from Brian Tracy, *Get Smart! How to Think and Act Like the Most Successful and Highest Paid People in Every Field* (New York: TarcherPerigee, 2016), Introduction; Cantwell, *Be a Free Range Human,* p. 12; and Barbara Sher, *I Could Do Anything: If I Only Knew What It Was* (New York: Dell, 1994), p. 33.

onto the cave wall. Until we see the reality itself, we'll always accept the reflections as the ultimate truth: the inevitable and only way to live.

This is a parable, not a creation story as such, so don't get hung up on Plato's take on the Origins of Everything. Instead, try to recognize his genius in describing, so vividly, a common human experience: The let-down (slight or massive) that we all feel when an imagined, desired, planned-for experience finally comes to pass; the slippage between what we hoped would be, and what actually is; and the universal human tendency to accept what *is* as what *must be*.

According to Plato, the way to get out of the prison is to learn, carefully and slowly, about the Ideal, so that the Copy will no longer satisfy. Here, we can take a slight left turn away from the *Republic*, since Plato's path to the solution involves studying a lot of highly abstract mathematics. Instead, let's skip to the end: The more clearly you can visualize the ideal, the *less* real—and the less inevitable—the Copy will seem.

So the final thought experiment for you: Describe X.

X has to equip your child to read, understand basic maths, and express herself (whether in writing or speech, I'll leave up to you).

You're doing a thought experiment, so everything else is up for grabs. The different subject areas we study in school have evolved in a haphazard and essentially unguided way over the last centuries, so don't get hung up on them.

But reading, mathematics, speaking, and writing are the ways in which civilized human beings have understood and transmitted culture since ancient times.

That's it.

X doesn't have to occupy twelve years. It doesn't have to use textbooks and teachers. It doesn't have to happen during a particular part of the day or year.

Forget about truancy laws and your work schedule. Forget about grades and college applications. You're not worrying about those things right now (they all *definitely* belong to the imperfect Copy).

Every time you think, "Well, that's impossible!" stop yourself and consciously dismiss the objection. If you could educate your child in *exactly the way that would best suit both of you*, free of all restrictions and fears, what would that look like?

"You know what I should have done?" a friend of mine (a qualified RN, mother of three boys, stepmother of two more) confided in me.

"Just let them work and earn money in sixth and seventh grade, and then go back. I don't think any learning happened those two years. Their brains were in the wrong place." In your thought experiment, no schooling has to happen when adolescent hormones are at their height. Those boys could pick fruit, or practice programming, or work on a ranch, or learn how to cook.

Let me repeat something one more time: *This has nothing to do with getting into college.* College is simply a future extension of the same artificial system that you're trying to think your way out of. (See my Postscript for more.) For the moment, put college out of your mind.

Here are four real parents trying this experiment out. Notice that X ranges from fairly traditional to completely nontraditional, from less to more detailed.

Except for learning to read, I wish compulsory formal schooling began at eight or ten. Those younger years could be filled with stories, crafts, music, maybe foreign language if the opportunity is there.

I would love a school that focused on academics for the morning, mainly the 3R's. I would picture it structured and with instructors. Then the afternoons could be for active, hands-on learning, particularly along the students' interests and gifts: life skills, music, arts and crafts, shop, computers, nature study and wildcraft, money management, drama, culinary arts, trade skills, athletics, community service, science projects, etc., etc. —BEN

I would fill the day with fun and interesting lessons in the early years and apprenticeships when they are older. Art classes, dance lessons, music lessons, martial arts, read-alouds, writing about what interests them. As they get older and interests start to get more evolved, apprenticeships and mentorships could take over. Developing skills that could be useful in life and jobs. Think Star Trek, where people could pursue interests simply because they believed it would better society and themselves. Not to check boxes for a degree for a job that doesn't even exist yet. —POLLY

I want my kids to have lots of time outdoors, playing and engaging in their natural environment. I have visions of kids being able to go out

and play by the creek for a few hours a day, just observing, playing, and doing nothing in particular.

Lessons would be short, and focused on core subjects—math and lots of varied reading. Our lessons would probably be in the late morning or early afternoon when we tend to be less active. I would ignore grade levels and where they are "supposed" to be, and focus on improving their academic skills: teaching them to read for deeper meaning, think logically, solve problems, and see connections in the world around them.

The kids would have lots of opportunities to learn interesting skills. My fifteen-year-old would spend part of her days playing ukulele, singing, weaving, and drawing. She'd probably learn a couple of languages, and study abroad, and she might even have the opportunity to quit math after algebra 1. The thirteen-year-old would spend a lot of time outside, building stuff, climbing trees, and talking to animals. He'd have a supply of building materials to create with—things for building sheds and treehouses, but also for building robots and computers. The younger kids would explore a variety of activities and discover what they love.

I envision community. I want my spouse home with the family, as my partner, teaching the kids how to live life happily and productively. I want to surround myself with people who love what they do. We need multiple generations, and a community that's just large enough that people can do what they love, help one another out, and teach each other.   —TRACY

It would look very different for each kid. My eldest would do math of all kinds, study history through music, read for hours, and learn at least eight languages. The only writing she would do would be in those foreign languages (because she hates writing but strangely doesn't mind it if she's doing it in Spanish). There might not be any science in her education except as part of her math studies.

My next kid would spend her afternoons drawing while listening to audio books. Each morning, she would either be working on writing a new book or editing an existing one. All her spelling and grammar learning would be through that editing. Her science would revolve around animals and nature. Her knowledge of history would *be through audio books and research for her children's books. She would learn no (more) math if she could get away with it.*

My youngest would be building, exploring, and visiting as his interests led him—lots of animals and robotics and science, learning the math as needed on the way. Everything would be done for the purpose of his interests, so it would be worthwhile to him. We would spend a lot of time investigating—talking to people in his fields of interest, finding hands-on animal adventures, visiting labs (like the ones where Mars rovers are being built or monitored). —ANN

Once again: This is not an idle exercise in fantasy. A thought experiment, in the words of Yale philosopher Tamar Szabó Gendler, is "a process of reasoning carried out within the context of a well-articulated imaginary scenario in order to answer a specific question about a non-imaginary situation."[2]

The nonimaginary situation: We have a fairly inflexible K–12 system that funnels into four-year college, which in turn funnels into our economic system; yet this system does not fit all students.

The specific question: What about this system *can* flex?

You may not be able to escape entirely from the box of our K–12 system (unless you leave the country) any more than you can indefinitely avoid paying your taxes (same exception applies).

But once you have a clearer vision of what X could be, you can begin to make a plan to put its most important elements into place.

This plan may lead you back to the previous two sections, as you use the actions and strategies I've suggested to bring your current schooling system closer to X.

Or it may lead you out of the system, toward homeschooling, which can give you (as Part V points out) more freedom to create an individual education for your child.

2 Tamar Szabó Gendler, *Intuition, Imagination, and Philosophical Methodology* (Oxford: Oxford University Press, 2010), p. 56.

THOUGHT EXPERIMENT 4

Describe X now, either in list form or as a written description.

You might want to take an initial run at this, and come back to it at various times as your thoughts continue to develop. But here are a few questions to get you started.

What skills will this education develop? Skills: what the child can do. Skills can be primarily mental (critical analysis, problem solving, synthesizing information), or primarily practical (building a shed, installing wiring or plumbing, rotating tires, baking the perfect cream puff). Or skills can be a mix of the two (programming, bookkeeping, nursing/doctoring).

What qualities? Qualities: who the child is.

Are there teachers, courses, external structures? Or does the child pursue his own learning?

Who directs this education? You? Another adult, or group of adults? The child?

Does this education involve travel? Where? For what purpose? (It's a big world. Remember, you don't have financial restrictions in this experiment.)

Is it primarily active or book-centered? Projects or written assignments?

What part does earning money play/not play in this scenario? Either is fine.

In what places does learning happen? Home, outdoors in woods and fields, in institutions? (Schools are institutions, but so are museums, libraries, hospitals, courthouses, and some businesses.)

Does this education involve any apprenticeships or internships? It's a thought experiment, so you can apprentice your kid to a Supreme Court justice, or a master welder, or Jeff Bezos, or Gordon Ramsay (although that would be mean).

What sort of relationship does the student have to other students? Does she study alone, together, with peers, with learners of all ages, with adults, with people of all generations?

How does evaluation happen? Does the student take tests, write essays, perform a hands-on demonstration?

What does the day look like? When does the child get up? What occupies the bulk of the day? When does time with family happen?

How does family culture play into this schooling? "Family culture" is simply a phrase for those things that are important to parents and passed on to kids as part of daily life: We read books before bed. We eat together. We take trips. We try new foods. We watch basketball. We raise sheep. We go to live concerts, plays, dance performances. We stay in bed on Saturday until we all wake up, and then Dad fixes pancakes with chocolate chips. These are important things; how are they related to what the child is doing for "education"?

How much unstructured time is there? When does the child play?

Answer any other questions that come to you, as the picture begins to sharpen into focus.

PART V

Opting Out

CHAPTER SEVENTEEN

Deciding to Homeschool

There comes a point when you've flexed the system as hard as you can—and it still doesn't fit.

If the fit is bad enough, have the courage to step out. Home education is legal in every American state, in every Canadian province, and in a healthy number of foreign countries. It's simply a reasonable choice when other options have failed.

We bought our home in a very nice district, one block from the elementary school, and just assumed our child would go there.

My son started reading a few months before he turned four and we realized we needed to start thinking about his education. We went to the elementary school and they told me that we needed to quit teaching him and hold him back a year. In their words, "If you hold him back, he will be more mature and able to sit quietly while we are teaching the other children to read." Clueless, I asked them, "But he's reading on a second-grade level now, what level will he be reading at if we hold him back?" They became insistent that we not teach him anything more, nor should we allow him access to books "above his age level."

Scratch going to the local elementary school.

At that point, we decided we would look at private schools. Every private school we looked at wanted to push our son up a grade. That would have been great, except he was a left-handed boy who couldn't sit still, and certainly couldn't hold a pencil well enough to write at a first-grade level.

Finally, we looked at each other and said in unison, "What do you think about homeschooling?" —GREG

I was a total anti-homeschooler. I'm the daughter of two retired public school teachers. My sisters are/were both public school teachers. Aunts, uncles, cousins? All but three are in public education. I am genetically predisposed to hate homeschooling.

When my oldest son entered kindergarten, he began struggling emotionally at school. We barely made it through kindergarten. First and second grades were just tolerable.

Third grade? Bullying, yelling, belittling from the teacher. My son was made fun of by other students for his interests (weather) and put down for his lack of interests (designer sneakers). When I talked calmly to the principal about some specific bullying issues, I was given parenting advice and a little pat on the head. My son was miserable, and no matter how much I tried to become involved and be present at school, there was just no way to push my way into the "in" crowd of parents who ran the place.

We decided to pull our two boys out (the younger had just finished kindergarten) and homeschool. Best decision we have ever made. —WREN

Not everyone can, or should, homeschool.

But if you do decide to pull your child out of the classroom, remember this: You've been parenting this child for his entire life. If you can parent, you can home educate.

Scores of wonderful curricula have been developed for home educators (I've developed a few myself). Online classes and tutorials abound. To home educate, you don't have to be an *educator*. You just have to put time and thought into providing, and organizing, a better educational experience for your child than the one she's currently in.

My homeschooling journey began when my brother and I turned out to be such classroom misfits, back in the early 1970s, that my schoolteacher mother took us to the local mental-health clinic to find out what was wrong with us.

The psychologist who tested us told her: They will never fit into that classroom. Teach them yourself.

It was the last thing my mother had even intended to do, but she knew that the school had failed us—and that she could do better.

In the homeschooling manual that my mother and I coauthored nearly twenty years ago, we wrote:

> Never mind educational rhetoric about the years of specialized training necessary for teachers. Forget everything you've heard about the need for classes in child development and educational psychology. These things are indeed necessary for the teacher faced with thirty squirming first graders or twenty-five turned-off adolescents. But you have an entirely different task: the education of your own child, one-on-one.
>
> You probably feel that you don't have the skills to teach your child at home. You aren't alone; every homeschooling parent has felt this way. But we have consulted with scores of parents—some college-educated, some without high-school diplomas—who have successfully guided their children's education. At conferences and seminars, we've met hundreds more. Home-education magazines overflow with stories of parent-taught teens who excel at reading, writing, science, and math.
>
> All you need to teach your child at home is dedication, some basic knowledge about how children learn, guidance in teaching the particular skills of each academic subject, and lots of books, CDs, posters, kits, and other resources.[1]

Home education is hard work. But if school is frightening your child, or boring her to tears; if he has to be medicated just to fit in; if she gets off the bus weeping or fighting, every single day; if school is conveying the clear message to your child that he is failing . . . then you're already spending tremendous amounts of energy fighting to change those things.

If you put that energy directly into teaching your child, amazing accomplishments are well within your reach.

---

1 Susan Wise Bauer and Jessie Wise, *The Well-Trained Mind: A Guide to Classical Education at Home*, 4th ed. (New York: W. W. Norton, 2016), p. xx.

HOMESCHOOLING STYLES

There are scores of different homeschooling methods, but in my experience, they fall into three basic styles, which I'll call:

> Home-organized schooling
> Conventional school at home.
> Nontraditional homeschooling

Home-organized schooling happens when parents register as homeschoolers, but use that freedom to piece together classes that actually fit the child. These might include individual classes taken *in* the local public school (in many areas, homeschoolers have the right to make use of some or all public-school facilities), online classes, individual tutorials, and community-college classes.

Rather than taking a child out of the K–12 system, home-organized schooling assembles a menu of classes and re-creates the system from them, in a way that better suits the child.

We actually did something like this one year with our youngest for ninth grade. We had been homeschooling, but the third of her three older brothers was heading off to college, and I didn't want her to suddenly be at home alone. The nearby Montessori school had upper grades (7, 8, and 9), so we enrolled her in eighth grade, planning on doing the two years before deciding on our next strategy.

Halfway through the eighth-grade year, the school suddenly decided to cut ninth grade and only offer middle school. My daughter had been prospering at the school, we didn't want to move her after just one year, and all of the ninth-grade resources were still in place. So I told the administrators that if she could do the ninth-grade-level work, I'd register her as a homeschooler, do my own testing, and keep the transcript myself. ("I love working with home educators," the head of school said. "They always can find great solutions to problems.")

Although we're primarily homeschooling, in my district we can take part in public-school classes. I have one son taking Drama 3/4 and doing cross country and track. My youngest is taking Drama I and TV Production I. He's also doing cross country and lacrosse, and will take driver's ed in the spring. My eldest is also dually enrolled at the community college and taking twelve hours there.   —AMY

The border between the next two styles is a fuzzy one—in fact, they shade into each other almost imperceptibly (which is fine, except when homeschoolers, who are as prone to infighting as any other group, start sniping at each other about which is better).

Conventional school at home happens when parents are perfectly comfortable with the standard K–12 model, with its age-grades, subject divisions, and progressions, but are creating it at home, at their own pace, with their own personally chosen resources, in a way that fits their child. They may use a single curriculum (or "school in a box"—such as the Calvert program, which provides all materials for all subjects in K–8), or they may piece together their own curricula from the many options out there.

In contrast, nontraditional homeschooling doesn't try to re-create a formal curriculum. It may even question why we have twelve grades; why we have subject divisions; why textbooks are necessary.

Nontraditional homeschooling steps outside of the artificial system and says: What parts of this are intrinsically useful? And which parts can we discard? "Unschooling," a philosophy that is child-led and learner-centered, is one type of nontraditional homeschooling, but nontraditional homeschooling can also be quite structured and directed—as, for example, in a family that decides to center a month of schooling around *Little House on the Prairie* and studies history, geography, science, and math as they relate to the world of the book, rather than pursuing separate courses of study in each subject.

And many families, of course, use some combination of these styles: nontraditional schooling along with a formal course or two, for example, or a boxed curriculum for the course skills in math and language arts along with a more experimental approach to literature, history, and science.

I use a boxed curriculum (Seton Home Study School), so I'm more in the conventional "school at home" style. But I never stand in front of a whiteboard or in front of my student at all. I sit with her wherever we land, and we talk through the material. I don't lecture, I don't assign homework, we don't really value standardized tests. We also do learn-

ing at the library, at the preserve, going to a farm to learn about ani-
mals, learn the chemistry of apple cider–making by going to an apple
farm, use DVDs when appropriate, carry out experiential learning in
a myriad of ways. —*SUSAN*

My older son went to public school for two years, and with his Asperg-
er's syndrome, he doesn't adapt well to change. He wanted to follow
a "schoolish" routine. So, I made a set of magnets with subjects and
activities on them, and every morning, he puts them up in order of
what we are going to do. He wanted break time to be called recess,
so we call it recess. We don't have a set time to start the day, usually
happens around 9 a.m., though. We don't have set times for subjects,
either. However long it takes to do math, or reading, or history is how
long it takes. Many times, we are cuddled on the couch, but I do have
a table where we sit and a whiteboard where I can put instructions. We
definitely use textbooks and other types of books, magazines, DVDs,
websites, etc. We do have a structure to our days, but it's much less
rigid than a traditional school setting. —*CHARLOTTE*

HOW TO INVESTIGATE

Remember that you don't have to make any immediate choices. You can
pull your kids out of school—or, for that matter, put them back in—at
any point during the year.

Take some time to explore your options. When the time is right to
make a decision, you'll know.

Find out what your local regulations are.

A number of homeschooling websites, including ours (welltrained
mind.com) maintain links to Department of Education policies in
all U.S. states and territories plus a number of foreign countries.
In the United States, policies range from fairly lax (in Virginia, if
you have a bachelor's degree, all you have to do is file an Intent to
Homeschool in the summer along with a list of the subjects you'll
be studying, and then administer a standardized test the following
spring) to quite detailed (Pennsylvania mandates specific subjects to

be taught, requires various types of affidavits and certificates, and insists that a yearly evaluation be done by a licensed psychologist or certified educator).

In most cases, though, regulations are relatively easy to follow, and the rising popularity of home education makes it very unlikely that your decision will be challenged.

You do not need to join any sort of association, state group, or legal defense fund in order to homeschool.

Read up.

Begin to investigate what homeschooling can look like.

Read through the guides suggested in Appendix C.

If you're already thinking ahead to high school, study the credit and transcript information in Appendix A so that you know you're headed in the right direction.

Visit homeschool message boards (we host one of the most active on the Web at forums.welltrainedmind.com).

Do a search for popular methods (a starting list: classical education, unit studies, Charlotte Mason approach, Waldorf method, "eclectic homeschooling," unschooling) and see which one resonates with you.

Find out your instructional options.

What level of participation in the public school is possible in your locality? In Washington State, children receiving home-based instruction are entitled to enroll in any ancillary course or extracurricular activities offered by the public schools. In New York, you're either in or out.

What classes are available, online and locally, for home-educated students?

A good shortcut to these answers is to check out the resources provided by a local or state homeschool group. Homeschool associations are an odd mixed bag. Since home education is a grassroots effort, there is no such thing as official state organizations (although many of them imply that they are). And since they are all privately run, they range from inclusive and welcoming to insular and tightly controlled. But even if your state association doesn't line up with your political or religious views, you can mine its website for answers.

CHAPTER EIGHTEEN

Getting Started in Five Steps

How do you take the plunge?
Follow these steps.

1. Make an instructional plan.

I frequently suggest to new homeschoolers that they start out with a boxed curriculum, online charter school, or some other highly structured program that provides very concrete goals and guidance.

If you're homeschooling for the first time, you are about to make a *lot* of major adjustments. Simply having your child at home is going to take some getting used to—as is playing the role of teacher as well as parent. If your academic plan is laid out for you already, that reduces one major source of angst.

As you homeschool, you'll get a sense of what's working and what's not. You may decide to stick with your original program for the entire year—or you might decide to jettison parts of it, or even all of it. And the following year, you'll have a much better sense of how to move forward.

On the other hand, if you're excited about planning your own program and *not* struggling with parental panic, go for it.

2. File your state's required papers and notify any necessary school personnel.

Most states tell you that intent has to be filed by a summer deadline. While technically that's true, you can pull your child out of school anytime during the year and file the intent at that point.

Filing the intent (whether or not by some "deadline") is important, particularly if you're leaving your current situation midyear. Without the intent, the child is technically truant. Having it on file protects you.

If you're taking your child out during the school year, it's wise (and kind) to have at least a brief conversation with the teacher. It will probably simplify things to either meet briefly with the principal as well (with a copy of your filed intent on hand), or send an email or letter with this information.

If you decide over the summer, there's no need to contact school personnel, particularly if you have an adversarial relationship with the school. Your level of communication is entirely up to you.

In California, you can file a private school affidavit, and set up a legal private school in your own home with zero hassle. So I picked a name for my school, filed my PSA, met with the principal and let him know my intentions, briefly met with the teacher and let her know my plan (we had met previously to discuss how my daughter's year was going, so it wasn't entirely out of the blue). Then I wrote a letter to the school, letting them know I was withdrawing my daughter and requesting that her file be sent to my private school name and address. The secretary at first didn't want to let go of the file, but after she called the district office they told her I was correct, and she sent it.

For me, because my younger daughter stayed in kindergarten at the school, it was really important to maintain good relationships. It worked out very well, and my older daughter was welcomed at school for parties and events that we attended because my kindergartener was taking part. —CHRIS

I withdrew my son midyear because (among many other things) his teacher criticized and picked on boys. I did not give the teacher any notice because I thought that she would surely do something mean to

my son in response. I followed my state's laws for withdrawing him, and then I told the school the first day of homeschooling that he was not going to attend any longer. I thought that was the safest plan for my son's situation.

—*Tracey*

Don't ask the school for advice on how to handle it—find out the laws in your state and follow the option that best fits your needs. When I pulled my children out of public school, I sent an e-mail to each of their teachers three days prior to their last day, simply out of respect. I didn't send a letter to the principal.

The office staff did call me a few days later and tried to tell me that I had to come sign papers with them in order to be able to homeschool my children. I told them that I knew that to be untrue, but if they wanted to mail them to me, certified mail, I'd be happy to have my attorney look them over and get back to them. They never sent anything.

—*April*

3. Consider taking some time to deschool.

If you're removing your child from a difficult situation, don't plunge directly into school the next day.

Gifted kids who need more challenges may be ready to leap into homeschooling immediately, but kids who've been frustrated or discouraged in the classroom usually need a "deschooling" period. If they've been struggling, they've often developed a mental habit of shutting down when faced with schoolwork. Putting schoolwork in front of them right away doesn't send the message that things have changed.

Take at least a month and do unstructured learning.

Go to museums and aquariums, concerts and plays, historic sites and art galleries.

Take field trips.

Read lots of books together, listen to audiobooks.

Bake and cook (take the opportunity to talk about measurements).

Watch documentaries together.

Do science experiments for fun (don't worry about documentation).

Establish a library habit.

Enroll in physical activities that the child enjoys—martial arts, dance.

Allow your child to pursue his interests.

Deschooling is *not* "doing nothing." Deschooling is planned and deliberate. Deschooling is reintroducing your child to the love of learning.

Deschooling reminds the child that education happens in every part of life, not just through worksheets and textbooks.

It's taken us a summer vacation (two and a half months) plus another two months, ultimately transitioning into a gentle routine and very light work schedule during October. After all that, my daughter is now beginning to regain her curiosity and love of learning that her school experience destroyed. I think that had I insisted on high academic standards right away, she'd never have made it totally back to that wonderful place of learning as a joyful endeavor. —SHEILA

We pulled the kids out in October and took a camping trip before we even thought about starting school. Then we eased into our schoolwork and did a lot of local field trips the first year. —MOIRA

My son went to a Montessori preschool, kindergarten, and first grade. We did not deschool, because as far as I could tell, my son was having a grand old time in school (although he didn't learn anything that last year, which is why we moved to homeschooling). —E.K.

4. Start with the basics.

When you begin academic work for the first time, don't leap into twelve subjects at once.

Start with just the core skills: math and language arts (that's phonics, spelling, and penmanship for K–2; spelling, grammar, writing, and literature for grades three and up). Find your feet in those subjects, do them well, and spend the rest of your time on the deschooling activities described on the previous page.

After a couple of weeks, add history and science.

And then, when that habit is established, include anything else you've planned to add: logic, foreign languages, fine arts, practical arts, projects.

5. Practice saying, "We're doing great. So what are your vacation plans this year?"

In other words, don't feel that you have to defend your choice to friends and family.

Or your pediatrician.

Or, for that matter, to random checkout clerks who ask why your kids are with you in the middle of a school day.

There is plenty of evidence that home education works. No, socialization isn't going to be a problem. No, they won't turn into misfits. Yes, they'll be able to get into college.

If you've done any of the reading suggested in Appendix C, you'll find good responses to all of these concerns and many more. But the only truly convincing proof that homeschooling is a good idea is that your child begins to flourish.

And that takes time.

You are the parent.

You get to make this decision without being second-guessed.

You don't have to defend yourself.

Change the subject, and keep homeschooling.

We quietly go about our business and when we're asked where our children attend school, we just respond that they're homeschooled. If the "why" question comes up, I respond that it works well for our family. I don't volunteer any additional information. Short, direct answers are the way to go. —KIM

What helped for me: to say, "Well, I think we're going to give it a try for one year. Let's see how it goes."

Over the course of the year I would update on things we were doing that were fun and educational. Family, etc., were very impressed. Also impressed by my son's results on his yearly achievement test, which I was careful to brag about.

The good thing about this approach, is that you can change your

mind. For us, we have decided that he'll be going to public school next year—a lot of effort went into this decision, and I am really at peace with it, because it is really what is best for our family—so nobody can say "I told you so! I told you homeschooling would not work out!" Because it clearly did work out for this year, yet we are free to make our own choices about what is best for our family each year.

—NYSSA

CHAPTER NINETEEN

Developing Independence

Stepping outside the K–12 classroom isn't just a move away from factory-model education; it's also a move away from factory-model supervision.

Elementary classrooms *have* to be tightly controlled, or else they'd dissolve into chaos. Most middle-school students, and the majority of high-school students, are also under strict direction: They are told what work to do, when to do it, when to study, when to eat; sometimes, whether or not they can go to the bathroom. The teacher is required to act as a foreman.

Cut adrift from this oversight, young learners often struggle.

The hardest thing for my girls was the transition to more freedom. I had two third-graders and a sixth-grader. They were conditioned to have every moment of their day scheduled and rules to follow for all of it. After several meltdowns, I ended up setting up a much more rigid schedule than I had planned at first, just to get them over the hump.
—MONA

At home, you have the opportunity to turn learning back into a self-directed pursuit, rather than a set of arbitrary assignments dictated from on high.

Teaching students to work independently is a central part of this realignment.

THE STAGES OF INDEPENDENT WORK

The Parent at Elbow Stage (from preschool through second or third grade or through about age eight)

At this stage, expect to be close to the child while she's working.

Young children need close guidance. Some of them need reassurance as they work: "Yes, good job on that sentence, you're doing a wonderful job!" Some of them need constant reminders to stay on track: "Time to stop looking out the window. Pick up your pencil. Get up off the floor—you can have a play break soon. Pick up your pencil." (That's me channeling my mother-of-three-boys persona.)

In the early years, home education is, inevitably, a parent-intensive activity. Some unusually mature elementary students may be able to work on their own for short periods of time, but you should plan to be either directly teaching, or else watching and helping, for most of the child's learning time.

The good news: When the child isn't in a classroom, all the academic work necessary for an excellent elementary education can be completed in four hours or less. Even in the best classrooms, teachers spend a good part of the day taking attendance, making announcements, dealing with students who may have been absent the day before, distributing materials, collecting materials, handing out assignments, and correcting bad behavior. Students who've finished assignments often find themselves doing busywork so that others can finish. Moving from one activity to another, standing in line for lunch and cleaning up after lunch, going to and from lockers all take time away from learning—not to mention the time wasted sharpening pencils, making unnecessary trips to the bathroom, and chatting with friends.

I was a classroom teacher (first grade) and when we first started homeschooling (third grade) I was shocked at how much more we got done in a day at home than in a week in the classroom.

It's not just the amount of work that gets done, it's the fact that you

*are providing your child with one-on-one tutoring, instant feedback,
and an appropriate challenge. You just can't do that in the classroom.
So, yes, my kids get more out of one single lesson than they would sitting in a classroom hearing/practicing that concept all week.*

*There is a lot of wasted time in schools. It's not just getting books
out, it's getting ready for lunch, getting ready for recess, cleaning,
dealing with behavior, stopping for assemblies/fire drills/guest speak-
ers, etc. However, many of those things have value. Kids are learning
patience, cooperation, and how to behave at school. They are having
unique experiences and getting to see the "outside" world.*

*Still: My daughter with special needs is able to get quality instruc-
tional time every day that is ten times more than she ever got in a
day in school, because of all the school things that prevented her from
really learning.*   —NORA

More good news: Teaching a fresh, rested child at home first thing
in the morning is a *much* simpler task than struggling through even the
simplest homework with a child who's been up since 6 a.m. and has
already been sitting inside and working for hours and hours.

Elementary-grade homework is often a huge fight—because it
probably shouldn't be given. Teaching at home is an entirely different
experience.

*Homeschooling is much easier than helping with homework. At the end
of the day kids are tired and not usually at their best, learning-wise.
Whereas I can teach my daughter at the time of the day when it is really
easiest for her to learn, and that goes much better.*   —CAROL

*I've had friends say, "I would like to homeschool but I am not cut out
to be my kid's teacher. We have it hard enough with daily homework
battles." Homeschool doesn't have to be as adversarial as doing busywork after a long day at school, but that is what parents envision and
why they feel they "can't do that."*   —SUNNY

So although you'll be at your child's elbow for most of the time
that he's doing schoolwork from preschool through second or third
grade, that time will *not* be seven or eight hours; nor will it be one
long fight.

The Hovering Parent Stage (third through fifth grades, or between ages eight and ten)

Sometime during third grade, you should begin the shift away from being Parent at Elbow for *every single subject*.

There will inevitably be some kinds of work where you have to give more help and support so that the child doesn't become frustrated or overwhelmed. (For one of my kids, it was always Latin. Even in high school, if I wasn't sitting with him and coaching, he got that deer-in-the-headlights look. He did *not* become a classics scholar.) But overall, you should be moving toward a new pattern: going over the material to be learned, talking about anything that needs to be processed through discussion, and then asking the child to complete the remaining work on his own.

For me, "hovering" means that you're off doing something else, but that you're usually within sight. Fourth- and fifth-graders normally have intellects that are ahead of their ability to resist distraction; if you send a child to complete work in their room, they're likely to find staring at the ceiling much more fascinating than finishing the job at hand.

Training a child to work independently means that, at first, you spend a fair amount of time watching them and saying, "Are you still thinking about your project? Because you look like you're staring out the window" and "I know you love the dog, but why don't you finish reading your chapter first and then scratch his ears as a break."

For kids who seem particularly dependent on your assistance, try to develop independence by delaying your arrival to help out. When they call you, say, "Try to solve that yourself for five more minutes, and then, if you still need me, call and I'll come help." Of course, you want to give as much aid as necessary, but you also want to break the automatic Mom or Dad call whenever things get difficult.

At this age, it's time to give kids a checklist of all the work to be done during the day; as far as you can, let them choose the order in which they do the work, and check each assignment off as it's finished. It's human nature: If you're denied control over an activity, you're much less likely to assume responsibility for it. Responsibility is the flip side of control.

And before students can move much further toward independence, they need to be taught how to take responsibility, not just for academic work, but for the whole day. I strongly suggest that by fifth grade, you begin to teach the child how to organize and keep a schedule.

Invest in a wall calendar or notebook planner for the student. (Or they can, of course, use a Web- or computer-based scheduling tool— it's just that, in my experience, middle-grade students get distracted fiddling with the technology, or find clicking onto social media irresistible once they're online.)

Help the student write in all academic deadlines: when essays need to be finished, for example, or when they need to finish reading a book. Also help them to write in appointments that affect them: babysitting jobs, family outings, vacations, doctor appointments.

Establish a regular morning check-in when the student actually *looks* at the calendar or planner and sees, not just what needs to be done *today,* but *this week* and even *this month.* It takes a long time to develop this habit, and you want it firmly in place before the freshman year of college.

By fifth grade, also make sure that the student begins to take on the responsibility of getting herself up *and* going to bed on time. Whether you're homeschooling or not, it's easy to get into the habit of being the child's alarm clock and curfew enforcer. Middle school is time to shift that job over to where it belongs.

The Assign-and-Check Stage (sixth grade and above, or from age eleven onward)

As children move toward the teen years, their ability to stay on task without direct supervision continues to increase. You can cut down on the hovering.

Train them to work responsibly and stay focused while *out* of your sight. By now, you should have a good idea of their natural working pace. Go over the material with them, give them a clear assignment, a reasonable timeframe, and a timer. Tell them to come check back in with you at the end of the timeframe, even if the work isn't done.

If the assignment *isn't* completed, investigate. Did the student run into unexpected difficulties? Or did he get distracted and tinker with a project, text a friend, leaf through a novel or comic book? If so, the consequence is that he has to sit right under your eyes and finish the work. If the work was completed on time, be sure to reward diligence: Have a break or a snack. He deserves it for doing a good job.

What if the work is finished, but not well?

Be very clear, when you're giving the assignment, about exactly what you expect. If you say, "Answer these questions and then show me," but you *don't* say, "Answer these questions in legible handwriting, in complete sentences, properly punctuated, on one side of the paper," don't be surprised if you get a series of scrawled phrases. If you're not specific, don't penalize the student for not reading your mind.

If you *do* give detailed instructions and they aren't followed, the work should be redone. Don't punish or penalize; having to repeat the assignment *is* the penalty.

There are two more important aspects to teaching middle-grade independence. First: A major challenge for most middle-grade students is properly storing books and finished assignments. The more work they do on their own, the more likely they are to end up in the middle of a crumpled sea of paper.

Establish a single shelf for all school-related books, or you'll waste hours hunting for lost texts. This is an area in which you probably *should* impose a penalty that fits your family's style: Every time you don't put your books back on the shelf, you get an extra household chore/lose screen time/give up a privilege.

The voice of experience regarding paper storage: Most kids will not stop to put papers in a binder or three-ring notebook, no matter how good the intention. A household organization book I read many years ago pointed out that while kids can be trained to toss socks into a drawer, requiring them to use small partitions within the drawer will result in them giving up. The same is true of papers. My advice is to give them boxes where they can drop papers with a minimum of effort; then, you can periodically sit down and sort the papers into a more permanent storage order.

Second: Surrender the teacher's book or answer key. For work that can be objectively checked, like math problems and grammar exercises, give the assignment, tell the student to check his own work and mark what he got wrong, and then report back to you and explain the errors. Making mistakes, understanding why, and correcting them is *how* learning happens. Don't let students abdicate this responsibility. It's *their* work, *their* learning, *their* education.

The On-Call Supervisor Stage (high school)

As students move into high school, you'll find yourself shifting roles: from teacher to administrator. Home-educated students become increasingly independent in their learning, but will also need outside teachers, tutors, and classes; your job is to organize and arrange their learning opportunities.

High-school students can earn their credits (see Appendix A) in a whole range of ways:

Independent work supervised by parent

Self-designed independent study

Course arranged and supervised by private tutor (we often used college juniors and seniors from the nearby university)

Independent course or learning module (such as a MOOC, an EdX course, or a Teaching Company or Coursera offering), supervised by parent or tutor

Online high-school-level course (we offer a full high school slate at the Well-Trained Mind Academy, wtmacademy.com)

Class taken at community college

Dual enrollment class taken at local college or university[1]

Class taken at local private or public school that allows homeschoolers to participate

There are hundreds and *hundreds* of options for high school at home. The homeschooling guides in Appendix C offer plans for scheduling and documenting high school; also visit the High School board at forums .welltrainedmind.com to find out what has succeeded for other parents.

We outsourced foreign language (two four-unit college semesters) as dual enrollment at the local community college, with each of our sons doing that in twelfth grade. To make educating high school at home

---

1 Dual enrollment, offered by universities and community colleges in many states, allows high school juniors and seniors to enroll in college classes and receive both high school *and* college credit for their academic work, thus allowing them to begin the freshman year of college with credits already completed.

not feel overwhelming, we also looked for some programs our sons would be able to do more independently: math with a DVD component, and a few courses based around a series of Teaching Company lectures. Sometimes we counted hours done in an extracurricular activity where learning occurred toward a class credit (for us, that was involvement in a youth and government program counting toward American government class). We also used homeschooling programs written directly to the student, and "scripted" programs for parents that have all of the questions and writing assignments laid out for us.

—LORI

We decided to completely outsource school for my eldest next year, with me supplementing several of the classes. Half of her high school classes will be at the community college. We have dual enrollment in Florida, so she will earn her AA degree there. Three of her classes will be through Florida Virtual School, which is free. The rest will be through a couple of online programs that offer classes we want that are not available through the other two schools. Most of my supplementing is in the form of literature/additional reading, lectures (Teaching Company or open courseware) and discussion. —MELISSA

For my older son, I became mostly just a mediator, because he wanted/ needed other voices than just mine. His ninth-grade year, he took three dual enrollment courses, two high school correspondence courses, and I had him in a homeschool co-op for some other things, like SAT test prep, theater company, journalism, etc. He accomplished phys-ed through his year-round swimming and a number of other sports-related lessons he took, too. —CONNOR

We decided that we wanted to do AP biology at home. So we used an AP recommended text (Campbell). My son performed, in real life or online, the twelve mandated College Board labs. He prepped for the test using two different prep books, then took the exam. On my son's transcript, I am listing biology along with his AP score. Since I did not have my syllabus approved by the College Board, I cannot call the class "AP biology." But this shows that he achieved at AP levels.

—JANE

As you approach high school, sit down with the student and, together, make a tentative four-year plan that fulfills transcript requirements (outlined in Appendix A). This plan is up for constant revision, but it's a good idea to know where foreign languages will fit in, what courses will be basic requirements and which will show advanced achievement, and where the student's primary energies will go (maths? literature? dance? engineering?). Then, year by year, you can decide how each course will be taken and taught.

Piecing together an excellent, personalized high-school plan for the student is your job; regularly checking to make sure the work is progressing, also your job; learning, the student's task.

I looked at the requirements for my town, the ones in The Well-Trained Mind, *and the ones for the sort of college my child might be interested in, and blended those together with my child's interests to make a beginning plan.*

At maximum, a college is probably going to want four years of foreign language (preferably the same one), four of language arts, four of math through at least calculus taken every year, four of science with at least three labs, one year each of world history, U.S. history, government, and economics, some fine arts, some computer skills, extra years of whatever the student is specializing in, and some outside verification of the transcript that you will make, like SAT scores or outside classes of some kind given by professionals. My town's requirements were less than that—still four years of math and language arts, but only two or three years of the other things. Most colleges land somewhere between my town and the maximum list.

I started out by aiming for the maximum, and wound up with less as we decided that things involving my son's interests were more important than, say, four years of the same language. It really helps to define your family's goals—start with your definition of a well-educated adult and work backward, trying to figure out how to get there.

Don't forget that getting into college is only half the battle. The other half is being able to do the work once there. That means your child has to have the study, organizational, and social skills to be able to learn in a classroom. Make sure you talk to your child a lot about what his interests are, and get him involved in the planning process.

—NAN

While you're planning high school, remember that there are other areas in which your child needs to develop independence.

As soon as the child is old enough, help her open a checking account (joint, with you, is a good starting place) with a debit card. Encourage her to *use* the debit card. Keeping track of those deductions without overdrawing is a vital life skill. (Better now, than as a college freshman.)

Teach basic cooking skills. Make him actually *use* them. He can cook dinner for the family occasionally. It doesn't have to be fancy.

Once children hit sixteen, consider dropping them at the doctor's office and letting them go through appointments alone (while you wait nearby in case they need help or advocacy). Negotiating a medical appointment is complicated for kids: They need some experience in producing the insurance card, explaining what's wrong, filling out the paperwork, talking to medical personnel. If they don't practice this now, they'll end up with the freshman plague in college and have to figure out how to get through a doctor's appointment *while* they already feel overwhelmed and lousy. My experience with getting three (so far) through the freshman year is that because it's intimidating, they just don't go until they're so sick that they need parental intervention.

Teaching them how to do their own laundry is great, but if you want them to be *really* independent, make them buy their own detergent. (You can provide the funds, just not the soap.) It's a bit of a shock for them to get to college and realize that they can't just grab the family detergent.

Make sure they know what to do if they get pulled over in traffic by police. I assumed this would be covered in driver's ed, but it often isn't. The first time this happened to one of my sons, he was so panicked that he called me from the car to find out what to do. Fortunately, the officer took young-driver nerves into account, but we were lucky.

The most helpful advice I received about planning for high school had to do with things outside of planning academics and credits: to make sure I planned for and scheduled time throughout the high school years for the things I wanted our sons to learn or experience before they graduated. Things like:

— *learning basic life skills (shopping / cooking; making a budget / taxes / finances; basic car maintenance; basic home upkeep; etc.)*

— *having meaningful conversations (about how to go about making choices; the opposite sex / dating / marriage; spiritual topics; sharing fears or dreams; etc.)*
— *developing good life habits*
— *enjoying some family vacations together*
— *allowing our kids time to fiddle around trying out hobbies and interests*
— *leaving "wiggle room" in the schedule to allow for them to pursue unexpected interests (as elective credits or as extracurricular activities)*

—LORI

CHAPTER TWENTY

Out-of-the-Box Teaching Strategies

We want our children to leap into their assignments with energy and complete them without nagging. We want them to have a thirst for knowledge. We want them to *love* learning.

If only that were reality.

You can create a learning environment that *fosters* a love for learning, but you can't create love for learning. You can offer your child resources to quench the thirst for knowledge, but you can't bring that thirst into being.

True appreciation of the value of education only comes with maturity. And often, when we're dealing with our children, we're waiting for that maturity to happen. For many children, something has to click in the brain before they become self-motivated, engaged learners. In the meantime, you may need to be a little bit crafty in how you teach.

Let me suggest some ways to get your kids to listen and learn while you're waiting for them to grow into the love of learning.

A CAVEAT

One caution, before you read on.

Everything below assumes a nonpathological family situation—

that, insofar as any family relationship is "normal," you have a normal parent-child relationship.

When I speak at large education conferences, I'm sometimes approached by parents who are considering homeschooling and ask, "What do you do if you tell your child to do his work and he just says, 'No'?" I never know quite what to say to this. When we did schoolwork, my kids sometimes whined, complained, dragged their feet, did careless work, and left stuff unfinished. That's what children do. But I can't really envision a scenario in which one of them would simply turn around and tell me, "No."

That's not our family dynamic. Defiance is a no-go area.

If you're dealing with a child who's so oppositional that you have no power to give assignments, nothing below is going to help you. I strongly recommend that you get professional counseling for the child and therapy for the family.

THE STRATEGIES

Strategy 1: Bribery

Bribery has a bad name. But be honest with yourself: When you do something difficult, or polish off a task you didn't really want to do, you reward yourself afterward—perhaps with food, or a Netflix break, or even just a walk around the office or a few minutes chatting to friends.

There's nothing wrong with giving a child a reward for doing something against their natural inclinations. You're not going to be able to convert them to a motivating love of grammar or math just because you tell them how important subordinate clauses and multiplication tables are going to be later in life. Tell them that when the worksheet's finished, they can have some chocolate chips. Or fifteen minutes to build with Legos. Or an outside play break.

Obviously, if you have to bribe a child to do *all* schoolwork, there's a problem. You need to rethink your curriculum, because it's clearly boring the child to tears. But there are some areas of learning that will always be a struggle. Give the child a concrete reason to buckle down to them.

I've had parents say to me, "But I want to develop character in my child. Shouldn't he learn to do work simply for the sake of doing it?" I'm a fan of character development, but I also think it's important that we teach well—and one principle of good teaching is that you never ask a child to do two new and difficult things simultaneously. If the spelling list is new and difficult, let the kid just struggle with the spelling list—not the spelling list *and* character development. There are plenty of nonacademic opportunities during the day when character development can take centerstage. The grammar lesson doesn't have to be one of them.

So use rewards. Everything is less dire when there's a cookie at the end.

Strategy 2: Nibbled to death by ducks

In case you don't live on a farm: It would take a duck a really long time to nibble anything to death. But if it keeps nibbling . . .

There is almost no subject in which there won't be progress if you work at it very hard for fifteen minutes, six days a week.

Sometimes, children become so frustrated by a subject that it is almost impossible to move forward. They simply refuse to try to understand. Make a bargain with them: You don't have to do the whole lesson, or read the whole chapter, or finish the whole exercise. I just want you to work as hard as you can for fifteen minutes. Then you can stop. (I highly suggest that you tell them this will have to be done on Saturdays also. Explain that this is a tradeoff: They no longer have to complete an hour-long lesson, but in return they have to be willing to do their fifteen minutes six days per week.)

You won't see weekly progress like this. But if you're diligent, you'll see progress over the course of several months. It takes patience on your part.

Kids who are natural multitaskers and whirl from one project to the next can benefit from this; it encourages them to focus hard over a manageable time period. If the child really is so burned out or frustrated that they've simply developed a loathing for the subject, fifteen minutes is not an eternity. And if a child is not quite old enough to find the subject easy (writing, for example, really *does* make little hands hurt), fifteen minutes per day will help any child grow slowly toward maturity.

Strategy 3: Drastically drop the difficulty level and expand the time

What if you know the child is capable of doing the work, but she's dragging her feet, constantly asking for help, stalling, leaving it unfinished?

It's possible that she's bumping up against her ability and maturity ceiling in the subject. The work's not completely out of her grasp—but it *almost* is. Working at that level is mentally exhausting. (A good question to ask: Has something changed? A child who is working at the extent of her ability can seem out of her depth if something else absorbs some of her energy—a lingering cold or a bout of allergies, a new sport or team or athletic practice session, puberty.)

Drop back to an earlier level, and expand the time spent. If Algebra I was trundling along but then became a constant battle, drop back two math levels and ask the child to spend twice as much time working. If that hour of high school literature is overwhelming, ask him to read middle-school novels for two hours every day instead. Do this for a month, and then make another run at the subject.

Think of this as a return to foundational skills. Any dancer will tell you that perfecting plies is an essential part of polishing advanced moves. The child may need more practice in basic, foundational skills before she can move on. And the drop back to an easier level will also remind her what it feels like to do the subject *well*, moving her out of the "I can't do it" space (in which no learning happens).

Strategy 4: Three-way teaching (hear, feel, see)

Don't get stuck on only one way of teaching. Remember that children learn visually, aurally, and physically. Try to teach the same material all three ways.

Difficult book? Have him read a chapter out loud to you. Then, you read the next chapter out loud to him. Then, send him out to walk around the house while he's reading the next.

Trouble with a math problem? Have her work it out on paper. Then, challenge her to demonstrate it with nothing but manipulatives—Cuisenaire rods, pattern blocks, or even just beans or toothpicks. Finally, ask her to solve the problem out loud without writing.

Can't remember a grammar rule? Chant it out loud a number of times with him. Then, assign a worksheet. Then ask him to draw a comic strip illustrating it.

Hear, feel, see.

Strategy 5: Use a timer

Poky children may need a time limit.

This may seem basic, but it only works well if you implement it properly. First, realize that every child has a natural pace. Some work quickly. Some have a much slower tempo. You're not going to be able to change that very much—and, in fact, one of the great strengths of teaching at home is that your child won't be artificially hurried or held back. But what you *can* do is teach the child to minimize wasted time and distractions.

Watch your child work, reminding him to stay on task, until you have some idea of what a reasonable timeframe would be for the task at hand. Then, put a timer or countdown clock next to the assignment and tell the child, "You have fifteen minutes to finish those problems." Make sure the timer is completely visible. The passage of time is *not* easy to sense. Nor does it come naturally. Even adults talk about time flying or dragging, and children have much less practice in gauging how much time is going by.

I'd also encourage you to use a timer that doesn't have a buzzer or bell. The prospect of the noise at the end will paralyze some children, particularly during the last two minutes or so, when all they can think about is when the alarm will go off.

Keeping an eye on the timer will begin to train the student to minimize distractions. At first, you can help by reminding them to track the time: "Are you going to the bathroom again? Look at the timer. I don't think you have enough time to finish those problems *and* go to the bathroom." Ultimately, you're training them to notice those distractions themselves and to stay on task.

One last tip: Use carrots, not sticks. Don't penalize if the child runs over time; just promise rewards if they finish before the time limit. Don't say, "If you don't finish, you lose your iPod for today." Instead, offer chocolate chips, or Lego time, or an outside break if they meet the goal. The prospect of punishment can be paralyzing, and doesn't allow for unexpected difficulties.

Strategy 6: Block scheduling

Studying five or six different subjects for forty-five minutes every day seems natural only because you're so familiar with it. It's probably how you were taught, so it's normal to set up your homeschool days in the same way.

This is *not* how many children naturally learn. Some of them learn best if they're allowed to obsessively focus on one thing at a time. Others just take a long time getting started, remembering previous work, orienting themselves to the task; they're like very heavily loaded freight trains that start very slowly and take a long time to get up to speed. If you stop one of these kids and move them to the next subject just as they're gaining momentum, you've halted learning.

You can do history one day, math the next, science the day after that, and allow the child to work for the entire day on one subject.

You can do a week of history, a week of math, a week of science . . .

You can spend a *month* on history, a *month* on math . . .

Don't be afraid to make drastic changes to that classroom schedule that's probably at the back of your mind. As long as you have a goal and you're moving toward it, you can do this in any set of time-frames you want.

My only caution: The younger a child is, the more often you need to revisit information so that it isn't forgotten. (If you don't do spelling with a first-grader for two weeks, he's likely to have no memory of what you did in the last lesson.)

Strategy 7: Speed bursts

Not a great long-term strategy, but a fun change of pace and good for subjects that need regular drill and practice: Place everything that needs to get done on the table, spaced evenly all around, and tell the child he gets ten minutes to get as far as he can on the first subject before you yell, "Switch!" Start the stopwatch. At ten minutes, he *has* to leave what he's doing and go on to the next subject.

Clearly this won't work very well for literature or history, or for science reading, but it can add a little fun to the day, particularly if there are workbook-type exercises that need doing. Competitive kids and natural multitaskers will love it. (Perfectionists and introverts won't. Don't even try.)

Strategy 8: The checklist

Some children need control over their day in order to learn well. This can be difficult to implement, particularly when they still need considerable help with the subject matter, but here's one way to give them this control: Make a checklist at the beginning of the day. Put everything that the child needs to do on it: subjects to be studied, independent assignments, chores, appointments. Insofar as possible, let the student choose the order in which these things will be done. As each is finished, the student should physically check it off.

With the checklist, a child knows that when everything on the list is finished, they will be *done*. The rest of the day is theirs.

That's motivation for independent-minded kids. It's also a good way to begin to hand some control of daily life over to children. Learning to order a day so that everything gets done in good time is a life skill—one that they often don't learn in the tightly controlled confines of the classroom.

A FINAL CAUTION

Keep this one in mind all the time, every day, no matter what you're teaching, or what methods you're using.

When you educate your child at home, parenting and teaching mix together. You become increasingly aware that your child is relying on *you* not just for academic achievement, and preparation for college, but also for preparation for life, and character development, and . . .

This sense of responsibility can tempt you to go global.

"Going global" begins with a small frustration:

You told me you finished your math problems, but I just found the crumpled paper shoved down next to the sofa cushion and it's not even half done.

And then it escalates.

You didn't do the work. I know it's hard. But you just quit. You don't know how to work hard.

And you lied to me! You didn't tell the truth.

If you can't tell the truth and work hard, you won't ever get out of this grade.

In fact, you won't be able to graduate from high school. And then what will you do? You'll never be able to go to college and get a job.

And you'll end up in a cardboard box.

Under a *bridge*.

With no health insurance.

That's going global.

I think most parents go global from time to time, over messy rooms, or chronic lateness, or chore evasion. But just keep in mind that when you're homeschooling, the opportunities for going global multiply. It's related to fear: Fear that you're not doing a good enough job to prepare them for life.

Here's the thing: Even if that were true (which it isn't), going global doesn't work. When kids hear that tone in your voice, they usually stop listening anyway. And as there's absolutely no causal connection that they can see between the math worksheet and the (far distant, unreal) homeless future, you're giving them no reason to change the behavior.

It's just a math worksheet, not a referendum on the rest of his life. He's not revealing a deep character flaw. He just doesn't want to do his math.

Try some of the other teaching strategies instead.

And don't panic.

CHAPTER TWENTY-ONE

Radical Alternatives

Life is full of boundaries and boxes.

Adult life is one long process of discovering and negotiating with the perimeters that hem us in: the unspoken rules that govern our roles as parents, partners, teachers, spouses, bosses, employees. We fit comfortably into some of those boxes. Other boundaries have to be tested, prodded, pushed, and changed before we can exist within them.

And others are so uncomfortable and unnatural that we try them out and abandon them—or are pushed by them into an increasingly distorted existence that becomes less and less sustainable.

Children encounter these same perimeters, with much less power to push against them.

Our K–12 framework is a *very* sturdy box. Even homeschooled students are working within borders that can't easily be transcended. Certain kinds of intellectual work must be performed at a prescribed level, competence in a series of culturally defined subjects must be attained, and this leads into a series of high-school credits and achievements that have to be mastered in order to unlock the path to adult life (usually, college; more rarely than should be the case, trades or crafts).

Most children eventually adapt—to a greater or lesser degree.

For some, education is a natural second skin. Others itch and agitate, but survive (with a variety of coping strategies, from apathy to rebellion) until they escape.

A few never fit in.

This is not a flaw. It's a reality, not a defect.

In his junior year of college, one of my sons said to me, in a rare moment of Christmas-vacation honesty, "I feel like I'm in this unending purgatory with no way to ever get out and it will never end." I should have stopped, years before, and pursued some sort of radical alternative for this child—but I didn't. I'm a natural academic, I have three graduate degrees, I taught college for fifteen years: This was my natural home, my native air. Even though I was homeschooling, I couldn't step out of the box and discard all of the books and techniques and projects and papers and subjects that were working so well for my other three children.

He wasn't flourishing inside that box, but I didn't know how to flex the walls.

And although we managed to muscle him into college (a brief phrase for a long and tortured process), he loathed it.

If I could do it again, I'd make some radical changes.

I'd figure out a way to meet the minimum state requirements, so as not to lay myself open to charges of truancy or child neglect, and I'd find a way to let that child travel, and volunteer, and work, and develop trade skills, instead of plugging away through assignments that were quickly forgotten, on the way to a destination he didn't want to find.

I wouldn't push traditional college.

In many ways, my odd-man-out child was my hardest worker: the one who never complained when I asked him to do a chore or run an errand. He was loving, sweet, kind, grateful. And he needed something else.

In case you're wondering, over that Christmas vacation, I told him to drop out, apply to trade schools, and look for apprenticeships.

I wish I'd made that decision four or five years earlier.

If you're the parent of a kid who needs a radical solution, you already know that all the teaching, disciplining, scolding, exhorting, and threatening in the world is not going to reshape that child so that she fits inside the box. Homeschooling can give you another framework, one within which your child might find that elusive way forward.

Don't let other people make you operate from a place of fear or view your child as "broken" or "damaged." As a homeschooler, you have the freedom to guide your son through his education in a way that respects his individuality. —E.K.

In Appendix C, I've listed additional resources for you to investigate, if you need to start thinking outside the box in a radical way.

The suggestions below are starting places.

DIFFERENT PATHS

Apprenticeships

Go back and reread Chapter 14. *Not everyone is a propositional learner.*

I'm a historian, so I'm most definitely *not* a fan of chronological snobbery: Things were *not* better in the Middle Ages. If you were a woman, just for example, you were more likely than not to die in child-birth. Whether male or female, you could die from a scratch, a tooth-ache, or a sore throat. Your children could be kidnapped as slaves, commandeered by your king, or enlisted in the army without your con-sent. You ate no vegetables in winter, and probably had scurvy. If you had a thirst for learning and didn't happen to be eligible for cathedral school learning, too bad: You didn't learn.

On the other hand, if you weren't a propositional learner, you could adopt a trade and become a well-respected professional with a good income (until you died for lack of antibiotics, that is).

Western modernity has many upsides, but it also has a downside: it channels *all* students into the same developmental path. That's not how people actually *are.*

Some of us should not be railroaded into college. We should take alternative paths: toward being stonemasons, shepherds, brewers, art-ists, costume designers, diesel mechanics, landscapers, weavers, elec-tricians, or plumbers.

All of these are professions that demand a high level of skill and a great deal of training. They also can pay very well. But the exit lanes that lead from our usual high-school-into-four-year-college interstate toward those alternative destinations are poorly marked, and (too often) littered with road blocks: chief among them, parental disappointment, and social stigma (vo-tech as the "stupid" track).

For a student who's not connecting with traditional K–12 learning, an apprenticeship can serve as a useful exit lane away from the four-year liberal arts degree. The goal is to move toward post-high-school apprenticeship programs, which typically offer both classroom instruction and on-the-job training in order to equip students to enter into a trade or craft.

I maintain a list with links to current possibilities for both high school and post-high-school apprenticeships at welltrainedmind.com.

Unschooling

I am not, generally, a fan of unschooling. Which isn't to say that it doesn't sometimes work.

Back in the early days of homeschooling (the 1970s or thereabouts), unschooling was just another word for home education: taking your child out of school and doing something different at home. But as the home-education movement gained shape and legitimacy, unschooling came to mean something narrower: pursuing an education without external requirements, grades, standards, curricula, or structure.

> Unschooling . . . means learning what one wants, when one wants, in the way one wants, where one wants, for one's own reasons. The learning is learner-directed; advisors or facilitators are sought out as desired by the learner.

> We live our lives and learn as we go. We have no teaching, no classes, no lesson plans, no grades, no curriculum, no textbooks, no tests. Basically, I don't pay particular attention to what the kids are learning; it is enough to see that they are growing as people, and gaining knowledge and experience as they go.[1]

> Unschooling is also known as natural, interest-led, and child-led learning. Unschoolers learn from everyday life experiences and do not use school schedules or formal lessons. Instead, unschooled

---

1 Both quotes from Mary Griffith, *The Unschooling Handbook: How to Use the Whole World as Your Child's Classroom*, 2nd ed. (New York: Three Rivers Press, 1998), Chapter 1.

children follow their interests and learn in much the same way as adults do—by pursuing an interest or curiosity.[2]

When unschooling is done well, it takes tremendous effort on the part of the parent. As the child shows interest, you have to provide active, careful follow-up; this requires not just the provision of the correct materials and resources, but the broad knowledge and insight to know how to point a fourteen-year-old who's obsessing about developing the perfect basketball shot toward the quadratic equations that would define the perfect parabola, or a twelve-year-old fascinated by wolves toward the most recent and accessible literature on pack behavior and the psychology of pack mentality.

Personally, I've never felt I had the wide-ranging knowledge to carry off unschooling; I'm very sure that without a structured guide to learning, my kids would have been massively short-changed in maths and science.

I've also found, in the last quarter-century of my involvement with homeschooling, that too many parents encounter the concept of unschooling, grab onto it without much research, and use it to jus- tify "nonschooling," which too often involves watching limitless TV or playing online games without restriction.[3]

But I won't say that it can't be done.

Unschooling principles *can* be of great help when you're looking for a way out of the K–12 box with a child who simply isn't fitting into any of the models you've tried. One parent writes:

> We centered a whole year around amusement parks.
> On the physics side: linear Gs vs. vertical Gs. Most coaster junkies,

---

2 Rebecca Kochenderfer and Elizabeth Kanna, *Homeschooling for Success: How Parents Can Create a Superior Education for Their Child* (New York: Grand Central Publishing, 2002), p. 45.

3 A typical quote from a popular unschooling site: "If a child is happily playing a computer game or watching TV for the *entire* time that that child would have been in school, that child is infinitely better off than if she was unhappily at school." That's a false distinction; you could remove the child from the unhappy school situation, impose a much shorter and very reasonable amount of "unhappy" time learning the basics of reading, writing, and mathematics, and then point her in productive direc- tions with the rest of that time (http://sandradodd.com/beginning, accessed Decem- ber 12, 2016).

like myself, usually have a preference. My daughter analyzed how they work, how they feel, the science behind them.

We looked at marketing: Why are Disney tickets frontloaded (more expensive) for the first few days but much less expensive to add days on to at the end? Why does Disney offer the Magical Express service to pick up resort guests from the airport and transport them straight to the resort? How does Disney attract customers year-round?

We examined tiered ticket prices and their effect on crowd levels.

We listened to presentations about how Christmas/winter holidays are done in the different "countries" at Disney's Epcot. We studied each country included, and interviewed the Epcot employees that are from the countries that they work in.

We looked at landscaping (topiary making is especially fascinating).

We examined safety plans that amusement parks have to have in place, in case of a natural disaster or other issues.

We talked about continuous load rides vs. non-continuous load rides, and how they affect capacity. And now, how Disney has changed the wait times and demands with their tiered Fastpass+ technology.

Fastpass+ technology alone is interesting. Biometrics is another option . . .

We studied psychological barriers vs physical barriers at amusement parks and zoos.

We did lots of animal behavior observation and individual animal observation and then research.

We made friends with Rachel Reenstra, who hosts The Wildlife Docs, *after meeting her at Busch Gardens. We interviewed her about how she went about entering the world of television hosting, and through Facebook we follow along on some of her gigs as she shares.*

—PAT

Single focus homeschooling

Focused kids don't want to do anything that doesn't relate to their primary obsession.

That's admirable in some ways, but unless you're dealing with an Olympic-level figure skater or BioGENEius Challenge award winner, students who won't do anything that they can't see the point of can be excruciatingly difficult to work with. *You* know that they need to be able to write, read, and understand mathematical concepts, so that they can go on to whatever the next stage may be. They don't agree.

Walking a single-focus child through the K–12 years is a very particular kind of unschooling: You have to constantly adapt and research in order to dovetail those basic skills with the obsession. You have to give the focused child a reason to learn.

> *I have a circus kid. She's an advanced aerialist and just joined a new performance company in January. She has two group classes on Tuesdays; one private and one partner lesson on Wednesdays; rehearsals on Friday; two classes and extra workshops on Saturday; one class and rehearsal on Sunday; and we are about to add another Monday private. She does silks, trapeze, lyra, rope, acro, plus other circus things like stilting (including acro stilting), unicycling, juggling, etc. She has two sets of stilts, all kinds of circus toys, unicycle, silks in the house, and we are probably buying a rig (I'm researching aerial ropes right now).*
>
> *Suffice to say that if it were up to her, that's all she would do all the time. We've done circus math, circus history, circus science. She's taken rigging classes (aka circus physics). One of our local instructors is also a physicist, and he just started a points of intersection/trigonometry class that she'll join after she completes algebra.* —DARLA

Designing a curriculum around a single interest *can* be done; just keep your focus on practical applications of knowledge to the student's primary focus.

Investigate the unschooling resources in Appendix C, and keep in mind Alfie Kohn's words in *The Schools Our Children Deserve:*

> Ultimately, we want to call into question the whole idea of a curriculum to be "covered" and to think instead about ideas to be discovered. . . . As much as possible, students ought to discover things directly rather than just reading or hearing about them. They ought to explore, do, see—and reflect on what they've explored, done, and seen . . . The common element is giving students a chance to *do*. If you want them to learn about the conduction of heat, ask them to design a restaurant take-out container that will keep a customer's dinner hot. If you want them to learn the geography of an

area (and why it matters), ask them to find the major cities on a map that contains physical features and natural resources but no place names. If you want them to understand how a story is structured, invite them to dissect an episode of their favorite TV situation comedy, paying attention to the way problems are introduced and resolved—and then to write their own scripts.[4]

What ideas can your child discover while she explores, sees, and *does* things that are related to her passion?

Step out of time

You don't have to finish K–12 schooling in twelve years. In fact, after reading this book you should immediately realize just how arbitrary twelve years is.

Some kids need more time.

For a child who *can* do the work, just needs to do it more slowly, homeschooling can offer the opportunity to step out of the twelve-year restriction.

Is that going to affect college admissions? Yes, of course it is. But be realistic: A student who needs fourteen or fifteen years to get through secondary school is not going to be a favored applicant for a spot in competitive universities.

Take a deep breath. That's not the only path toward success. (See the Postscript.)

A student who eventually does finish the required high school credits for graduation, even if it takes five or six (or more) years, can then earn a two-year associate's degree at community college and use that degree as a stepping stone into a regular four-year program, if desired.

Or, go to trade school or enter an apprenticeship (see pages 215–16).

Or go directly into work that doesn't require a four-year degree.

Have an adventure

If you're homeschooling, you can actually take a year off.

Sometimes, kids need a year to process, think, experiment, work, live abroad, volunteer, try something else. A gap year (see pages 31–32)

---

4 Alfie Kohn, *The Schools Our Children Deserve: Moving Beyond Traditional Classrooms and "Tougher Standards"* (Boston: Houghton Mifflin Harcourt, 2000), p. 143.

is an accepted post-high-school institution, but if you're the one who's recording subjects and grades and documenting those high-school credits, there's absolutely no reason not to allow a gap year *before* graduation.

Have a goal for the gap year: to travel, learn a language, experience another culture, master a skill, try out potential careers before committing to a college, experiment with another way of living.

Keep a record of what the student actually did during that gap year. Ask her to maintain a written journal, make a video blog, or do a regular podcast.

Remember that education is intended to benefit the child, not the other way around.

Don't panic.

Last year was a radical year, and everyone turned out just fine. I sent them to German public school a grade level behind, so literally the only thing they learned was German. No history, science, math, or literature since they couldn't understand it, and the math was a repeat. The cultural experience was completely worth it. And I also learned that a year doing little to no school is not the end of the world.

—HEIDI

About College

My mother decided to homeschool us when my sister was four, I was five, and my brother was seven.

On hearing the news that we'd been withdrawn from our kindergarten and second-grade classrooms, my grandparents burst into tears: "Now they'll never get into college!" they wailed.

Neither of them had been to college, which made them keenly aware of the "thick line" that journalist Nicholas Lemann describes in his 1999 study *The Big Test: The Secret History of the American Meritocracy:*

> Here is what American society looks like today. A thick line runs through the country, with people who have been to college on one side of it and people who haven't on the other. . . . Whether a person is on one side of the line or the other is now more indicative of income, attitudes, and of political behavior than any other line one might draw: region, race, age, religion, sex, class. As people plan their lives and their children's lives, higher education is the main focus of their aspirations (and the possibility of getting into the elite end of higher education is the focus of their very dearest aspirations).[1]

1 Nicholas Lemann, *The Big Test: The Secret History of the American Meritocracy* (New York: Farrar, Straus & Giroux, 1999), p. 6.

This thick line is what makes a third-grade inability to understand multiplication, or a D in ninth-grade history, so fraught: not the *current* problem that your eight-year-old or fourteen-year-old may be having, but the fear that it's a portent, the first in a falling line of dominoes that will doom your child's chances of admission to a good college.

Because in the United States, the end game of our K–12 system is the college degree—and *getting my kid into college* (ideally, an Ivy League college) is the prime preoccupation of almost every parent with aspirations.

This is an exhausting mindset—and a damaging one.

If, while you're making decisions about homework, standardized testing, gap years, acceleration, and all the other issues I've been addressing, the question *Yes, but will they get into a good college?* is constantly rattling around in your head, you will *not* make the decisions that are right for your child *at this time.* Instead, you'll make choices based on fear—fear of what might happen down the road, fear for your child's hypothetical academical future, fear of what that college decision will mean for the rest of your child's life.

As a parent of grown children, a grandparent, and a lifelong academic, I can tell you that almost every parenting and educational decision I made out of fear turned out to be wrong.

Yes, plan ahead. Of course you want your child to get into college— if that turns out to be the right path. (Increasingly, I've begun to think that apprenticeships in crafts, internships in service professions, and certificate programs can be a better option than college for many young people.)

But should you be holding on to the dream of Stanford or Yale, I beg you, for your child's wellbeing, to let go of your elite college hopes.

The college-admissions racket has been exposed over and over again: "Selective" is merely a measure of applications against acceptances, and selective universities maintain their cachet by encouraging applications from students who have no chance of being admitted. Frank Bruni's book on college admissions, which should be read by every parent of a secondary-school student, points this out:

> Somewhere along the way, a school's selectiveness—measured in large part by its acceptance rate—became synonymous with its

worth. Acceptance rates are prominently featured in the profiles of schools that appear in various reference books and surveys, including the raptly monitored one by *U.S. News & World Report*. . . . Colleges know that many prospective applicants equate a lower acceptance rate with a more coveted, special and brag-worthy experience, and these colleges endeavor to bring their rates down by ratcheting up the number of young people who apply.[2]

The overall acceptance rate of the Ivy League schools, plus MIT and Stanford is, as of this writing, 8.47 percent. What does that mean? That out of nearly 350,000 applicants, many of whom had over 4.0 grade averages (thanks to AP and honors classes), 26,677 were accepted—which works out to fewer than one in ten, overall. Stanford's acceptance rate was below 5 percent in 2016. Harvard's, 5.2 percent. Columbia, 6.0 percent.[3]

In her book *The Overachievers,* journalist Alexandra Robbins describes watching as high-school senior Julie—a standout distance runner, co-captain of the varsity cross country and track teams, honors student, class officer, top scorer on both the SATs and a range of AP tests, community activist—meets with her private college counselor. Julie wants to apply to Stanford, but the counselor tells her not to bother: She won't get in.

Julie was crushed. She hadn't been dreaming of the California campus for so many years only to be told that even sending in an application was a waste of time.

"What . . . what would it take for me to get into Stanford?" she stammered.

"You would have to have lived in Mongolia for two years or have been in a civil war," Vera replied.[4]

2 Frank Bruni, *Where You Go Is Not Who You'll Be: An Antidote to the College Admissions Mania* (New York: Grand Central Publishing, 2015), p. 75.

3 "2020 Ivy League Admissions Statistics," https://www.ivycoach.com/2020-ivy-league-admissions-statistics/ (accessed December 12, 2016).

4 Alexandra Robbins, *The Overachievers: The Secret Lives of Driven Kids* (New York: Hachette Books, 2006), p. 3.

There are, perhaps, fifty brand-name colleges out there that everyone wants to get into. But there are *thousands* of colleges where your child can thrive, flower, mature, and learn the life lessons that matter.

Sure, go ahead and apply anywhere (or everywhere). Just realize that getting into any particular university is a complete crapshoot.

And, further, realize that *it doesn't matter.*

■ ■ ■

Let me offer my own experience.

I went to a *dreadful* college. My bachelor's degree was accredited, but I'm so embarrassed by my undergraduate alma mater that I don't even put it on my résumé. (You'd be surprised how few people ask.) I went there because my parents, to be frank, didn't know that I should aim higher; because they were very conservative, and thought it would be a safe place for a sixteen-year-old freshman; because my grandfather loved the school; because we were broke, and the school offered me a full tuition plus room and board scholarship.

Just a few things I learned at my tenth-rate college:

A lousy school can teach you fantastic things. I had a couple of amazing professors. I grew up. I had my heart broken. I discovered I was smart. I read Wallace Stevens and W. H. Auden and T. S. Eliot and Tom Stoppard for the first time. I learned Greek. I learned how to negotiate a world that didn't agree with me.

I'm a good writer. I didn't know that until I went to my lousy school.

A dreadful college still offers windows into another world. I got a passport, went overseas, visited the Bodleian, and first glimpsed Oxford, all thanks to my dreadful college.

My lousy school didn't keep me from getting into graduate school. It paved the way for me to earn two master's degrees and a Ph.D. and teach for fifteen years at the College of William & Mary in Virginia.

I discovered that most of the civilized world doesn't care where you went to college. If you don't go to graduate school, it doesn't matter, because you're not in the academic world where people put stock in such things. And if you go to graduate school, it doesn't matter, because people who put stock in such things look at your graduate degree instead.

A debt-free bachelor's degree is, as it turns out, priceless: As Jane Austen might put it, it sets you up forever. My friends were still paying off school loans into their forties. I never had any school debt at all. Because I had no debt, I could choose my life, and choose my adventure.

I didn't want my children to go to a dreadful college, but I also didn't want them to shoulder debt that would shape every post-graduation life decision. And we're in the vast American middle class: too well-off to qualify for aid, absolutely incapable of shelling out fifty grand or more (far, far more) per year for a college education per kid (let alone, per kid times four).

So we told them: You can apply anywhere you want, but you can only go to schools that we can afford.

We live in Virginia, which has amazing public universities, and that's where my children have flourished. Our very best experience, to date, has been with a public university that was a community college not too many years ago, but as a new four-year university has poured money into its performing arts department—and provided our budding composer with astounding opportunities to learn and listen and practice and perform and hear his work brought to life.

This book is about the K–12 years, not about college. Choosing a college, applying to college, going to college, and paying for college: These are topics that need an entire book of their own. Those books have been written, and you should read them. See Appendix C.

But as you make decisions about *now,* keep repeating this to yourself: *Where my child goes to college doesn't matter.*

What matters?

That your child moves toward maturity.

That he has the chance to try out some new directions, subjects, activities.

That she finds her footing.

That they learn how to *live.*

High School and the Transcript

Over the course of four years, high-school students are expected to complete a certain number of credits in several different areas. Let's start with some definitions:

Credit

Generally speaking, one high school credit equals one year of work in a subject. This is considered to be 120 full hours of instruction (that's approximately 160 forty-five-minute class periods).

This standard was established in 1906 by the Carnegie Foundation for the Advancement of Teaching, so you'll sometimes see 1 credit/120 hours referred to as one Carnegie unit.

So remember: 120 hours/160 class periods/1 credit/1 Carnegie unit.[1] (A half credit is one semester, or around 60 hours/80 class periods.)[2]

---

1 Broken down into fifty-minute class periods, that's 144 "class hours," or approximately four fifty-minute class periods per week in a thirty-six-week school year. If a high school does block scheduling (with ninety-minute class periods), one Carnegie unit can be completed if the class meets an average of 2¼ times per week.

2 Another parenthetical remark: As I write this, some states are stumbling toward competency tests rather than Carnegie units, but Carnegie units remain the overwhelming measure. As you plan, you can consider a Carnegie unit as the average number of hours a student needs to study in order to reach the level required by a standard competency test over the material (average, meaning that your particular student might need much more or much less).

One semester of college work is usually considered to be the equivalent of one year of high-school work. So students who take a regular level college class (*not* a remedial class) can be awarded one credit for a one-semester course. One year of a college language, for example, can serve as two foreign language credits in high school.

Areas and subjects

Each subject studied in high school falls within an area.

The core areas of content (every student must take them, sooner or later) are language arts, maths, social sciences, natural sciences, foreign languages, and physical education.

The elective areas (not necessarily required in order to graduate from the K–12 system) are fine arts, practical arts, and business.

Core Areas	**Subjects**
Language Arts	
	Reading
	Phonics
	Literature
	Writing
	Handwriting
	Composition
	Rhetoric
	Grammar
	Spelling
	Vocabulary
Maths	
	Arithmetic (calculations: anything that can be done with concrete numbers, or *integers*)
	Operations (addition, subtraction, multiplication, division)
	Geometry
	Mathematics (the larger field of numeric work)
	Algebra
	Pre-calculus and calculus
	Trigonometry
Social Sciences	
	History (including state history, in the U.S.)
	Geography
	Government

"Social studies"
Citizenship
Civics
Economics (including personal finance)

Natural Sciences

Biology
Chemistry
Physics
Earth science
Geology
Environmental science
Oceanography
Meteorology (sometimes combined with earth science and/or geology)
Labs (hands-on)

Foreign Language

Study of any language other than English

Physical Education

Instruction in sports
General fitness
Health
Nutrition

Elective Areas

Fine Arts

Music
Art
Theater
Dance
Graphic design

Practical Arts

Shop
Driver's education
Technology

Business

Accounting

Other

Computer programming
Logic/thinking skills
Test preparation

Required high school

The following table shows a list of the courses that most students are expected to complete over four years of high school. Each credit represents one year of work.

This table is a compilation that exceeds graduation requirements in almost every U.S. state, and represents the average credit accumulation that most college admissions offices hope for. But always check with your local department of education for graduation requirements, and always check with colleges that your child might want to apply to for their admission requirements.

Area	Required Credits/C-Units	Subjects
Language Arts	4	Literature, writing, grammar, composition, rhetoric
Mathematics	3–4	Algebra, geometry, advanced maths
Foreign Language	2–4	Ancient or modern languages
Social Sciences	4	
	1	World history
	1	American history
	1	American government
	1	State history
Natural Sciences	3–4, at least 2 of which include lab work	Biology, chemistry, physics, etc.
Physical Education	2	
Electives	4–8	Any area

How does this relate to actual academic work?

Time spent on reading, writing, grammar, spelling, and vocabulary can all count toward the language arts credits. The actual classes taken can be literature classes, or rhetoric/expository writing/creative writing classes, or other classes centered around reading and responding in written prose.

Algebra 1, geometry, algebra II, and upper-level mathematics all count toward the mathematics credits. Pre-algebra isn't counted for high-school credit, even if taken in ninth grade. (Some states allow pre-algebra to be an elective, but not a math credit; no college admissions officer will give pre-algebra much weight.)

Foreign language credits can be any modern or ancient language, and the two (plus) credits should be two consecutive years (or more) of the same language. Some universities accept ASL or another sign language as a foreign language, as long as it meets the two-consecutive-years standard. Some will also accept programming languages as fulfilling the foreign language requirement, but as of this writing, that policy is still unusual.

World history can be ancient, medieval, Renaissance, or modern.

Science can be biology, chemistry, physics, meteorology, oceanography, environmental science, or any topics that are subsets of those. Generally speaking, "physical science" and "earth science" are not considered to be high-school level, even when taken in ninth grade or later. They are considered lower levels, respectively, of physics and meteorology/oceanography/environmental science.

Physical education credits range from physical fitness, to instruction on nutrition and fitness training, to training in team sports and the dreaded dodgeball.

Electives are made up of additional high-school credits beyond those listed in the core areas. For example, if a high-school student takes expository writing and American literature, she would earn two language arts credits on the high school transcript. One credit would fulfill the language arts requirement for that year; the other could go either toward an additional language arts credit, if needed, or be placed in the electives total.

Transcript

A transcript is simply a document that shows the subjects, credits, and grades taken by the student each year in grades 9–12.

There is no single universally accepted form for high school transcripts. If you're preparing your own, you can just use a word processor to create a document that demonstrates the above. If you'd like a more "official" looking form, you can download software from the sources listed at http://welltrainedmind.com/a/high-school-transcript-forms (examples of actual high school transcripts are also shown).

Skills vs. Content

Common Core and state standards of learning can create confusion. These standards seem to dictate that certain *courses* be taken.

In fact, standards are almost exclusively focused on *skills,* not *content.* Keep these important definitions in mind.

Skills are the tools that the student needs in order to keep on learning. A grasp of the principles of grammar, phonics and spelling, of the mechanics of sentence and paragraph construction; of mathematical operations (from addition to complex equations) and why they work; the ability to keep accurate records, to read graphs, to care for scientific instruments, to set up a valid experiment; the enormous heap of analytical abilities generally labeled "critical thinking" (awareness of such things as point of view, validity of information, untested assumptions, etc.): all these are skills.

Content is subject-specific. Literature, history, topics in the sciences, mathematical thinking and understanding, written composition, art, music: These fields of study are open-ended. You can become literate in them, but you can never truly master them—never learn all of history, never comprehend every aspect of biological life, never listen to all of the important musical compositions, or read all of the great books.

Subjects, as in "You have to take a course in American government before you can graduate from high school" and "One semester of personal finance is required by the state of Virginia," are generally defined by schools according to their content, not the skills they develop.

Most standards of learning are skill and *not* content focused.

In the United States, the closest thing to an elementary-school national organization that exists is the National Association of Elementary School Principals, which offers no road map of content *or* skills for elementary education (the association is focused on administration, with its current hot topics ranging from bullying prevention to seasonal flu). Even those goals that are proposed—not mandated, mind you—by various national organizations can be reached without any formal courses attached to them.

Consider these National Council for the Social Studies recommendations for young students:

> Even though young children find the concept of time difficult, they need to understand how the present has come about and to develop an appreciation for the heritage of this country.
> Children need to develop an understanding of and an appreciation for their physical and cultural environments and to consider how resources will be allocated in the future.
> Children need to recognize the contributions of each culture and to explore its value system.
> Economic content in the early years should relate to events in children's lives as they examine buying, selling, and trading transactions, the process of making goods and services, and the origin of materials and products in their everyday lives.[1]

1 NCSS Task Force on Early Childhood/Elementary Social Studies, "Social Studies for Early Childhood and Elementary School Children: Preparing for the 21st Century," http://www.socialstudies.org/positions/elementary (accessed November 8, 2016). These four requirements are the core of a 6,500-word document, which can be accessed at the website above, that provides much more detail.

All of these goals could be met by reading nonfiction picture books, biographies, and historical novels; visiting museums and parks; helping with the grocery shopping.

Or consider the National Science Education Standards set by the National Research Council for K–4 education in biology:

> During the elementary grades, children build understanding of biological concepts through direct experience with living things, their life cycles, and their habitats. These experiences emerge from the sense of wonder and natural interests of children who ask questions such as: "How do plants get food? How many different animals are there? Why do some animals eat other animals? What is the largest plant? Where did the dinosaurs go?" . . . Because the child's world at grades K–4 is closely associated with the home, school, and immediate environment, the study of organisms should include observations and interactions within the natural world of the child.[2]

Which could be paraphrased: "Read picture books, watch nature documentaries, play outside, go for nature walks, take care of a pet."

The guide provided by the Association for Middle Level Education[3] for middle-school curriculum development lists *no content requirements* as necessary, or even desirable. No academic *subjects* are described— neither content-centered *nor* skill-focused. The chapter devoted to Curriculum Characteristics lists, and describes (at length), five central requirements for middle-school curricula:

> Educators value young adolescents and are prepared to teach them.
> Students and teachers are engaged in active, purposeful learning.
> Curriculum is challenging, exploratory, integrative, and relevant.
> Educators use multiple learning and teaching approaches.

2 National Research Council, "National Science Education Standards," http://www .csun.edu/science/ref/curriculum/reforms/nses/ (accessed November 8, 2016).
3 Formerly known as the National Middle School Association.

> Varied and ongoing assessments advance learning as well as measure it.[4]

None of those requirements mandate any particular courses.

Common Core standards, in the states that still hold to them, are skill-centered, but not content/class/subject specific. The standards lay out a series of thinking goals, not subject recommendations.

Here, for example, are Common Core "English Language Arts Standards » History/Social Studies » Grades 6–8":

CCSS.ELA-LITERACY.RH.6–8.2

Determine the central ideas or information of a primary or secondary source; provide an accurate summary of the source distinct from prior knowledge or opinions.

CCSS.ELA-LITERACY.RH.6–8.4

Determine the meaning of words and phrases as they are used in a text, including vocabulary specific to domains related to history/social studies.

CCSS.ELA-LITERACY.RH.6–8.7

Integrate visual information (e.g., in charts, graphs, photographs, videos, or maps) with other information in print and digital texts.

CCSS.ELA-LITERACY.RH.6–8.10

By the end of grade 8, read and comprehend history/social studies texts in the grades 6–8 text complexity band independently and proficiently.[5]

With apologies to Key and Peele, let me offer an actual English translator version. In history and social studies, middle-school students should:

4 Association for Middle Level Education, *This We Believe: Keys to Educating Young Adolescents,* Kindle ed. (National Middle School Association, 2010), loc. 290–400.

5 Common Core State Standards Initiative, "English Language Arts Standards » History/Social Studies » Grades 6–8," http://www.corestandards.org/ELA-Literacy/RH/6-8/ (accessed November 7, 2016).

Be able to read and understand texts written at grade level.

Know how to summarize.

Understand illustrations as well as text.

Those are skills, not content requirements. A middle-school student could achieve them without ever actually taking a history course.

The same is true of high-school standards of learning.

For example, American high-school students are expected, in all fifty states, to take one year of American history (that's a content requirement). However, the Common Core standards for eleventh- and twelfth-grade history decree that students should learn to "analyze in detail how a complex primary source is structured, including how key sentences, paragraphs, and larger portions of the text contribute to the whole," and be able to "evaluate authors' differing points of view on the same historical event or issue by assessing the authors' claims, reasoning, and evidence."[6] This is entirely skill-focused.

Colleges look at transcripts to see whether students have completed appropriate content courses, but skill is generally only measured through achievement test scores, admissions essays, and other non-transcript parts of the application.

Here's your takeaway: Don't get hung up on the "courses" your student is taking in grades K–8. Instead, focus on skill development and the achievement of a wide range of content knowledge. And for high school, think about the transcript, not Common Core or state standards.

6 Common Core State Standards Initiative, "English Language Arts Standards » History/Social Studies » Grades 11–12," http://www.corestandards.org/ELA-Literacy/RH/11-12/#CCSS.ELA-Literacy.RH.11-12.10 (accessed November 7, 2016).

APPENDIX C

A Brief Essential Bibliography

Acceleration

Assouline, Susan G., Nicholas Colangelo, Joyce VanTassel-Baska, and Ann Lupkowski-Shoplik. *A Nation Empowered: Evidence Trumps the Excuses Holding Back America's Brightest Students*, Vol. 1 and Vol. 2. Iowa City, Iowa: Connie Belin & Jacqueline N. Blank International Center for Gifted Education and Talent Development, University of Iowa, 2015.

> The first volume of this study, initially published in 2005, highlighted the extent to which school systems resist identifying students as gifted; the second volume, published along with a revision of the first, offers specific action plans to overcome that resistance.

College

Bruni, Frank. *Where You Go Is Not Who You'll Be: An Antidote to the College Admissions Mania*. New York: Grand Central Publishing, 2015.

> Bruni exposes the inhumanity of a selective system that maintains itself by whipping up applications in order to keep its acceptance stats low.

Marcus, David L. *Acceptance: A Legendary Guidance Counselor Helps Seven Kids Find the Right Colleges—And Find Themselves*. New York: Penguin, 2010.

A guidance counselor focuses on finding the correct fit for each student, rather than the most prestigious school.

Robbins, Alexandra. *The Overachievers: The Secret Lives of Driven Kids.* New York: Hachette, 2006.
As she follows a series of accomplished high-school students through the college application process, Robbins throws a stark light on the assumptions behind getting into a "good" school.

Curricula

Bauer, Susan Wise, and Jessie Wise. *The Well-Trained Mind: A Guide to Classical Education at Home,* 4th ed. New York: W. W. Norton, 2016.
Detailed and specific curricula recommendations for every grade and subject.

Duffy, Cathy. *102 Top Picks for Homeschool Curriculum.* Westminster, CA: Grove Publishing, 2015.
A guide to time-tested resources across the curriculum. (Duffy evaluates programs from a Christian point of view, but this handbook is useful for all parents searching for specific programs in math, writing, phonics, and other skills.)

Homeschooling

Bauer, Susan Wise, and Jessie Wise. *The Well-Trained Mind: A Guide to Classical Education at Home,* 4th ed. New York: W. W. Norton, 2016.
Guidance on getting started, choosing programs, designing and documenting a high-school program, and more.

Guterson, David. *Family Matters: Why Homeschooling Makes Sense.* San Diego: Harvest Books, 1993.
Novelist and (Washington State) public school teacher Guterson writes about his decision to homeschool and provides a useful survey of the movement.

Kuhl, Kathy. *Homeschooling Your Struggling Learner.* Herndon, VA: Learn Differently, 2009.

Kuhl outlines strategies for home-educating children with learning differences, offers creative teaching strategies, and lists scores of valuable resources.

Homework

Bennett, Sara, and Nancy Kalish. *The Case Against Homework: How Homework Is Hurting Our Children and What We Can Do About It.* New York: Crown Publishers, 2006.

A survey of the research showing that homework doesn't add to achievement, along with practical suggestions for managing homework overloads.

Kralovec, Etta, and John Buell. *The End of Homework: How Homework Disrupts Families, Overburdens Children, and Limits Learning.* Boston: Beacon Press, 2001.

A well-researched and convincing argument against the efficacy of homework for improving learning.

Learning Differences and Disabilities

Danforth, Scot. *The Incomplete Child: An Intellectual History of Learning Disabilities.* New York: Peter Lang, 2009.

A scholarly but readable account of how the concept of learning disabilities was created in the 1970s.

Dawson, Peg, and Richard Guare. *Smart but Scattered: The Revolutionary "Executive Skills" Approach to Helping Kids Reach Their Potential.* New York: Guilford Press, 2009.

A guide to coaching differently abled children in the skills they need to succeed at learning.

Eide, Brock, and Fernette Eide. *The Mislabeled Child: Looking Beyond Behavior to Find the True Sources and Solutions for Children's Learning Challenges.* New York: Hyperion, 2006.

Two clinical psychologists evaluate eleven different brain systems and how they affect learning.

Freed, Jeffrey, and Laurie Parsons. *Right-Brained Children in a Left-Brained World: Unlocking the Potential of Your ADD Child.* New York: Simon & Schuster, 1998.

> A guide to rethinking ADD as a series of strengths rather than weaknesses.

Homayoun, Ana. *That Crumpled Paper Was Due Last Week: Helping Disorganized and Distracted Boys Succeed in School and Life.* New York: Perigee, 2010.

> Designed specifically for use with preteen and teen boys, this is a guide to organizational techniques for children who might otherwise be diagnosed with executive function disabilities or ADHD.

Lauer, Vaughn. *When the School Says No, How to Get the Yes! Securing Special Education Services for Your Child.* Philadelphia: Jessica Kingsley Publishers, 2014.

> A detailed plan for securing IEPs and other specialized service from school districts.

Olenchak, F. Richard, Jean Goerss, Paul Beljan, James T. Webb, Nadia E. Webb, and Edward R. Amend. *Misdiagnosis and Dual Diagnoses of Gifted Children and Adults: ADHD, Bipolar, OCD, Asperger's, Depression, and Other Disorders.* Scottsdale, AZ: Great Potential Press, 2005.

> A team of healthcare professionals outlines the ways in which learning differences can be mistaken for disease.

Shaywitz, Sally. *Overcoming Dyslexia: A New and Complete Science-Based Program for Reading Problems at Any Level.* New York: Vintage Books, 2005.

> A neuroscientist outlines methods for dealing with the strengths and weaknesses of the dyslexic brain.

Spears, Dana, and Ron Braund. *Strong-Willed Child or Dreamer?* Nashville: Thomas Nelson, 1996.

> This exploration of a common gifted personality type is a parenting guide, but highly useful for negotiating school difficulties as well.

Radical Alternatives

Farr, Michael, and Laurence Shatkin. *200 Best Jobs Through Apprentice-ships,* 2nd ed. Indianapolis: Jist Publishing, 2009.
> A regularly updated guide to finding apprenticeships in a wide array of fields.

Frost, Maya. *The New Global Student: Skip the SAT, Save Thousands on Tuition, and Get a Truly International Education.* New York: Three Rivers Press, 2009.
> Frost suggests a travel-centered alternative to the traditional high school/college progression.

Griffith, Mary. *The Unschooling Handbook: How to Use the Whole World as Your Child's Classroom,* 2nd ed. New York: Three Rivers Press, 1998.
> Along with the *Teenage Liberation Handbook* (below), one of the foundational texts on unschooling methods and styles.

Guillebeau, Chris. *The Art of Non-Conformity: Set Your Own Rules, Live the Life You Want, and Change the World.* New York: Perigee, 2010.
> This outside-the-box guide questions not only traditional educational styles, but also traditional employment and other life choices.

Llewellyn, Grace. *The Teenage Liberation Handbook: How to Quit School and Get a Real Life and Education,* 2nd ed. Eugene, OR: Lowry House, 1998.
> The original unschooling manifesto.

Rethinking Our K–12 System

Gatto, John Taylor. *The Underground History of American Education: A Schoolteacher's Intimate Investigation into the Problem of Modern Schooling.* New York: Oxford Village Press, 2000.
> Gatto, New York State and New York City Teacher of the Year, offers a contrarian history of American public education that highlights its factory-model development.

Robinson, Ken, and Lou Aronica. *Creative Schools: The Grassroots Revolution That's Transforming Education.* New York: Penguin, 2015.

246 A Brief Essential Bibliography

Robinson expands on his 2006 TED talk questioning the ways in which our K–12 system enforces standardization and conformity and suppresses individuality, imagination, and creativity.

Taylor, James. *Poetic Knowledge: The Recovery of Education.* Albany: State University of New York Press, 1997.

Taylor establishes a philosophical base for education that is less propositional, less test-based, and more experiential.

Willingham, Daniel T. *Why Don't Students Like School? A Cognitive Scientist Answers Questions About How the Mind Works and What It Means for Your Classroom.* San Francisco: Jossey-Bass, 2009.

Willingham applies cognitive psychology to current school practices and points out the disconnect.

Teachers

Schwartz, Natalie. *The Teacher Chronicles: Confronting the Demands of Students, Parents, Administrators and Society.* Millwood, NY: Laurelton Media, 2008.

An invaluable guide to understanding the teacher's point of view.

Testing

Koretz, Daniel. *The Testing Charade: Pretending to Make Schools Better.* Chicago: University of Chicago Press, 2017.

An insightful study of the essential unreliability of current standardized testing, along with an examination of the development of standards such as Common Core (and their drawbacks).

Murdoch, Stephen. *IQ: A Smart History of a Failed Idea.* New York: John Wiley, 2009.

A history of the development of IQ testing that casts serious doubt on the accuracy and value of standardized evaluations.

Perlstein, Linda. *Tested: One American School Struggles to Make the Grade.* New York: Holt, 2008.

Education reporter Perlstein examines the effect of standardized testing on a school's mission to educate.

Sacks, Peter. *Standardized Minds: The High Price of America's Testing Culture and What We Can Do to Change It*. New York: Da Capo Press, 2000.
Sacks argues that standardized testing encourages superficial thinking and ruins learning.

Toxic Classrooms

Coloroso, Barbara. *The Bully, the Bullied, and the Not-So-Innocent Bystander: From Preschool to High School and Beyond: Breaking the Cycle of Violence and Creating More Deeply Caring Communities*, revised and expanded ed. New York: William Morrow, 2016.
A classic guide to confronting bad behavior.

Works Cited

Alexander, Kern, and M. David Alexander. *The Law of Schools, Students and Teachers in a Nutshell,* 5th ed. St. Paul, MN: West Academic Publishing, 2015.

Armstrong, Thomas. *Multiple Intelligences in the Classroom,* 3rd ed. Alexandria, VA: ASCD Publishing, 2009.

Association for Middle Level Education. *This We Believe: Keys to Educating Young Adolescents,* 4th ed. Westerville, OH: National Middle School Association, 2010.

Barkley, Russell A. *Taking Charge of ADHD: The Complete, Authoritative Guide for Parents.* New York: Guilford Press, 2013.

Barrow, Robin. *The Philosophy of Schooling.* New York: Routledge, 2015.

Bauer, Susan Wise, and Jessie Wise. *The Well-Trained Mind: A Guide to Classical Education at Home,* 4th ed. New York: W. W. Norton, 2016.

Baum, Susan, Julie Viens, and Barbara Slatin. *Multiple Intelligences in the Elementary Classroom: A Teacher's Toolkit.* New York: Teachers College Press, 2005.

Benchley, Robert. "The Most Popular Book of the Month: An Extremely Literary Review of the Latest Edition of the New York City Telephone Directory." *Vanity Fair,* February 1920.

Ben-Sasson, A., A. S. Carter, and M. J. Briggs-Gowan. "Sensory Over-Responsivity in Elementary School: Prevalence and Social-Emotional Correlates." *Journal of Abnormal Child Psychology* 37 (2009).

Campbell, Linda, and Bruce Campbell. *Multiple Intelligences and Student Achievement: Success Stories from Six Schools.* Alexandria, VA: ASCD Publishing, 1999.

Cantwell, Marianne. *Be a Free Range Human: Escape the 9–5, Create a Life You Love and Still Pay the Bills.* Philadelphia: Kogan, 2013.

Commager, Henry Steele. "Our Schools Have Kept Us Free." *Life*, October 16, 1950.

Darling-Hammond, Linda. *The Flat World and Education: How America's Commitment to Equity Will Determine Our Future.* New York: Teachers College Press, 2015.

Divoky, Diane. "Learning-Disability 'Epidemic.'" *The New York Times,* January 15, 1975.

Fisher, Dorothy Canfield. *Understood Betsy.* New York: Henry Holt, 1917.

Gendler, Tamar Szabó. *Intuition, Imagination, and Philosophical Methodology.* Oxford: Oxford University Press, 2010.

Hallinan, Maureen T., ed. *Handbook of the Sociology of Education.* New York: Springer, 2000.

Hergenhahn, B. R., and Tracy Henley. *An Introduction to the History of Psychology*, 7th ed. Boston: Wadsworth Cengage Learning, 2014.

Hess, Frederick M. *The Same Thing Over and Over: How School Reformers Get Stuck in Yesterday's Ideas.* Cambridge: Harvard University Press, 2010.

Holmes, Mark. "The Secondary School in Contemporary Western Society: Constraints, Imperatives, and Prospects." *Curriculum Inquiry* 15, no. 1 (1985).

Holt, John. *How Children Fail.* New York: Pitman, 1964.

———. *How Children Learn.* New York: Pitman, 1967.

"How Good Is Your School?" *Life*, October 16, 1950.

Hunt, Thomas C. *Encyclopedia of Educational Reform and Dissent,* Vol. 1. Thousand Oaks, CA: SAGE, 2010.

Kohn, Alfie. *The Schools Our Children Deserve: Moving Beyond Traditional Classrooms and "Tougher Standards."* Boston: Houghton Mifflin Harcourt, 2000.

Koretz, Daniel. *The Testing Charade: Pretending to Make Schools Better.* Chicago: University of Chicago Press, 2017.

Lang, Harry G., and Bonnie Meath-Lang. *Deaf Persons in the Arts and Sciences: A Biographical Dictionary.* Westport, CT: Greenwood Press, 1995.

Loudenback, Jeremy. "ADHD Diagnosis Three Times More Likely for Children in Foster Care." *Chronicle of Social Change,* November 3, 2015.

McClusky, Frederick Dean. "Introduction of Grading into the Public Schools of New England." *The Elementary School Journal* 21 (September 1920–June 1921).

Nieto, Sonia. *Language, Culture, and Teaching: Critical Perspectives,* 2nd ed. New York: Routledge, 2009.

Robbins, Alexandra. *The Overachievers: The Secret Lives of Driven Kids.* New York: Hachette, 2006.

Robinson, Ken, and Lou Aronica. *Creative Schools: The Grassroots Revolution That's Transforming Education*. New York: Penguin, 2016.

Rocco, Tonette S., ed. *Challenging Ableism, Understanding Disability, Including Adults with Disabilities in Workplaces and Learning Spaces*. San Francisco: Jossey-Bass, 2012.

Roth, Robert A., ed. *The Role of the University in the Preparation of Teachers*. Philadelphia: Taylor & Francis, 1999.

Sher, Barbara. *I Could Do Anything If I Only Knew What It Was*. New York: Dell, 1994.

Shurtleff, Nathaniel B., ed. *Records of the Governor and Company of the Massachusetts Bay in New England*, Vol. II (1642–1649). Boston: William White, 1853.

Smith, Corinne, and Lisa Strick. *Learning Disabilities: A to Z: A Parent's Complete Guide to Learning Disabilities from Preschool to Adulthood*. New York: Free Press, 1999.

Soled, Suzanne Wegener. *Assessment, Testing, and Evaluation in Teacher Education*. Westport, CT: Praeger, 1995.

Sornson, Bob, ed. *Preventing Early Learning Failure*. Alexandria, VA: ASCD Publishing, 2001.

Spear-Swerling, Louise, and Robert J. Sternberg. "Curing Our 'Epidemic' of Learning Disabilities." *The Phi Delta Kappan* 79, no. 5 (1998).

Stowe, Calvin Ellis. *The Prussian System of Public Instruction: And Its Applicability to the United States*. Cincinnati: Truman and Smith, 1836.

Swanson, H. Lee. "Issues Facing the Field of Learning Disabilities." *Learning Disability Quarterly* 23, no. 1 (2000).

Tracy, Brian. *Get Smart! How to Think and Act Like the Most Successful and Highest-Paid People in Every Field*. New York: TarcherPerigee, 2016.

van der Stel, M., and M. V. J. Veenman. "Metacognitive Skills and Intellectual Ability of Young Adolescents: A Longitudinal Study from a Developmental Perspective." *European Journal of Psychology of Education* 29, no. 117 (2014).

Webb, James T., Edward R. Amend, Nadia E. Webb, Jean Goerss, Paul Beljan, and F. Richard Olenchak. *Misdiagnosis and Dual Diagnoses of Gifted Children and Adults: ADHD, Bipolar, OCD, Asperger's, Depression, and Other Disorders*. Tucson, AZ: Great Potential Press, 2005.

Weil, Leonora G., Stephen M. Fleming, et al. "The Development of Metacognitive Ability in Adolescence." *Consciousness and Cognition* 22, no. 1 (2013).

Willingham, Daniel T. *Why Don't Students Like School? A Cognitive Scientist Answers Questions About How the Mind Works and What It Means for the Classroom*. San Francisco: Jossey-Bass, 2009.

Wong, Bernice, and Deborah L. Butler, eds. *Learning About Learning Disabilities*, 4th ed. San Diego: Academic Press, 2012.

Index

Note: Page numbers in *italics* refer to charts and tables.

age:
  and grade/year, 22–24, 34, 128
  and size, 27–28
All About Reading (Rippel), 140–41
allergies, 37, 54, 55
alternatives:
  radical, 213–21
  suggesting, 95–97
anxiety, 58
apprenticeships, 169, 177, 215–16
Armstrong, Thomas, 132
articulation disorder, *45*
Assign-and-Check Stage of home-
    schooling, 198–99
Association for Middle Level Educa-
    tion, 237–38
Association for Supervision and
    Curriculum Development
    (ASCD), 48
asthma, 54
asynchronous development, 25–27,
    66–67, 73, 129
attendance, compulsory, 23, 24
attention span, short, 38, *45*
audiology, 54
auditory processing disorder, *45*
autism, 41, 50–52
autism spectrum disorder (ASD),
    46, 50–52
  ASD-1, 51
  restricted, repetitive behaviors, 51
  social communication, 51

back-to-school events, 93
Barrow, Robin, 168
Bauer, Pete, 8–9
behavioral problems, medication
    for, 9, 60, 169
behavioral therapy, 59
Benchley, Robert, 157–58
Big Test, The (Lemann), 222
Binet, Alfred, 55

block scheduling, 210
Bloom, Benjamin, 156*n*
Bloom's taxonomy, 156*n*
boundaries, testing, 213
brain dysfunctions, 9, 40
brain imaging tests, 39
bribery, 206–7
Buell, John, 118
bulletin boards, 94
bullying, 80, 82–83, 169
  action plan, 84–87
business, 213

California Achievement Test (CAT),
    109
Cantwell, Marianne, 152
Cappelli, Peter, 149
Carnegie units, 229
cerebral palsy, 39, 41
chain of command, 86–87, 94–95
checking account, opening, 203
checklists, 211
childcare, need for, 164, 169
clinical psychologist, 57
Cognitive Abilities Test (CogAT), *106*
cognitive discrepancies, significant,
    69
college, 222–27
  academic preparation for, 164
  dual enrollment in, 200
  fears of failing to get into, 75
  as future extension of school sys-
      tem, 174
  one semester of, 230
  and test scores, 115
colleges:
  acceptance rates in, 225
  needless worries about, 226–27
  selective, 125
  and transcripts, 239
Commager, Henry Steele, 165–66,
    167